MASTER THE
U.S. BORDER
PATROL EXAM

PETERSON'S

A **nelnet** COMPANY

About Peterson's, a Nelnet company

To succeed on your lifelong educational journey, you will need accurate, dependable, and practical tools and resources. That is why Peterson's is everywhere education happens. Because whenever and however you need education content delivered, you can rely on Peterson's to provide the information, know-how, and guidance to help you reach your goals. Tools to match the right students with the right school. It's here. Personalized resources and expert guidance. It's here. Comprehensive and dependable education content— delivered whenever and however you need it. It's all here.

For more information, contact Peterson's, 2000 Lenox Drive, Lawrenceville, NJ 08648; 800-338-3282.

Stephen Clemente, Managing Director, Publishing and Institutional Research; Bernadette Webster, Director of Publishing; Mark D. Snider, Editor; Ray Golaszewski, Publishing Operations Manager; Linda M. Williams, Composition Manager

ISBN-13: 978-0-7689-2910-2
ISBN-10: 0-7689-2910-5

Printed in the United States of America

10 9 8 7 6 5 4 3 2 1   12   11   10

First Edition

By printing this book on recycled paper (40% post-consumer waste) 70 trees were saved.

Petersonspublishing.com/publishingupdates

Check out our Web site at www.petersonspublishing.com/publishingupdates to see if there is any new information regarding the test and any revisions or corrections to the content of this book. We've made sure the information in this book is accurate and up-to-date; however, the test format or content may have changed since the time of publication.

Certified Chain of Custody

60% Certified Fiber Sourcing and
40% Post-Consumer Recycled

www.sfiprogram.org

*This label applies to the text stock.

Sustainability—Its Importance to Peterson's, a Nelnet company

What does sustainability mean to Peterson's? As a leading publisher, we are aware that our business has a direct impact on vital resources—most especially the trees that are used to make our books. Peterson's is proud that its products are certified by the Sustainable Forestry Initiative (SFI) and that all of its books are printed on paper that is 40 percent post-consumer waste.

Being a part of the Sustainable Forestry Initiative (SFI) means that all of our vendors—from paper suppliers to printers—have undergone rigorous audits to demonstrate that they are maintaining a sustainable environment.

Peterson's continually strives to find new ways to incorporate sustainability throughout all aspects of its business.

OTHER RECOMMENDED TITLES

Peterson's Master the Corrections Officer Exam
Peterson's Civil Service Handbook

Contents

PART II: DIAGNOSING STRENGTHS AND WEAKNESSES

PART III: PREPARING FOR THE BORDER PATROL EXAM

PART IV: TWO PRACTICE TESTS

APPENDIX

Before You Begin

Now, more than ever before, our nation needs qualified and dedicated individuals to join the U.S. Border Patrol. The men and women of the Border Patrol not only prevent illegal aliens and contraband from entering the United States, but they also protect our country from terrorists and their weapons. This book was carefully researched and written to help you navigate the Border Patrol screening process. The information provided will prepare you for the written exam, educate you on the physical skills you need, and give you valuable tips to help you succeed during your oral interview. Knowing what to expect along the way will help you feel confident in your chances of becoming a Border Patrol Agent.

HOW THIS BOOK IS ORGANIZED

To get the most out of this book, take the time to read each section carefully and thoroughly.

- **Part I** provides an overview of the duties of Border Patrol Agents and the qualifications required. It also offers information about the history of the U.S. Border Patrol, the working conditions that Border Patrol Agents face every day, and the benefits that they enjoy. This information will give you a sense of a Border Patrol Agent's responsibilities and the various opportunities for advancement within the Department of Homeland Security (DHS). Part I also provides a detailed explanation of the Border Patrol screening process. The book offers step-by-step instructions for registering for the written test, undergoing the structured oral interview, and preparing for the fitness test and background investigation. Notes and tips are given to help you understand each step of the process.

- **Part II** is a preview of the written examination. This section introduces you to the kinds of questions you will see on the Logical Reasoning Test, the Spanish Language Proficiency Test, and the Artificial Language Test (ALT). Part II was designed to help you assess your strengths and weaknesses so that you can concentrate on the areas that need improvement. This section will also help you determine if you should take the Spanish Language Proficiency Test or the Artificial Language Test.

- **Part III** is a comprehensive overview of the types of questions you will see on the Logical Reasoning Test, the Spanish Language Proficiency Test, and the Artificial Language Test. This section offers tips for understanding and completing each section of the test. Feel free to highlight tips you find useful and make notes in the margins. Each chapter in this part begins with a detailed explanation of the kinds of questions you will encounter on each test, and it offers practical suggestions about how to answer the questions. Read the instructions in each chapter and try the practice questions. Then study the answer explanations. You can learn a great deal from them. Even if you answer the question correctly, take the time to review the answer explanation. You may discover a new tip that will help you answer other questions. The answer explanations also reinforce your understanding of the questions.

- When you feel that you are well prepared, move on to **Part IV**—the Practice Tests. These practice examinations contain new questions modeled after the samples provided in the Custom and Border Protection's *Preparation Manual for the U.S. Border Patrol Test*. It is important to note that these are merely samples of the types of questions you may encounter on the Border Patrol Test. They are not the actual questions that you will see on the exam. If possible, try to work through an entire exam in one sitting. If you must divide your time, divide it into no more than two sessions per exam. You do not need to take the first exam first. You may want to save the longer exam for a period when you have a stretch of uninterrupted time available. When you do take the exams, time yourself accurately. This will help you assess the amount of time you can devote to each question. Do not look at the correct answers until you have completed the exam. Remember, these tests are for practice, and they will not be scored. Take the time to learn from any mistakes you may make.

- The **Appendix** offers a detailed overview of the fellowships, internships, and student programs offered by the Department of Homeland Security (DHS). This section discusses the Student Temporary Employment Program (STEP), the Student Career Experience Program (SCEP), Student Volunteers (SV), the Bureau of Customs and Border Protection (CBP) Explorer Program, Federal Career Intern Program (FCIP), and the Presidential Management Fellowship (PMF).

Remember to carefully read each chapter in this book. This will give you a better understanding of the responsibilities of a Border Patrol Agent and help you prepare for the written examination.

SPECIAL STUDY FEATURES

Master the U.S. Border Patrol Exam is designed to be as user friendly as it is complete. To this end, it includes several features to make your preparation more efficient.

Overview

Each chapter begins with a bulleted overview listing the topics covered in the chapter. This allows you to target the areas in which you are most interested.

Summing It Up

Each chapter ends with a point-by-point summary that reviews the most important items in the chapter. The summaries offer a convenient way to review key points.

NOTE

Notes highlight need-to-know information about the Border Patrol Exam, whether it is details about application and scoring or the structure of the question type.

TIP

Tips provide valuable strategies and insider information to help you score your best on the Border Patrol Exam.

YOU'RE WELL ON YOUR WAY TO SUCCESS

You have made the decision to become a Border Patrol Agent and have taken a very important step in that process. *Master the U.S. Border Patrol Exam* will help you score high on the exam and prepare you for everything you need to know on the day of the exam and beyond it. Good luck!

FIND US ON FACEBOOK®

Join the Border Patrol conversation on Facebook® at www.facebook.com/borderexam and receive additional test-prep tips and advice. Peterson's resources are available to help you do your best on this important exam—and others in your future.

Peterson's publishes a full line of books—test prep, education exploration, financial aid, and career preparation. Peterson's publications can be found at high school guidance offices, college libraries and career centers, and your local bookstore and library. Peterson's books are now also available as eBooks.

We welcome any comments or suggestions you may have about this publication. Your feedback will help us make educational dreams possible for you—and others like you.

PART I

A CAREER AS A BORDER PATROL AGENT

What Border Patrol Agents Do

chapter 1

OVERVIEW

- Bureau of Customs and Border Protection
- History of the U.S. Border Patrol
- Duties of a Border Patrol Agent
- Working conditions
- Where Border Patrol Agents work
- Traits of a Border Patrol Agent
- Requirements
- Automatic disqualifications
- CBP conditions of employment
- Salary
- Benefits
- Special operations groups
- Advancement opportunities
- Other jobs within the DHS
- For more information
- Summing it up

The job of a Border Patrol Agent is difficult and sometimes dangerous, but it is also rewarding. Border Patrol Agents play an important role in keeping America safe from those trying to enter the country illegally. They must be on the lookout for terrorists, drug smugglers, and "coyotes," that is, people smuggling undocumented immigrants into the country. Border Patrol Agents patrol the nearly 7,000 miles of land separating the United States from Mexico and Canada. Many agents work alone in remote areas, using surveillance equipment to help them perform their job.

BUREAU OF CUSTOMS AND BORDER PROTECTION

The Bureau of Customs and Border Protection (CBP), which is under the direction of the Department of Homeland Security (DHS), employs all Border Patrol Agents. Before the DHS was established in 2003, CBP was essentially two organizations: the U.S. Customs Service and the Immigration and Naturalization Service (INS). The main goal of CBP is to prevent terrorists and weapons of mass destruction from entering the country. The CBP also enforces trade and immigration laws.

NOTE

Though most of the illegal aliens who cross the border are simply looking for opportunities in the United States, Border Patrol Agents do encounter dangerous criminals. This is why proper training is so important.

On a typical day, CBP officers welcome more than 1 million visitors into the country and apprehend thousands trying to enter illegally. The U.S. Border Patrol is the mobile, uniformed law enforcement division of the CBP. The CBP employs nearly 30,000 employees who work at borders and other points of entry around the United States. In addition to Border Patrol Agents, the CBP also employs Deportation Officers, Customs and Border Patrol Officers (CBPOs), Immigration Enforcement Agents, Detention Enforcement Officers, Adjudications Officers, and Criminal Investigators.

HISTORY OF THE U.S. BORDER PATROL

Have you ever heard the expression, "To understand the present, you need to understand the past"? This is true of the Border Patrol. Before the establishment of the U.S. Border Patrol, mounted guards from the U.S. Immigration Service and the Texas Rangers worked to secure the border between the United States and Mexico. These groups, however, lacked the resources and organization to prevent most illegal immigrants and smugglers from entering the country. To better control the flow of immigrants and to prevent contraband from entering the United States, Congress established the U.S. Border Patrol with the Labor Appropriations Act of 1924. The Border Patrol was a mobile, uniformed law enforcement branch of the Immigration Bureau and had bases in El Paso, Texas, and Detroit, Michigan. The new agency hired 450 Border Patrol Inspectors to secure the United States' northern and southern borders.

NOTE

The government provided the first Border Patrol Inspectors with badges and revolvers, but the men had to supply their own horses and saddles.

The creation of the Border Patrol coincided with Prohibition, a period in U.S. history during which it was illegal to manufacture, sell, and distribute alcohol for consumption. Border Patrol Inspectors faced increased danger as criminals attempted to smuggle alcohol over the border from Mexico and Canada. Gunfights between Border Patrol Inspectors and smugglers were common. After losing several inspectors during heavy fighting in 1927, government officials realized that they needed to expand the Border Patrol program. Today, the Border Patrol has 18,000 agents working in regions throughout the United States.

Since its creation, the Border Patrol has worked to prevent undocumented immigrants—also called illegal aliens—and contraband from entering the United States. The events following the terrorist attacks of September 11, 2001, however, changed the Border Patrol's mission. In March 2003, the Border Patrol became a part of the Bureau of Customs and Border Protection (CBP) under the direction of the Department of Homeland Security (DHS). Border Patrol Agents now have the added responsibility of identifying and apprehending terrorists, which makes their job even more dangerous. As the threat to our nation's safety increases, the Border Patrol develops innovative technology to aid in detecting and capturing terrorists, undocumented immigrants, and criminals.

NOTE

Created in 2003, the Department of Homeland Security merged twenty-two government agencies into one organization.

DUTIES OF A BORDER PATROL AGENT

The tasks a Border Patrol Agent performs each day vary, depending on the situations an agent encounters. Since the primary mission is to observe those entering or trying to enter the United States, Border Patrol Agents often engage in covert surveillance of the border. This is called **line watch.** They use information from aircraft, electronic sensors, infrared scopes, and low-light television systems to detect motion. Agents who perform these duties while working along the Rio Grande River, which forms part of the border between the United States and Mexico, are involved in **river**

watch. Border Patrol Agents also pursue leads and interpret and follow tracks, marks, and other physical evidence that could lead to the apprehension of undocumented immigrants. Looking for signs that indicate the presence of people is called **signcutting.** The duties of a Border Patrol Agent are not always exciting. Border Patrol Agents sometimes sit in SUVs and Jeeps watching the border for long periods. When Border Patrol Agents apprehend undocumented immigrants or criminals, they must process detainees to determine their country of origin and find out if they have criminal records in the United States.

Other duties of Border Patrol Agents include inspecting cargo, participating in search-and-rescue missions, and conducting traffic and transportation checks at traffic checkpoints. Border Patrol Agents work at transportation terminals, inspecting freight and passenger trains and buses. They periodically perform background checks on those working on farms, on ranches, and in businesses. Border Patrol Agents patrol cities, gather intelligence, perform administrative duties, and work with other law enforcement agencies. They testify in court and before grand juries, and they even advise courts on matters concerning immigration.

WORKING CONDITIONS

Border Patrol Agents must endure extremely difficult working conditions. They are almost always outdoors, often during harsh weather. Most new hires work along the Mexican border, so they must be able to withstand high temperatures. In some areas of California, the temperature reaches 104°F in the summer. A recent policy change allows new hires to report for duty directly to the northern border, so Border Patrol Agents must be equally prepared for the challenges presented by cold weather. The terrain that Border Patrol Agents work in can also be difficult. For example, a search-and-rescue mission might take agents into places such as Arizona's treacherous Sonoran Desert.

Most agents work 40 hours per week, plus an additional 9 or more hours of what is called Administratively Uncontrollable Overtime (AUO). These extra hours are used for activities that can't be scheduled, such as the length of time it takes to process illegal immigrants and delays in shift changes. Border Patrol Agents work rotating shifts, some of which take place at night, on weekends, and on holidays.

While other law enforcement officers, such as police officers, work in pairs, Border Patrol Agents usually work alone. This is one element that makes the job potentially so dangerous. Armed with only a .40 caliber pistol and optional long arms, agents must face drug smugglers and gang members. Because they work in remote locations, it is difficult to receive backup. The position of U.S. Border Patrol Agent has become the most dangerous job in federal law enforcement. Before you apply to become a Border Patrol Agent, you should be aware of the risks.

In addition to working in harsh weather and facing danger, Border Patrol Agents must be ready for physical exertion. Keep in mind that in some places, "the border" is a barely discernable line that runs through deserts, canyons, and mountains. Patrolling the border in these areas is no easy task. A Border Patrol Agent might have to climb unstable structures, wade through water, cut through heavy brush, and even chase criminals.

NOTE

Border Patrol Agents must also complete Time and Attendance reports, which record the number of hours and days the agent has worked during a pay period.

WHERE BORDER PATROL AGENTS WORK

Border Patrol Agents are assigned to a **sector,** which is a region within the United States. Each region has a sector headquarters. Border Patrol stations within a sector communicate with the sector headquarters. For example, sectors in Texas include the Marfa Sector, the Del Rio Sector, the McAllen Sector, and the Laredo Sector. The Marfa Sector has Border Patrol Stations in Alpine, Amarillo, Big Bend, Marfa, Pecos, and in several other cities. The sector headquarters are in Marfa.

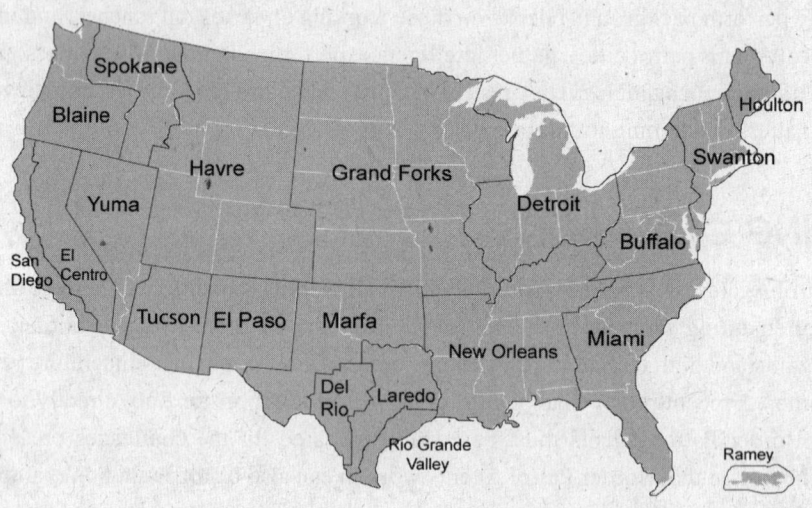

Once a Border Patrol Agent is assigned to a sector, he or she may patrol the border or work at checkpoints away from the border. As you learned, new Border Patrol Agents most often perform line watch along the Mexican border. This border is nearly 2,000 miles long and runs from San Diego, California, and Tijuana, Baja California (a state in Mexico) in the west to Matamoros, Tamaulipas, and Brownsville, Texas, in the east. This area covers a variety of terrains from harsh deserts to large cities. From the Gulf of Mexico heading west, the border follows the Rio Grande River to the border crossing at El Paso, Texas, and Ciudad Juárez, Chihuahua. While many parts of the border are marked with fencing, some parts are more difficult for agents to detect. As you learned, in other places, the Rio Grande serves as the border.

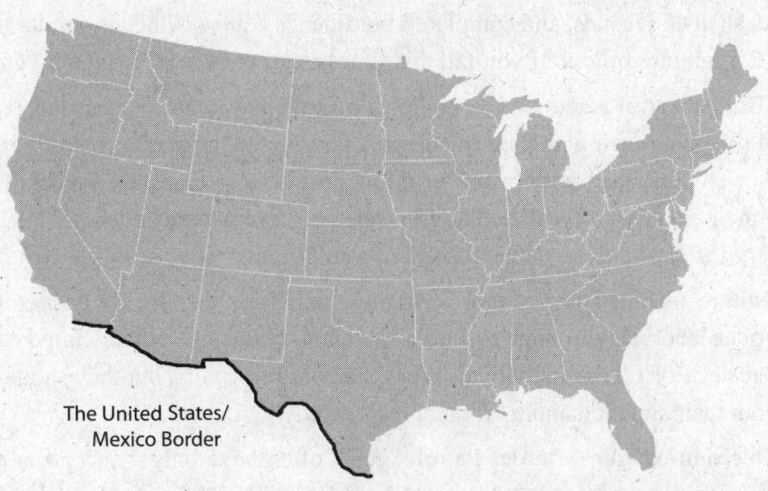

The United States/
Mexico Border

Those considering a career as a Border Patrol Agent should weigh the pros and cons of working and living near the Mexican border, especially if they have families. Most Border Patrol Agents work in New Mexico, Texas, and Arizona, and new recruits are often assigned to remote, rural areas, far from entertainment and shopping centers. The schools in these areas are usually poor, and there may be no access to health care. Employment opportunities for spouses may be scarce. Spanish may be the predominant language spoken. Other times, Border Patrol Agents are assigned to areas such as San Diego, where the cost of living is very high and the culture is very different from other areas of the country.

TRAITS OF A BORDER PATROL AGENT

It takes a special kind of person to succeed as a Border Patrol Agent. To gain employment as a Border Patrol Agent and to succeed once you are on the job, you must possess the following traits:

- **Committed**—Passing the Border Patrol exam is not easy. Only about 40 percent of those who take it pass. As you will learn in the next chapter, the higher your score, the higher your name will be placed on a hiring list, which means you will have a better chance of landing a job. You need to commit to study time. Once you get a job, you will complete fifty-five to ninety-five days of intense training at the CBP Border Patrol Academy in Artesia, New Mexico. You must be committed to make it through this training, which includes learning to speak Spanish, comprehending immigration and nationality laws, and learning how to use a firearm.

- **Physically Fit**—Border Patrol Agents must be in excellent physical condition to perform their jobs effectively. They spend much of their day on foot and may have to make their way across difficult terrain. Being physically fit also makes it easier to apprehend violators of immigration and nationality laws. Furthermore, to become a Border Patrol Agent, you must pass an initial fitness test plus a second physical fitness test just prior to entering on duty. The first timed test requires you to do push-ups, do sit-ups, and climb steps. The second test includes a 220-yard sprint, push-ups, sit-ups, and a 1.5-mile run. At the CBP Border Patrol Academy, you will undergo another fitness test. For this test, you must run 1.5 miles in 13 minutes or less, run a

220-yard dash in 46 seconds, and complete a confidence course, which is similar to an obstacle course, in 2.5 minutes or less. If you fail this fitness test, you are allowed only one more try.

- **Honest**—Border Patrol Agents often apprehend drugs and other contraband. They must be honest and follow through with their intentions of turning their findings over to the authorities. They cannot be persuaded with bribes or allow criminals to cross the border. They must be faithful to their country and realize that drug seizures save American lives. This is one reason why military veterans make excellent Border Patrol Agents.

- **Compassionate**—While some of those crossing the border illegally are dangerous criminals, many are poor laborers who hope to find a job and a better life in the United States. Border Patrol Agents can't let these individuals cross the border illegally, but they should be compassionate about their situation and treat them respectfully.

- **A Good Decision-Maker**—Border Patrol Agents often have only a second or two to make a decision, so they must have good decision-making skills. They need to apply the laws and regulations they learned at the CBP Border Patrol Academy. They may even have to defend their actions during court proceedings.

- **Flexible**—Border Patrol Agents perform many duties and often receive short notice for temporary assignments. They must be flexible and willing to shift from one task to another. Border Patrol Agents also work rotating shifts, so they must be willing to work whenever they are needed.

- **Tough**—How would you like to work long hours in the hot sun or pouring rain? Border Patrol Agents work outdoors in all kinds of weather. They must be tough enough to endure such conditions.

- **Brave**—Border Patrol Agents bravely serve their country by protecting its borders. They are often thrust into dangerous situations, such as confronting Mexican drug cartels with access to assault weapons. Many Border Patrol Agents have been killed or wounded.

- **A Good Communicator**—In addition to observing those individuals crossing the border, Border Patrol Agents must question them, so they must have good oral communication skills. They must also complete written reports, so good written communication skills are a plus.

REQUIREMENTS

The Bureau of Customs and Border Protection (CBP) has a list of qualifications or requirements individuals must meet to become Border Patrol Agents. Following is a summary of this list.

General Qualifications

- You must be a U.S. citizen.
- You must possess a valid driver's license.
- You must pass a urine drug test.
- You must be younger than 40 at the time of selection. This limitation is sometimes waived for applicants who are presently in a federal civilian law enforcement position or who have held such positions in the past:

- You must have experience in a job that requires you to take charge, make decisions, and maintain composure in stressful situation. This job does not have to have been in law enforcement.

- You should have either a 4-year college degree or enough education and experience to show that you can make decisions under stressful situations. Your degree may be in any field.

- You should be fluent in Spanish or have the ability to learn the Spanish language.

- You must be willing to carry and use a firearm.

- You must pass a written examination containing three parts: Logical Reasoning Test, Spanish Language Proficiency Test, and Artificial Language Test. You will take either the Spanish Language Proficiency Test or the Artificial Language Test. If you are proficient in Spanish, you should take the Spanish Language Proficiency Test. If not, take the Artificial Language Test, which measures your capacity to master the Spanish language.

Medical Requirements

Because Border Patrol Agents undergo physical exertion and endure extreme weather conditions, they must meet specific medical requirements.

Fitness/Physical Requirements

To become a Border Patrol Agent, you must be able to perform the following physical requirements:

- Run long distances
- Swim, spring, climb walls, ropes, and ladders
- Crawl through a simulated culvert, or drain
- Jump ditches
- Stand and stoop for long periods of time

Vision Requirements

You must meet these requirements in terms of vision:

- Your uncorrected distance vision must be equal to or better than 20/100 in each eye.
- Your binocular distant vision must be correctable to 20/20.
- Your depth perception must be equal to or better than 70 seconds of arc.
- You must have normal peripheral vision.
- You must have normal color vision.
- You can't have monocular vision or any other disease that interferes with vision.
- If you have undergone refractive surgery, such as LASIK, your post-surgery vision must meet the above requirements.

NOTE

The Border Patrol recently increased the maximum age of new recruits from 37 to 40, but this could change at any time.

NOTE

The Border Patrol will also review all medications you take to ensure that they will not adversely affect your safety or job performance.

Hearing Requirements

According to the CBP, your unaided hearing deficit can't exceed 30 dB at the 500 Hz, 1,000 Hz, and 2,000 Hz frequencies. At 3,000 Hz, the deficit in each ear should not exceed 40 decibels. You can't use a hearing aid to meet these medical standards.

Speech Requirements

You will be disqualified if you have a disease or a condition that interferes with your speech or breathing; however, this is reviewed on a case-by-case basis.

Respiratory System Requirements

You will be disqualified if you have a disease or a condition that interferes with respiratory function, though respiratory system requirements are also reviewed on a case-by-case basis. If you have asthma controlled by medication, you will likely be disqualified.

Cardiovascular System Requirements

You will be disqualified if you have a disease or condition that interferes with cardiac function, such as, coronary artery disease, a history of myocardial infarction, cardiomyopathy, or congestive heart failure. You will also be disqualified if you wear a pacemaker or have a prosthetic valve. Very high blood pressure might also result in disqualification.

Psychiatric Requirements

You may be disqualified if you have any of the following:
- Major depression
- Anxiety disorder
- Schizophrenia
- A personality disorder such as paranoia

Musculoskeletal Requirements

Any medical condition that interferes with movement may be a disqualification. This includes, but isn't limited to, the following:
- Arthritis that limits joint motion and/or causes pain
- Amputations of an extremity
- Degenerative disk disease
- Fractures that limit movement
- Chronic back pain

The following limitations will be reviewed on a case-by-case basis:

- Prosthetic devices
- Fewer than five fingers on each hand

Endocrine and Metabolic System Requirements

Most conditions affecting normal hormonal/metabolic functioning are reviewed on a case-by-case basis. They include, but are not limited to, the following:

- Insulin-dependent diabetes mellitus
- Adrenal dysfunction
- Thyroid disease
- Hyperglycemia

Gastrointestinal System Requirements

Some gastrointestinal disorders might make an individual suddenly incapacitated and unable to work. Because Border Patrol Agents face danger, these might be grounds for disqualification. These disorders include the following:

- Chronic diarrhea
- Crohn's disease/ulcerative colitis
- Irritable bowel syndrome
- A colostomy
- Chronic or recurrent ileitis

Other Medical Disqualifications

Disorders of the blood, such as hemophilia and anemia, may be grounds for disqualification if they interfere with an individual's ability to perform his or her job.

AUTOMATIC DISQUALIFICATIONS

You will be automatically disqualified during the selection process if you have been convicted of a misdemeanor crime of domestic violence, because it is then illegal for you to possess a firearm or ammunition. Other reasons for disqualification are:

- A poor driving record
- A poor employment record
- Excessive alcohol consumption
- Use of illegal drugs
- Sale or distribution of illegal drugs

NOTE

The use of anabolic steroids is prohibited by the Border Patrol and may lead to disqualification.

- An arrest record
- Excessive debt or serious financial problems

CBP CONDITIONS OF EMPLOYMENT

The CBP cautions that to become a Border Patrol Agent, you must be willing to do the following:

- Undergo an extensive background investigation
- Accept appointments at any location along the border
- Work rotating shifts, many at night
- Work long and irregular hours, including weekends and holidays
- Work alone
- Learn the Spanish language
- Adhere to grooming and dress standards
- Carry, maintain, and use a firearm
- Work under hazardous conditions such as inclement weather, rough terrain, heights, moving trains, high-speed chases, and armed encounters
- Operate a variety of motor vehicles
- Submit to a physical examination
- Fly as a passenger and an observer in various types of aircraft
- Maintain composure and self-control under extremely stressful conditions
- Bear initial travel and uniform costs (a uniform allowance is provided after entrance on duty)
- Undergo intensive physical and academic training, which includes 55 to 95 days of study at the CBP Border Patrol Academy, and subsequent training throughout the year
- Work on operational details away from home for extended periods of 35 days or more

SALARY

The Border Patrol bases new agents' salaries on their education and experience. Border Patrol places new hires in the GL-5, GL-7, or GL-9 pay grades. Note that GS stands for General Service pay scale, and GL stands for Law Enforcement Officer (LEO) pay scale. The GL pay scale is generally higher than the GS pay scale. The U.S. Border Patrol uses a combination of these pay scales.

GL-5

To begin at the GL-5 pay grade with an annual salary of $36,658, you must have one of the following:

- Substantial work experience in fields such as journalism, security, claims adjusting, or interviewing
- A bachelor's degree
- A combination of education and experience

GL-7

To begin at the GL-7 pay grade with an annual salary of $41,729, you must meet the GL-5 requirements and demonstrate the following abilities:

- Make arrests and exercise sound judgment when using firearms
- Deal "courteously, tactfully, and effectively" in law enforcement matters
- Quickly analyze information and act appropriately according to laws, court decisions, and law enforcement procedures
- Develop and maintain contact with a network of informants

GL-9

To begin at the GL-9 pay scale, you must meet the GL-7 requirements and demonstrate the following abilities:

- Develop cases, conduct interviews or interrogations, and make apprehensions and arrests
- Prepare cases and appear as a professional witness in court
- Exercise sound judgment using firearms and conduct training or qualifications exercises in the proper care and use of firearms
- Deal effectively with individuals in their detention, control, or interrogation, and promote community outreach and public relations
- Analyze and disseminate intelligence information and data, and apply law enforcement concepts and techniques
- Develop and maintain a network of informants, social and political organizations, local law enforcement agencies, and citizens
- Prepare legal reports and documents concerning illegal activity

Additional Information About Salary

Once Border Patrol Agents have passed the probationary exam after six and a half months of work, those hired at the GL-5 level are eligible for promotion to the GL-7 level. Likewise, those hired at the GL-7 level are eligible for promotion to the GL-9 level. Individuals hired at the GL-9 level may progress to the GS-11 level after one year at the GL-9 level. You can only progress to the GS-12 level through merit promotion competition.

Border Patrol Agents at any level may earn from 10 percent to 25 percent additional pay for overtime. They also receive night deferential pay, Sunday pay, and holiday pay.

BENEFITS

As federal employees, Border Patrol Agents receive excellent benefits. Border Patrol Agents may choose from a variety of health care plans and have sixty days to select and enroll in a plan. In addition to health care, Border Patrol Agents may choose to enroll in the following:

NOTE

Recruits receive full pay while attending the Border Patrol Academy.

- Federal Employees Group Life Insurance (FEGLI) Program
- Federal Employees Dental and Vision Insurance Program (FEDVIP)
- Federal Flexible Spending Accounts (FSAFEDS) Program
- Federal Long-Term Care Insurance Program (FLTCIP)
- SAMBA Employee Benevolent Fund (EBF)
- Thrift Savings Plan (TSP)

New employees also receive a $1,500 uniform allowance in the form of credits while at the Border Patrol Academy. Border Patrol Agents also receive free lodging and meals at the Border Patrol Academy.

Vacation Leave

Border Patrol Agents earn vacation days in proportion to their years of service, as shown here:

Less than three years of service	4 hours for every pay period
Three years of service but less than fifteen years	6 hours for every pay period
Fifteen years of service of more	8 hours for every pay period

Sick Leave

All Border Patrol Agents earn thirteen days of sick leave per year. Unused sick leave can be accumulated from year to year.

Retirement

Border Patrol Agents who have at least 20 years of service are eligible for retirement at age 50. Retirement is mandatory at age 57 with 20 years of service, but employees may work beyond age 57 if they still haven't met the requirements of service to retire.

SPECIAL OPERATIONS GROUPS

Some Border Patrol Agents join special operations groups that require specialized training. These units are made up of Border Patrol Agents who volunteer to learn skills beyond those required for regular duty and to undergo specialized training.

BORSTAR

A premier special operations group of the Bureau of Customs and Border Protection (CBP), BORSTAR teams specialize in emergency search-and-rescue missions. BORSTAR stands for Border Patrol Search, Trauma, and Rescue. These highly skilled agents travel throughout the country, sometimes rappelling out of helicopters or down cliffs and into canyons to help those in need. They ride dune buggies, ATVs, hovercrafts, and specially retrofitted hummers and work with search-and-rescue canines.

BORSTAR agents primarily rescue undocumented immigrants suffering from heat-related conditions such as heatstroke and dehydration, or cold-related conditions such as hypothermia, which can occur in individuals who become stranded in water. BORSTAR agents also rescue U.S. citizens and other Border Patrol Agents in distress.

Being on a BORSTAR team requires incredible physical exertion and dedication. BORSTAR teams work year-round throughout the United States in various climates and terrains, participating in rescues lasting up to five days. While some rescues only require an agent to locate victims and provide them with water, others require agents to travel many miles over the course of days to rescue dozens of individuals. In the hot summer months, BORSTAR teams participate in at least three rescue missions per day.

Considered the "supermen" of search and rescue, BORSTAR agents undergo intense training in physical fitness, medical skills, technical rescue, navigation, communication, swiftwater rescue, and air operations. The rigorous selection process has three phases: a physical evaluation, a field evaluation, and an oral interview. For the physical evaluation, agents must run 1.5 miles in 12 minutes or less, be able to do at least 40 push-ups and 60 sit-ups, and bench press 85 percent of their body weight. During the field evaluation, a 6- to 8-person team must successfully carry a stretcher over 4 to 5 miles of rugged terrain. Once selected, BORSTAR agents complete a 5-week training course at the BORSTAR Academy. The organization then assigns each agent a specialty and provides agents with advanced training. BORSTAR is headquartered in El Paso, Texas.

BORTAC

BORTAC is the U.S. Border Patrol Tactical Unit, the special-response team for the CBP. Its mission is to respond to terrorist threats throughout the world to keep America and its interests safe. Agents on this team are considered among the nation's most highly trained and dedicated defenders. BORTAC agents complete assignments involving counterterrorism operations, counternarcotics operations, international training and advisory functions, airmobile operations, maritime operations, and precision marksmen operations.

Unlike other special operations groups, BORTAC agents are trained both in the United States and abroad. Many full-time BORTAC agents work at the unit's headquarters in El Paso, Texas. Part-time members often work in other parts of the country and travel to various locations when the agency has need.

Following the September 11, 2001, terrorist attacks on the United States, BORTAC agents worked throughout the world to prevent future attacks. BORTAC agents also performed tactical relief operations (TRO) to help victims of Hurricane Katrina.

Becoming a BORTAC agent is not easy. The BORTAC Operator Training Course (BOTC) may last more than a month. In addition to passing the course, to become a BORTAC agent, an individual must receive a score of at least 90 percent on the Border Patrol Physical Efficient Battery (PEB) and the firearms qualification course of fire. He or she must pass an oral interview and must have served at least three continuous years as a Border Patrol Agent.

NOTE

The San Diego Sector was the first to request permission to develop a BORSTAR team in 1998.

NOTE

BORTAC teams have provided additional support to the U.S. Armed Forces in Iraq and Afghanistan.

SRT

The U.S. Special Response Team (SRT) provides immediate tactical assistance to Border Patrol Agents when the need arises. SRT members must effectively resolve a situation while reducing the risk of death or injury to those involved. They also assist law enforcement agencies at the local, state, county, and federal levels, and they frequently assist BORTAC agents with national emergencies such as Hurricane Katrina. SRTs must be ready to take action at any time. They might engage in close-quarters combat, participate in a mobile field force, offer protection to dignitaries, and serve as a precision marksman observer. They must pass an annual physical ability test and demonstrate a high level of proficiency with firearms.

To become a member of an SRT, an individual must have at least two years of continuous service as a Border Patrol Agent, must obtain a score of at least 85 percent on the Border Patrol Physical Efficiency Batter (PEB) and the firearms qualification course of fire, pass an oral interview, and successfully complete an SRT Selection Course.

AMU

Members of the Air Mobile Unit (AMU) fly helicopters and assist Border Patrol Agents in locating both undocumented immigrants and smugglers. They also assist in search-and-rescue missions. Because the pilots of helicopters have a "bird's eye view," they can often spot illegal aliens who manage to flee after being detected by Border Patrol Agents. Pilots also provide photographic evidence of criminal activity that can be used in court proceedings.

Canine Unit

NOTE

Border Patrol canines and their handlers often participate in public relations programs to help communities understand what the Border Patrol does.

The U.S. Border Patrol uses canines to help locate illegal aliens, to aid in search-and-rescue missions, and to detect illegal drugs, such as marijuana, heroin, cocaine, and methamphetamines. If you become part of a canine unit, you'll take your canine home with you when you're not working. This fosters a bond between a Border Patrol Agent and a dog. The CBP explains that some handlers become so attached to their dogs that they remain in the program until the dog retires, even if it means passing on a promotion.

Very few dogs have what it takes become a Border Patrol Canine. All dogs are imported from Europe and are either Belgian Malinois or German Dutch Shepherds. Only 1 out of every 100 dogs passes the U.S. Border Patrol selection test and is eligible for training. Border Patrol Canines are trained at the National Canine Facility in El Paso, Texas. Once they are matched with a Border Patrol Agent, canines and their handlers undergo an intensive 6-week course. Once trained, Border Patrol Canines even rappel out of helicopters with their handlers.

Horse Patrol

Horses have played an important role in the U.S. Border Patrol since its inception. A horse can travel to places that an ATV or SUV cannot—and it can often travel faster. Horses are quieter than motorized vehicles and less likely to be heard by undocumented immigrants. Agents on Horse Patrol usually travel in groups of three or four, so they share a camaraderie not enjoyed by Border Patrol Agents working alone.

Members of the Horse Patrol usually begin their day grooming their horses and inspecting them for bruises and injuries. Then they "tack up," which means they put a saddle, a bridle, and reins on their horses. Horses are driven in a trailer to a place near the border where suspected activity has taken place. Border Patrol Agents on horseback look for footprints and other signs of human activity. While interesting, riding a horse is physically demanding. Riders might spend their entire shift in the saddle, often riding in the hot sun.

Border Patrol Agents volunteer to become members of the Horse Patrol and then participate in a two-phase selection process. They will first complete an oral interview and then demonstrate their riding skills. Even those with limited experience may be selected if they demonstrate potential for learning to ride. Once selected, riders train for about 8 weeks with the CBP and then attend a riding course.

ATV Unit

ATVs are ideal for border patrol because they are fast, are unlikely to get stuck, and can access areas that SUVs cannot, such as canyons and ridges. ATVs are great for signcutting because they are low to the ground and allow Border Patrol Agents to easily spot tracks and other evidence of human activity. The sight of a Border Patrol Agent on an ATV often deters undocumented immigrants from crossing the border, as they know it will be difficult for them to escape.

To become a member of an ATV Unit, a Border Patrol Agent must complete a mandatory 2-week rider safety course. During this course, agents are taught the basics of an ATV, the principles to maintain control, and how to identify obstacles within a terrain. Agents must pass this course before they will be allowed to drive an ATV.

Other Specialized Units

The CBP has other specialized units, including:
- Marine Unit
- Bike Patrol Unit
- Infrared Scope Units
- Snowmobile Unit

ADVANCEMENT OPPORTUNITIES

Border Patrol Agents have the opportunity to earn a higher salary based on years of service and job performance. Once they reach the journeyman grade level of GS-11, they earn about $70,000 per year, including overtime, night, weekend, and holiday pay. Supervisory positions to GS-12 are available to those who qualify.

OTHER JOBS WITHIN THE DHS

The Department of Homeland Security (DHS) offers many other positions in addition to Border Patrol Agents. While some are law enforcement positions, others are non-enforcement positions. Following are descriptions of some of the many entry-level jobs within the DHS.

Law Enforcement Positions

- **Criminal Investigator (CI)**—Also called Special Agents or CIs, Criminal Investigators are involved in criminal and civil investigations, which might involve terrorism and other threats to national security. Other tasks include investigating crimes such as drug smuggling, human trafficking, illegal exportation of firearms, child exploitation, and commercial fraud.

- **Deportation Officer (DO)**—A Deportation Officer conducts legal research to support decisions regarding the deportation of individuals and assists attorneys who represent the government in such cases. With the assistance of other law enforcement officials, DOs locate and arrest undocumented immigrants and oversee their removal from the country. They also conduct investigations, perform surveillance work, and write reports.

- **Detentions and Deportation Officer (DDO)**—Detentions and Deportation Officers take criminals and illegal aliens into custody and direct, coordinate, and execute their detention and removal from the country. They also assist in criminal proceedings and advise others as to regulations and requirements for detention and deportation. DDOs might also prepare budgets.

- **Immigration Enforcement Agent (IEA)**—Like Border Patrol Agents, Immigration Enforcement Agents wear uniforms. They investigate, identify, arrest, prosecute, detain, and deport undocumented immigrants and assist in removing them to their country of citizenship.

Non-Enforcement Positions

- **Immigration Information Officer (IIO)**—An Immigration Information Officer provides the public with technical information about immigration and nationality laws and regulations. The main responsibility of all IIOs is to assist clients in completing required forms, explain which benefits are available to clients, and screen applications and petitions for completeness and authenticity. Immigration Information Officers may also compile trend reports for various law enforcement units.

- **Adjudications Officer (AO)**—Adjudications Officers use their knowledge of immigration and nationality laws and regulations to examine and rule on applications and petitions. These officers determine if an applicant is eligible for various benefits. Adjudications Officers may also conduct background investigations on applicants.

- **Asylum Officer**—Asylum Officers (also called AOs) use their knowledge of immigration and nationality laws to review and rule on applications for asylum from around the world. The United States offers asylum to certain individuals who are persecuted or fear they will be persecuted because of their race, religion, political beliefs, nationality, or social background. Asylum Officers often conduct interviews with asylum applicants, research relevant laws and country conditions, and conduct security checks when necessary. Officers also compose written reports for various agencies and provide testimony for individual cases.

FOR MORE INFORMATION

For more information about the Border Patrol, contact the U.S. Bureau of Customs and Border Protection at www.cbp.gov. You can also contact the Department of Homeland Security at www.dhs. gov. For information about job openings, you can log on to the Office of Personnel Management's Web site at www.opm.gov, or the USAJOBS Web site at www.usajobs.gov.

NOTE

The Department of Homeland Security also employs attorneys, analysts, and technicians.

SUMMING IT UP

- The Border Patrol is part of the Bureau of Customs and Border Protection (CBP), which is a branch of the Department of Homeland Security (DHS). The main goal of the CBP is to prevent terrorists and terrorist weapons from entering the country. The CBP is also responsible for enforcing trade and immigration regulations. This agency employs more than 30,000 employees who work at various points of entry across the United States.

- The Border Patrol works to prevent terrorists, illegal aliens, criminals, and contraband from entering the United States.

- Congress created the Border Patrol to control the flow of immigrants following the passage of the Immigration Act of 1924. The Border Patrol began as a branch of the Immigration Bureau. The agency had 450 inspectors working out of bases in El Paso, Texas, and Detroit, Michigan. The government expanded the program after Prohibition led to an increase in violent skirmishes between alcohol smugglers and Border Patrol Inspectors. Today, the Border Patrol employs 18,000 agents in twenty sectors across the United States and its outlying territories.

- The primary responsibility of Border Patrol Agents is to observe people crossing the border and apprehend any aliens who enter the country illegally. Agents use aircraft, electronic sensors, and specialized television systems to conduct covert surveillance of the border. Other duties include investigating signs of human activity along the border, conducting traffic and cargo inspections, and participating in search-and-rescue missions. There's no such thing as a typical day with the Border Patrol.

- Border Patrol Agents usually work outdoors under harsh environmental conditions. These agents also work by themselves in remote locations, making it difficult to call for backup in an emergency. These factors make a Border Patrol Agent's job one of the most difficult in all of federal law enforcement.

- Border Patrol Agents must be committed, physically fit, honest, compassionate, good decision-makers, flexible, brave, and tough. They must display good oral and written communications skills. To apply for the Border Patrol, a candidate must be a U.S. citizen under the age of 40 with a valid driver's license. An applicant must also have a 4-year college degree or enough educational experience to show adequate decision-making skills. Experience in a leadership position is also a positive. All Border Patrol Agents must speak Spanish, though it is not necessary to be fluent before applying for the Border Patrol.

- The Border Patrol hiring process requires applicants to pass a written exam. The exam comprises three parts: the Logical Reasoning Test, the Spanish Language Proficiency Test, and the Artificial Language Test. The Logical Reasoning Test assesses the candidate's decision-making skills. The Spanish Language Proficiency Test tells officials how well the candidate understands the Spanish language. Candidates who are not proficient in Spanish will take the Artificial Language Test, which measures a candidate's ability to learn a language. Some test questions are also designed to assess a candidate's job experience.

- Applicants who pass the Border Patrol Exam are placed on a register, which is organized in score order. The candidates who are selected for tentative employment must pass a medical exam, a fitness test, an oral interview, and an extensive background check before moving on to the Border Patrol Academy.

- The Border Patrol Academy is an intensive program where interns learn the skills needed to succeed with the Border Patrol. Interns spend 55 days taking courses in police science, weapons handling, anti-terrorism training, and driving techniques. Interns who do not know Spanish spend an additional 40 days at the academy in an intense language course.

- The Border Patrol offers a competitive salary and benefits package, which includes sick leave, vacation, medical insurance, and retirement packages. All new agents start out at either the GL-5 or GL-7—and in certain exceptional cases, GL-9—pay levels. After normal intervals, employees who pass probationary exams and demonstrate exceptional skills on the job may qualify for promotions to the GS-11 level. Promotions beyond this level are based on merit promotion competition.

- Border Patrol Agents have the opportunity to join special operations groups, including BORSTAR, the canine unit, and BORTAC. Other specialized units within the CBP include the Marine Unit, Bike Patrol Unit, Infrared Scope Units, and Snowmobile Unit.

- Many positions within the Department of Homeland Security are available to Border Patrol Agents. Those interested in law enforcement positions may apply for jobs as Criminal Investigators, Deportation Officers, Detentions and Deportations Officers, and Immigration Enforcement Agents. Non-enforcement positions within Homeland Security include Immigration Information Officer, Adjudications Officer, and Asylum Officer.

Becoming a Border Patrol Agent

chapter 2

OVERVIEW

- Understanding the Border Patrol screening process
- The written test
- The inventory of potential candidates
- The structured oral interview
- Other tests
- Background investigation
- A job offer from the CBP
- Attending the U.S. Border Patrol Academy
- The probationary period
- Summing it up

UNDERSTANDING THE BORDER PATROL SCREENING PROCESS

Because Americans depend on Border Patrol Agents to keep them safe, only the best candidates are selected for the job. Border Patrol Agents undergo a lengthy screening process. Depending on the number of applications received and the agency's hiring needs, this screening process may take four months or an entire year. To become a Border Patrol Agent, you must complete these steps:

- Register online for the written test
- Schedule the written test
- Prepare for the written test
- Take the written test
- Wait while your name is on the inventory
- Undergo the structured oral interview
- Pass other tests, including a drug test, a medical examination, a fitness test, and a background investigation
- Receive a job offer
- Take a second physical fitness test
- Attend the U.S. Border Patrol Academy
- Complete the probationary period

THE WRITTEN TEST

Register Online

The first step to becoming a Border Patrol Agent is to register online for the written examination by accessing the Web site of the U.S. Customs and Border Patrol (CBP) (http://www.cbp.gov) and completing an application. You can register for the exam during any open hiring period. The Border Patrol only accepts applications and gives the written examination at certain times, usually when additional agents are needed. If it is not an open hiring period, you will not be able to access and complete an application. During an open hiring period, you may complete an application 24 hours a day, seven days a week.

To become a Border Patrol Agent, you must be a U.S. citizen under the age of 40 with a valid driver's license, a sufficient education or combination of education and work experience, and an adequate level of physical fitness. When you complete the online application, you will answer several questions to help CBP officials determine your suitability for a position with the Border Patrol. You must also respond to hypothetical situations that will determine your ability and willingness to perform the essential job tasks of a Border Patrol Agent.

Schedule the Written Test

When you complete an application, you will select a geographical location, a place where you would like to work if the Border Patrol offers you a job. Keep in mind, however, that the Border Patrol cannot honor every location request. Where you are stationed depends on a number of factors, including agency need and the number of applicants who have requested the same location. As a rule, the Border Patrol generally assigns new agents to the Mexican border. After you have been with the Border Patrol for several years, you may request a transfer to a sector along the northern border—but again, there is no guarantee that your request will be honored.

You will also select a date and a location to take the written examination. Try to select a location close to home. The Border Patrol will not reimburse you for travel expenses. After you register for the exam, print your test admission notice, which contains the date, location, and time of your exam. At this time, you will also receive a user ID and password that allows you to log on to the USA Test Manager Web site (http://www.usatestmanager.gov). Here, you can reprint your test admission notice, find useful study guides, and reschedule your test session, if necessary.

Prepare for the Written Test

The Border Patrol Exam has three parts: the Logical Reasoning Test, the Spanish Language Proficiency Test, and the Artificial Language Test. Note that you will take *either* the Spanish Language Proficiency Test *or* the Artificial Language Test, not both. The entire test takes about 4.5 hours to complete. You can increase your chances of doing well by studying well in advance of your test date. This book is designed to prepare you for each section of the Border Patrol Exam. The CBP Web site also has several manuals, study guides, and practice tests that you may find useful while preparing for the exam.

 www.facebook.com/borderexam

Logical Reasoning Test

The Logical Reasoning Test assesses your logic and decision-making skills and determines your ability to solve complex problems on the job. Border Patrol officials also use this test to see which applicants have the best chance of succeeding at the Border Patrol Academy. The Logical Reasoning Test is one of the most important factors in determining an applicant's suitability for a career with the Border Patrol.

This test contains sixteen questions. Each is based on a paragraph describing a hypothetical situation related to working for the Border Patrol or the federal government. Be sure to accept all information in these paragraphs as factual. Although there may be factual errors in these paragraphs, remember that you are being tested only on what you have read. The test does not assess your knowledge of Border Patrol or law enforcement. Each paragraph is followed by five answer choices, which are labeled (A) through (E).

The Logical Reasoning Test contains two types of questions. The first is a positive lead-in question. This question asks you to choose the only valid conclusion out of the five answer choices. Remember, you must base your answer only on what you have read in the paragraph. Following is an example of what a positive lead-in question looks like.

Example 1

Border Patrol Agents were led to believe that some weapons sold at a hunting store were sold illegally. Upon investigating the lead, the Border Patrol learned that all weapons made by Brown Rifle that were sold at the store were sold legally. Also, none of the illegally sold weapons were revolvers.

From the information given above, it can be validly concluded that, concerning the weapons sold at the store,

- **(A)** some of the weapons made by Brown Rifle were sold illegally.
- **(B)** none of the revolvers were made by Brown Rifle.
- **(C)** all of the revolvers were made by Brown Rifle.
- **(D)** all of the revolvers were sold legally.
- **(E)** some of the weapons made by Brown Rifle were revolvers.

This is the only conclusion you can make based on the information in the paragraph. Since the paragraph says that none of the illegally sold weapons were revolvers, the revolvers were sold legally. Choice (A) is incorrect because the paragraph says that all weapons made by Brown Rifle were sold legally. The paragraph does not contain enough information to conclude that Brown Rifle does not make revolvers, so choice (B) is incorrect. It also does not provide enough information to conclude that all revolvers were made by Brown Rifle, so choice (C) is incorrect. The paragraph does not indicate if Brown Rifle makes revolvers, so choice (E) is incorrect. **The correct answer is choice (D).**

The second type of question is a negative lead-in question. This question asks you to choose the only invalid conclusion out of the five answer choices. The following is an example of a negative lead-in question.

Example 2

Forty-two Border Patrol Agents patrol the border in a certain sector in Arizona. Of these, half patrol on ATVs. Some of those who patrol on ATVs also patrol in SUVs. Eight of the Border Patrol Agents patrol only on foot. All Border Patrol Agents who drive ATVs have received special training.

From the information given above, it CANNOT be validly concluded that

    (A) some Border Patrol Agents in this sector patrol in SUVs.

    (B) some Border Patrol Agents in this sector patrol only on foot.

    (C) all Border Patrol Agents in this sector have received special training.

    (D) all Border Patrol Agents in this sector work in Nevada.

    (E) some of the Border Patrol Agents who drive SUVs have received special training.

This question asks you to choose the answer choice that *cannot* be concluded based on the information in the paragraph. Because some of the Border Patrol Agents in this sector patrol in SUVs, choice (A) is true and therefore not the correct answer. Eight Border Patrol Agents in this sector patrol only on foot, so choice (B) is also not a correct choice. The paragraph says that Border Patrol Agents who drive ATVs have received special training, but only some agents drive ATVs, so choice (C) is correct. Choice (D) only states a fact in the paragraph: All Border Patrol Agents in this sector work in Arizona. Therefore, this is not the correct answer choice. Since Border Patrol Agents who drive ATVs have received special training and some of these agents also patrol in SUVs, some drivers of SUVs have received special training. So, the statement in choice (E) is true and therefore not the correct answer. **The correct answer is choice (C).**

You will learn more about Logical Reasoning Test questions in Chapter 4.

Spanish Language Proficiency Test

Only take the Spanish
Language Proficiency
Test if you are sure that
you are fluent in the
language because
this test is difficult.

All Border Patrol Agents must know the Spanish language. This, however, is no reason to panic. If you cannot read and speak Spanish fluently, you will take the Artificial Language Test instead of the Spanish Language Proficiency Test and learn the language at the U.S. Border Patrol Academy. The Spanish Language Proficiency Test has two parts: vocabulary and grammar. All questions are multiple-choice, with either four or five answer choices.

Following is a sample vocabulary question.

Example 1

In the question below, indicate which answer most closely relates to the underlined word.

Eran como las tres de la tarde y nos <u>disponíamos</u> a regresar.

    (A) rehusábamos

    (B) demorábamos

    (C) dispersábamos

    (D) preparábamos

    (E) tardábamos

The word *disponer* has several meanings, but in this sentence it means to <u>be ready</u> or <u>about to</u> do something. Consequently, the best synonym is *preparábamos* ("prepared"). Choices (A) ("refused") and (C) ("scattered") are unrelated to the meaning of *disponer*. Choices (B) ("delayed") and (E) ("were late") mean the opposite of being ready or prepared. **The correct answer is choice (D).**

Here is a sample grammar question.

Example 2

Read each sentence carefully. Select the one sentence that is correct.

    (A) La misión de los agentes fronterizos es proteger nuestro país y defenderlo.

    (B) El misión de los agentes fronterizos es para proteger nuestro país y para defender.

    (C) La misión de los frontera agentes es a proteger nuestro país ya defenderlo.

    (D) La misión es proteger y defenderlo los agentes de nuestro país fronterizo.

This sentence has the proper sentence structure and contains no errors. Choices (B), (C), and (D) contain various errors, including illogical structures, misplaced clauses, improper articles, and incorrect prepositions. Hence, none of these choices can be the correct answer. **The correct answer is choice (A).**

You will learn more about the Spanish Language Proficiency Test in Chapter 5.

Artificial Language Test

If you do not know the Spanish language, or you cannot yet speak and read Spanish well, take the Artificial Language Test, which predicts your ability to learn the Spanish language. This test contains fifty multiple-choice questions. The artificial language—the make-believe language in this test—has grammatical rules that are similar to those in the Spanish language. If you take this test, you will receive a vocabulary list, a list of grammatical rules, and a glossary of grammatical terms that you may refer to during the test. It is a good idea to study these materials well in advance of taking the exam. If you do this, you will be able to complete the test questions quickly and more accurately, and you will have time to check your work before the exam ends. A question on the Artificial Language Test might look like this:

Example 1

Sentence	Translation
1. The inspector skillfully drove the jeep.	Wire <u>zell</u> janlek <u>arzotem</u> wir <u>daqlek.</u> 1 2 3

    Mark:

    (A) if <u>only</u> the word numbered 1 is correctly translated

    (B) if <u>only</u> the word numbered 2 is correctly translated

    (C) if <u>only</u> the word numbered 3 is correctly translated

    (D) if <u>two</u> or <u>more</u> of the numbered words are correctly translated

    (E) if <u>none</u> of the numbered words is correctly translated

You will learn more about the Artificial Language Test and strategies for answering the questions in Chapter 6. Once you have reviewed Chapter 6, you will know that in the example above, the word numbered 1 is translated incorrectly. **The correct answer is choice (D).**

Take the Written Test

You must pass the written exam with a minimum score of 70 percent. Although this may seem daunting, you will increase your chances of success by remaining calm. If you feel nervous during the exam, take a few deep breaths and try to relax. This will help you maintain your composure. Use the following test-taking tips to help you on the day of the exam:

- Read all directions carefully before you begin the test.
- Read the entire question and all response options before choosing a final answer.
- There is no penalty for guessing. Your score is based only on the number of questions you answer correctly. Therefore, respond to every question, even if you are unsure of the correct answer.
- If you do not know the answer, eliminate obviously wrong answer choices before choosing an answer. This increases your chances of choosing the correct answer.
- Mark your answers clearly on the answer sheet. If you change an answer, erase your first response completely before entering a new answer.
- Do not assume that there is a pattern to the letters on your answer sheet. You may have several As or Bs in a row. Do not use these letters as a strategy to determine the next answer.
- Answer the easy questions first and come back to the difficult questions later.
- If you finish before time is up, go back and check your answers.
- Periodically check to be certain you are on the correct answer sheet number.

THE INVENTORY OF POTENTIAL CANDIDATES

About four to six weeks after you take the exam, you will receive a Notice of Results (NOR) in the mail. If you do not pass the exam, you will be restricted from retaking it for one year. After a year, you may retest during another open hiring period. If you pass the exam, the Border Patrol will place your name on an inventory of potential candidates. The inventory is arranged in score order, so the higher you score, the better your chance is of receiving a job offer. Those with honorable records with the U.S. military during certain timeframes receive extra points for their service. These extra points are called veterans preference points.

Passing the written exam does not guarantee you a job with the Border Patrol. Selection also depends on other factors, such as a review of your initial application.

If the Border Patrol does not select you during this hiring period, your test results are good for one year. You may reapply during another open hiring period using the same test results. If the Border Patrol selects you, you will receive a tentative selection package in the mail. This package includes information about scheduling appointments for the oral interview, the medical examination, the fitness test, and other important meetings. You will also receive several forms that you must complete and send back to the Office of Personnel Management (OPM).

THE STRUCTURED ORAL INTERVIEW

If you receive a tentative offer of employment, you must complete a structured oral interview. This interview is conducted by three Border Patrol Agents. These agents, who are called the oral board, will ask you a series of situational questions designed to assess your judgment skills, decision-making skills, willingness to work with others, emotional maturity, and compassion—qualities the Border Patrol looks for in its agents. The oral board rates you on a pass-fail basis. You have to pass to continue in the hiring process.

TIP

Try to leave for your interview as early as possible to ensure you get there on time.

OTHER TESTS

After passing the oral interview, you must complete a drug test, a medical examination, and a fitness test. The Border Patrol will also thoroughly investigate your background.

Drug Test

In 1986, Executive Order 12564 established the drug-free federal workplace. This made it an actionable offense for a federal employee to use illegal and illicit drugs, whether on or off duty. Since Border Patrol Agents are federal employees, you must take and pass a drug test. The agency can administer the drug test at any point during the screening process. If you fail the drug test, you will likely be disqualified from the Border Patrol and any other job with the federal government.

Medical Examination

As you learned in Chapter 1, certain medical conditions can disqualify you from working for the Border Patrol. You must complete the medical examination to determine if you are physically capable of performing the duties of a Border Patrol Agent. About two weeks after receiving your tentative selection package, Comprehensive Health Services (CHS) will contact you to arrange the medical examination. CHS will make every attempt to schedule the exam at a clinic close to your home. Before your scheduled exam, the Border Patrol will ask you to complete a detailed medical history. The medical examination itself includes an electrocardiogram (EKG), a vision test, a hearing test, and a physical examination.

Following your medical exam, CHS will contact you about any health issues that may disqualify you from working as a Border Patrol Agent. You will have the opportunity to provide the CHS with medical evidence and records needed to clarify any issues. CHS uses this information to determine if you are able to perform the duties of a Border Patrol Agent safely.

NOTE

The Border Patrol will not accept medical examinations conducted by personal physicians.

Fitness Test

The job of a Border Patrol Agent is physically demanding. To ensure that you are up to the task, you must take and pass a pre-employment fitness test. This test is administered on the same day and at the same location as the medical examination. The Border Patrol will not accept fitness tests conducted by outside organizations.

On the day of the medical examination and fitness test, wear or bring clothing that you would normally wear to work out. The Border Patrol recommends that you bring shorts or sweatpants, a T-shirt, athletic shoes, and sweat socks. You may also bring any athletic braces that you regularly use, such as a back or knee brace. Bring documentation of any medical condition that could hinder your physical performance, so the examining physician can determine if you are capable of taking the test. Staying hydrated is important, so remember to bring a bottle of water.

The fitness test has three parts: a push-up test, a sit-up test, and a cardiovascular step test. You must take and pass all three parts of the exam. You will be given a 3-minute break between each test, during which the administrator will provide directions for the next test. Failure to complete any part of the fitness test results in an immediate end to the test. Failing the test voids your conditional offer of employment with the Border Patrol. While you are not allowed to retest if you fail, you can improve your level of fitness and reapply during future open hiring periods.

Push-Up Test

NOTE

Rest between push-ups, if necessary, must be taken in the up position.

The push-up test is a timed test requiring you to do 20 proper-form push-ups in 60 seconds. You must start in the up position. The test administrator will place an 8-inch foam block directly under your sternum (breastbone). When the administrator tells you to start, drop down until your chest touches the block, and then push up until your elbows are straight. This completes one push-up.

The test administrator will assess your form. Your push-ups will not count if you spread your feet too far apart, raise your buttocks, or allow your back to sag. You must perform each push-up with your back and buttocks in a straight line and your feet close together. Touching your knees to the floor at any time will end the test and result in a failure. When the administrator confirms that you have done 20 proper-form push-ups, you will have passed this part of the fitness test.

Sit-Up Test

The sit-up test is a timed test requiring you to do 25 correct-form sit-ups in 60 seconds. You will start in the down position with your back on the floor and your knees at a 90-degree angle. Your hands should be behind your head, cupping your ears. When the test administrator tells you to start, contract your abdominal muscles to pull your upper body off the floor until your elbows touch your knees or upper thighs. Return to the starting position. This completes one sit-up.

The administrator will assess your form during the test. Raised buttocks are a sign of improper form. Improper sit-ups do not count. You will fail the test if you stop before the administrator counts to 25. The test ends when the administrator counts 25 correct-form sit-ups. Then, you will have passed this part of the fitness test.

Cardiovascular Step Test

The cardiovascular step test measures endurance. To complete this test, you will step on and off a bench for 5 minutes with no rest. You are allowed to practice before the test begins.

The test administrator will play an audio tape to help you keep your rhythm during the test. The test requires you to step up with your left leg, up with your right leg, down with your left leg, and down with your right leg. You must maintain this cadence (up, up, down, down) for more than six consecutive sequences to pass the test. You should only stop when instructed to do so by the administrator or the audio tape.

If you stop before the administrator or audio tape tells you to, fail to maintain the stepping cadence, or use your arms to assist you in stepping up, you will fail the test.

If you feel that your level of physical fitness needs improvement, consult with your physician about starting or intensifying your workout program, which should include aerobic exercise, strength training, core exercises, and stretching. Remember to get enough rest before your fitness test. You should also drink water before, during, and after your workout.

NOTE

In January 2010, the Border Patrol raised the height of the bench used for the step test from 12 inches to 14 inches.

BACKGROUND INVESTIGATION

CBP thoroughly investigates the background of all Border Patrol candidates to ensure that they are reliable, trustworthy, of good moral character, and loyal to the United States. Evidence to the contrary may disqualify you from future employment in any occupation with the federal government.

Expect the CBP to investigate your citizenship, place of birth, education, military history, and employment history. Investigators will also perform credit checks to verify that you do not have debt problems and that you pay your bills on time. The CBP checks public records for evidence of arrests, criminal or civil lawsuits, and bankruptcies. The CBP may interview your family, spouse (current or former), and former employers. The agency interviews such individuals to compile a profile of your character. The CBP may also interview your friends, coworkers, and neighbors to resolve any discrepancies that have arisen during the investigations. All candidates are also subject to interviews with CBP investigators at any time during the process.

NOTE

All applicants, including those who have been employed by the federal government in the past, must successfully pass the background check to continue in the hiring process.

Once the investigators gather all pertinent information, they pass this information on to CBP Internal Security for the adjudication process. During this process, the adjudicators examine all evidence to determine whether a candidate is suitable for employment with the Border Patrol. A poor credit score, a criminal record, a history of drug use, and an association with inappropriate individuals may make you unsuitable for employment. After the investigators complete the adjudication process, they will inform you of the results. Some applicants might receive an NOPA (Notice of Proposed Action). This is a notification that something negative has come up during the adjudication process. These applicants will not be hired unless they can provide information that refutes the evidence against them. Other applicants may receive a message from the adjudicator stating that their case has been flagged for special attention. At this time, the adjudicator will give the applicant the opportunity to withdraw his or her application. This prevents the applicant from receiving a negative adjudication, which could cause the applicant to be barred from federal employment.

A JOB OFFER FROM THE CBP

If you pass all tests, the CBP will place your name on an inventory for a position with the Border Patrol. The agency will contact you with a firm offer of employment when a position becomes available. Keep in mind that the job offer will be at a specific duty station that may not be in your preferred geographical location. The agency does not recommend turning down your first offer of employment even if it is not in your preferred geographical location. If you are considering turning down an offer, you should know that you would have to start the hiring process over again from the beginning. Remember that a job offer does not guarantee you a job. You have two more steps to complete: (1) graduation from the Border Patrol Academy and (2) completion of a mandatory probationary period. As part of your offer, you will have to report, at your own expense, to the nearest Border Patrol Sector for a second physical fitness test, known as the PFT-2. This test consists of four timed elements. All recruits must complete a 220-yard dash in 46 seconds or less, 25 correct-form sit-ups in 1 minute or less, 20 correct-form push-ups in 1 minute or less, and a 1.5-mile run in 15 minutes or less. Border Patrol Agents will conduct the tests. If you fail any part of the tests, you will be removed from consideration and your offer will be withdrawn. Your blood pressure and pulse will be taken before you take the PFT-2. If your blood pressure is higher than 140/90 or your heart rate is greater than 100 beats per minute, you will not be permitted to take the PFT-2.

ATTENDING THE U.S. BORDER PATROL ACADEMY

In 2004, the U.S. Border Patrol Academy moved to the Federal Law Enforcement Training Center in Artesia, New Mexico. Prior to this move, Border Patrol recruits trained at various facilities in New Mexico, Texas, Alabama, Georgia, and South Carolina. The Border Patrol believes that merging these facilities allows the agency to provide Border Patrol candidates with higher-quality courses and training.

Recruits at the U.S. Border Patrol Academy undergo one of the most demanding training programs in federal law enforcement. Because of this, the academy has an unusually high dropout rate. While some recruits drop out for personal reasons, most cannot meet the high physical and academic demands of training. Only the most dedicated recruits graduate from the academy, and many of these graduates do not make it through the mandatory probationary period. You must receive a grade of 70 percent or higher in each subject to graduate from the U.S. Border Patrol Academy.

All recruits must complete 55 days of training. If you are not fluent in Spanish, you must complete an additional 40 days of language instruction. During this time, you will receive your regular salary and benefits. In addition, the Border Patrol will provide your room and board and give you a small allowance for other expenses. The academy also provides bed linens, towels, and workout uniforms. While you must pay the initial travel costs to your assigned sector, the Border Patrol will pay your travel expenses to get to the academy.

Do not bring family members with you to the academy. The Border Patrol cannot accommodate spouses, children, or other family members. The Border Patrol also recommends waiting to move to your permanent duty station until after you have completed your training. Do not bring a vehicle with you to the academy; recruits rarely have time to leave the base. You will most likely spend your free time studying, training, or resting. If you wish to explore the area during your free time, you can rent a car.

While at the academy, you will take courses in law, physical training, firearms instruction, and driver training.

Learning About the Law

The academy's law program consists of five courses: Nationality Law, Immigration Law, Applied Authority, and Operations 1 and 2. You must earn a grade of 70 percent or higher in each course to graduate from the academy.

In Nationality Law, you will learn how to determine whether a detainee is an illegal alien, a U.S. citizen, or a U.S. national. You will learn the importance of using proper questioning techniques. In Immigration Law, you will learn how to verify an alien's legal status. The course also teaches you to recognize immigration violations and explains the appropriate actions to take in various situations. In Applied Authority, you will learn how to identify violations of federal criminal statutes. Operations 1 and 2 teach you the skills and techniques you will use every day on the job. These courses include practical labs that will give you hands-on experience.

Physical Techniques

All recruits must complete the Border Patrol Academy's Physical Techniques Program. The Border Patrol designed this program to condition you to handle the daily physical demands of patrolling the border. You will learn how to overcome environmental and man-made obstacles. Most importantly, you will learn how to stay safe in dangerous situations—important instruction for a new agent.

Your instructors at the academy will try to instill in you the importance of physical fitness. Border Patrol Agents face danger; being physically fit may save your life. Your safety and the safety of those you are protecting may depend on your conditioning and stamina. This is why all agents must maintain a rigorous fitness regime even after they graduate from the academy.

Before graduation, you must pass a final physical fitness test with three timed components. You must pass all three components in one class period to pass the course. This means that you must run 1.5 miles in 13 minutes or less, complete a confidence course in 2.5 minutes or less, and run a 220-yard dash in less than 46 seconds.

Firearms Training

All trainees receive instruction in range safety, survival shooting techniques, judgment pistol shooting, quick point shooting, and instinctive reaction shooting. You will train both in the classroom and on the firing range. You will learn how to handle the Heckler and Koch P2000 handgun, the Remington 870 shotgun, and the Colt Arms M4 carbine rifle.

Driver Training

In the Driver Training Program, you will learn how to safely operate various motor vehicles. This course begins with classroom instruction in van/utility operations, skid control, and emergency response driving. After this instruction, you will receive advanced instruction in pursuit driving, low- and

TIP

It is important to arrive at the academy in good physical condition, so you should continue your training routine once you pass all of the pre-employment fitness tests.

NOTE

Do not bring your own firearm with you to the academy because it will be confiscated after your arrival on base.

high-risk vehicle stops, night driving, 4 × 4 off-road driving, and SUV/van evasive driving—all skills that you will use to stay safe when you begin working as a Border Patrol Agent.

Spanish Task-Based Language Training (TBLT) Program

An estimated 90 percent of all illegal aliens who cross the U.S. border speak only Spanish. Because of this, Border Patrol recruits must become fluent in Spanish. Shortly after arriving at the U.S. Border Patrol Academy, you will take a test that measures your Spanish-language abilities. If you pass this test, you will report to your permanent duty stations after graduation. If you fail, you will remain at the academy to complete the Spanish Task-Based Language Training (TBLT) Program. The Spanish TBLT is an intensive training program that focuses on the words, phrases, and expressions that Border Patrol Agents must understand to perform their jobs successfully.

Spanish experts have developed a rigorous course that employs creative methods to help new agents understand and speak the language in a short time. The course immerses you in the law enforcement-specific words and phrases that you will frequently use on the job. You must pass this course before you can move on to your permanent duty station.

THE PROBATIONARY PERIOD

New agent training continues long after graduation from the U.S. Border Patrol Academy. After you arrive at your permanent duty station, the Border Patrol will assign you to a training unit. You will continue training in the classroom, but you will also train in the field. During this time, trainees must pass a series of tests to secure permanent employment after the probationary period.

While completing your probationary period, limit your use of vacation time and focus your energy on your job. This will show your supervisors that you are committed to completing your training. Once you complete the probationary period, you will be eligible for permanent employment with the Border Patrol.

SUMMING IT UP

- Because the job of Border Patrol Agent is important, candidates are carefully screened. This screening process may last a year and includes these steps: registering online for the written test during an open hiring period; scheduling the written test online; preparing for the written test; taking the written test; waiting while your name is on an inventory; undergoing a structured oral interview; and passing other tests, such as a drug test, a medical examination, a fitness test, and a background investigation.

- The written test has three parts: the Logical Reasoning Test, the Spanish Language Proficiency Test, and the Artificial Language Test. For each question on the Logical Reasoning Test, you will read a short paragraph describing a scenario and choose the best conclusion based on the information in this scenario. If you can speak and read Spanish well, you will take the Spanish Language Proficiency Test. If you are not fluent in Spanish, you will take the Artificial Language Test. For this test, you will learn a make-believe language with a grammatical structure that is similar to Spanish. Then, you will choose the answer choice that uses this language correctly.

- After taking and passing the written examination, the Border Patrol places candidates on a score-ordered inventory for potential employment. The higher your score, the better your chances of receiving a job offer.

- If the Border Patrol is interested in you, someone will contact you and schedule an oral interview. This interview is conducted by three Border Patrol Agents who will ask you situational questions designed to assess your judgment and decision-making skills. You must pass this interview to continue with the selection process.

- Once you receive a tentative offer of employment, you must complete a medical exam and fitness test on the same day. The Border Patrol can administer a random drug test at any point during the pre-employment period. Failing any of these tests will result in the termination of your tentative employment agreement.

- The background investigation examines every aspect of your life. The investigators will interview your friends, family members, and coworkers to determine if you meet the moral and ethical standards of the Border Patrol.

- After receiving a firm offer of employment, you will train at the U.S. Border Patrol Academy. The training program at this academy is rigorous. You will study and undergo physical training for 55 days. If you do not understand the Spanish language, you will stay an additional 40 days for the Spanish Task-Based Language Training (TBLT) Program. You must graduate from the academy to keep your position within the Border Patrol.

- All new agents must complete a probationary period to be eligible for permanent employment with the Border Patrol.

PART II

DIAGNOSING STRENGTHS AND WEAKNESSES

ANSWER SHEET PRACTICE TEST 1: DIAGNOSTIC

Logical Reasoning

1. Ⓐ Ⓑ Ⓒ Ⓓ Ⓔ   5. Ⓐ Ⓑ Ⓒ Ⓓ Ⓔ   8. Ⓐ Ⓑ Ⓒ Ⓓ Ⓔ   11. Ⓐ Ⓑ Ⓒ Ⓓ Ⓔ   14. Ⓐ Ⓑ Ⓒ Ⓓ Ⓔ

2. Ⓐ Ⓑ Ⓒ Ⓓ Ⓔ   6. Ⓐ Ⓑ Ⓒ Ⓓ Ⓔ   9. Ⓐ Ⓑ Ⓒ Ⓓ Ⓔ   12. Ⓐ Ⓑ Ⓒ Ⓓ Ⓔ   15. Ⓐ Ⓑ Ⓒ Ⓓ Ⓔ

3. Ⓐ Ⓑ Ⓒ Ⓓ Ⓔ   7. Ⓐ Ⓑ Ⓒ Ⓓ Ⓔ   10. Ⓐ Ⓑ Ⓒ Ⓓ Ⓔ   13. Ⓐ Ⓑ Ⓒ Ⓓ Ⓔ   16. Ⓐ Ⓑ Ⓒ Ⓓ Ⓔ

4. Ⓐ Ⓑ Ⓒ Ⓓ Ⓔ

Spanish Language Proficiency

Part I

1. Ⓐ Ⓑ Ⓒ Ⓓ Ⓔ   5. Ⓐ Ⓑ Ⓒ Ⓓ Ⓔ   9. Ⓐ Ⓑ Ⓒ Ⓓ Ⓔ   13. Ⓐ Ⓑ Ⓒ Ⓓ Ⓔ   17. Ⓐ Ⓑ Ⓒ Ⓓ Ⓔ

2. Ⓐ Ⓑ Ⓒ Ⓓ Ⓔ   6. Ⓐ Ⓑ Ⓒ Ⓓ Ⓔ   10. Ⓐ Ⓑ Ⓒ Ⓓ Ⓔ   14. Ⓐ Ⓑ Ⓒ Ⓓ Ⓔ   18. Ⓐ Ⓑ Ⓒ Ⓓ Ⓔ

3. Ⓐ Ⓑ Ⓒ Ⓓ Ⓔ   7. Ⓐ Ⓑ Ⓒ Ⓓ Ⓔ   11. Ⓐ Ⓑ Ⓒ Ⓓ Ⓔ   15. Ⓐ Ⓑ Ⓒ Ⓓ Ⓔ   19. Ⓐ Ⓑ Ⓒ Ⓓ Ⓔ

4. Ⓐ Ⓑ Ⓒ Ⓓ Ⓔ   8. Ⓐ Ⓑ Ⓒ Ⓓ Ⓔ   12. Ⓐ Ⓑ Ⓒ Ⓓ Ⓔ   16. Ⓐ Ⓑ Ⓒ Ⓓ Ⓔ   20. Ⓐ Ⓑ Ⓒ Ⓓ Ⓔ

Part II Section I

1. Ⓐ Ⓑ Ⓒ Ⓓ Ⓔ   3. Ⓐ Ⓑ Ⓒ Ⓓ Ⓔ   5. Ⓐ Ⓑ Ⓒ Ⓓ Ⓔ   6. Ⓐ Ⓑ Ⓒ Ⓓ Ⓔ   7. Ⓐ Ⓑ Ⓒ Ⓓ Ⓔ

2. Ⓐ Ⓑ Ⓒ Ⓓ Ⓔ   4. Ⓐ Ⓑ Ⓒ Ⓓ Ⓔ

Part II Section II

1. Ⓐ Ⓑ Ⓒ Ⓓ   3. Ⓐ Ⓑ Ⓒ Ⓓ   5. Ⓐ Ⓑ Ⓒ Ⓓ   6. Ⓐ Ⓑ Ⓒ Ⓓ   7. Ⓐ Ⓑ Ⓒ Ⓓ

2. Ⓐ Ⓑ Ⓒ Ⓓ   4. Ⓐ Ⓑ Ⓒ Ⓓ

Part II Section III

1. Ⓐ Ⓑ Ⓒ Ⓓ Ⓔ   3. Ⓐ Ⓑ Ⓒ Ⓓ Ⓔ   5. Ⓐ Ⓑ Ⓒ Ⓓ Ⓔ   6. Ⓐ Ⓑ Ⓒ Ⓓ Ⓔ   7. Ⓐ Ⓑ Ⓒ Ⓓ Ⓔ

2. Ⓐ Ⓑ Ⓒ Ⓓ Ⓔ   4. Ⓐ Ⓑ Ⓒ Ⓓ Ⓔ

Artificial Language

Set 1

1. Ⓐ Ⓑ Ⓒ Ⓓ Ⓔ   5. Ⓐ Ⓑ Ⓒ Ⓓ Ⓔ   9. Ⓐ Ⓑ Ⓒ Ⓓ Ⓔ   13. Ⓐ Ⓑ Ⓒ Ⓓ Ⓔ   17. Ⓐ Ⓑ Ⓒ Ⓓ Ⓔ
2. Ⓐ Ⓑ Ⓒ Ⓓ Ⓔ   6. Ⓐ Ⓑ Ⓒ Ⓓ Ⓔ   10. Ⓐ Ⓑ Ⓒ Ⓓ Ⓔ   14. Ⓐ Ⓑ Ⓒ Ⓓ Ⓔ   18. Ⓐ Ⓑ Ⓒ Ⓓ Ⓔ
3. Ⓐ Ⓑ Ⓒ Ⓓ Ⓔ   7. Ⓐ Ⓑ Ⓒ Ⓓ Ⓔ   11. Ⓐ Ⓑ Ⓒ Ⓓ Ⓔ   15. Ⓐ Ⓑ Ⓒ Ⓓ Ⓔ   19. Ⓐ Ⓑ Ⓒ Ⓓ Ⓔ
4. Ⓐ Ⓑ Ⓒ Ⓓ Ⓔ   8. Ⓐ Ⓑ Ⓒ Ⓓ Ⓔ   12. Ⓐ Ⓑ Ⓒ Ⓓ Ⓔ   16. Ⓐ Ⓑ Ⓒ Ⓓ Ⓔ   20. Ⓐ Ⓑ Ⓒ Ⓓ Ⓔ

Set 2

21. Ⓐ Ⓑ Ⓒ Ⓓ Ⓔ   23. Ⓐ Ⓑ Ⓒ Ⓓ Ⓔ   25. Ⓐ Ⓑ Ⓒ Ⓓ Ⓔ   27. Ⓐ Ⓑ Ⓒ Ⓓ Ⓔ   29. Ⓐ Ⓑ Ⓒ Ⓓ Ⓔ
22. Ⓐ Ⓑ Ⓒ Ⓓ Ⓔ   24. Ⓐ Ⓑ Ⓒ Ⓓ Ⓔ   26. Ⓐ Ⓑ Ⓒ Ⓓ Ⓔ   28. Ⓐ Ⓑ Ⓒ Ⓓ Ⓔ   30. Ⓐ Ⓑ Ⓒ Ⓓ Ⓔ

Set 3

31. Ⓐ Ⓑ Ⓒ Ⓓ Ⓔ   34. Ⓐ Ⓑ Ⓒ Ⓓ Ⓔ   37. Ⓐ Ⓑ Ⓒ Ⓓ Ⓔ   39. Ⓐ Ⓑ Ⓒ Ⓓ Ⓔ   41. Ⓐ Ⓑ Ⓒ Ⓓ Ⓔ
32. Ⓐ Ⓑ Ⓒ Ⓓ Ⓔ   35. Ⓐ Ⓑ Ⓒ Ⓓ Ⓔ   38. Ⓐ Ⓑ Ⓒ Ⓓ Ⓔ   40. Ⓐ Ⓑ Ⓒ Ⓓ Ⓔ   42. Ⓐ Ⓑ Ⓒ Ⓓ Ⓔ
33. Ⓐ Ⓑ Ⓒ Ⓓ Ⓔ   36. Ⓐ Ⓑ Ⓒ Ⓓ Ⓔ

Set 4

43. Ⓐ Ⓑ Ⓒ Ⓓ Ⓔ   45. Ⓐ Ⓑ Ⓒ Ⓓ Ⓔ   47. Ⓐ Ⓑ Ⓒ Ⓓ Ⓔ   49. Ⓐ Ⓑ Ⓒ Ⓓ Ⓔ   50. Ⓐ Ⓑ Ⓒ Ⓓ Ⓔ
44. Ⓐ Ⓑ Ⓒ Ⓓ Ⓔ   46. Ⓐ Ⓑ Ⓒ Ⓓ Ⓔ   48. Ⓐ Ⓑ Ⓒ Ⓓ Ⓔ

Practice Test 1: Diagnostic

LOGICAL REASONING

Directions: In Questions 1 through 16, some questions will ask you to select the only answer that can be validly concluded from the paragraph. These questions include a paragraph followed by five answer choices. Preceding the five answer choices will be the phrase "From the information given above, it can be validly concluded that…" In other questions, you may be asked to select the only answer that **cannot** be validly concluded from the paragraph. These questions include a paragraph followed by five answer choices. Preceding the five answer choices will be the phrase "From the information given above, it **CANNOT** be validly concluded that…"

You must use only the information provided in the paragraph, without using any outside information whatsoever.

1. Karen T. was convicted of selling arms illegally to another country. She received a sentence of ten years in prison, but the President of the United States pardoned her after five years. A pardon is the forgiving of a crime and the penalty associated with it. Presidents sometimes offer pardons when they feel that individuals have fulfilled their debt to society. Karen T. claims that she is innocent and was wrongfully convicted.

    From the information given above, it can validly concluded that

    (A) if Karen T. was pardoned, she was wrongfully convicted.

    (B) if Karen T. was pardoned, she has fulfilled her debt to society.

    (C) if the President pardoned Karen T., she is innocent of the crime.

    (D) if the President did not pardon Karen T., she was wrongfully convicted of the crime.

    (E) if the President did not pardon Karen T., she would have served only five years.

2. The U.S. Federal government aims to ensure that workplaces are drug free. Federal employees in safety and security positions may be subject to random drug testing. Furthermore, if supervisors suspect that an employee is under the influence of drugs, the employee may have to undergo a drug test. Federal regulations require the owners of trucking companies to screen truck drivers for both drugs and alcohol. In addition to random drug tests, truck drivers also have to undergo random alcohol tests.

    From the information given above, it CANNOT be validly concluded that

    (A) some Federal employees must undergo random drug tests.

    (B) employees suspected of drug use may have to undergo a drug test.

    (C) all trucking companies must test drivers for drugs.

    (D) all trucking companies must test drivers for alcohol.

    (E) all Federal employees must undergo random alcohol tests.

41

3. Criminals often use underground tunnels to smuggle illegal immigrants, drugs, weapons, and even explosives across the border. Because these tunnels can begin and end anywhere, they are difficult for Border Patrol Agents to detect. The entrances and exits of tunnels might be in warehouses or under trees growing in heavy brush. The Department of Homeland Security (DHS) is developing technology to assist Border Patrol Agents in detecting tunnels. This technology will allow Border Patrol Agents to use a truck to tow a trailer containing radar antennae. These antennae will shoot a signal into the ground. When this signal appears in a certain color, such as red, Border Patrol Agents will know there is a tunnel underneath them.

From the information given above, it can validly concluded that

(A) the DHS is mainly responsible for detecting tunnels under the border.

(B) most Border Patrol Agents know when there is a tunnel underneath them.

(C) most Border Patrol Agents ride in trucks when patrolling the border.

(D) criminals most often use tunnels to smuggle drugs across the border.

(E) in the future, it will be easier for Border Patrol Agents to detect tunnels.

4. Recently, Border Patrol Agents in West Palm Beach, Florida, were contacted by the sheriff's office and asked to investigate a vessel in the mangroves of Hutchinson Island. The agents discovered 4 illegal immigrants from Haiti on the vessel and 1 illegal immigrant from the Dominican Republic. Agents seized the vessel and processed the illegal immigrants. A U.S. citizen has been charged with smuggling the 5 immigrants into the United States.

From the information given above, it can validly concluded that

(A) most illegal immigrants in Florida are Haitian or Dominican.

(B) many illegal immigrants enter the country on vessels.

(C) U.S. citizens often smuggle illegal aliens into the United States.

(D) Border Patrol Agents may work with other law enforcement personnel.

(E) Border Patrol Agents in West Palm Beach work for a sheriff.

5. All police officers in a sector in Texas are allowed to earn overtime pay if they patrol the border during their time off. Half of the police officers in this sector participate in this program. All police officers who participate in this program must complete a training course on Border Patrol. Rita K. is a police officer in this sector.

From the information given above, it can validly concluded that

(A) if Rita K. participates in this program, then she completed a special training course.

(B) if Rita K. earns overtime pay during her time off, then she patrols the border.

(C) if Rita K. patrols the border, then she works in this sector in Texas.

(D) if Rita K. is a police officer in this sector, then she is also a Border Patrol Agent.

(E) if Rita K. earns overtime pay during her time off, then she works in this sector.

6. Nearly half of Border Patrol Agents in a certain sector in California reported being shot at during the last year by members of a Mexican drug cartel. Four of these Border Patrol Agents were injured from these shots. Two Border Patrol Agents were killed from these shots. A few Border Patrol Agents in other sectors also reported being shot at by members of this cartel. Emmanuel T. is a Border Patrol Agent in this sector.

From the information given above, it can validly concluded that

(A) Border Patrol Agents in other sectors have been killed by this cartel.

(B) Emmanuel T. has been shot at by a member of this drug cartel.

(C) many Border Patrol Agents in this sector have been killed.

(D) Emmanuel T. has been injured by a member of this drug cartel.

(E) agents in this sector are at a high risk of being shot at by this cartel.

7. The government routinely pinpoints the location of criminals by obtaining logs from mobile phone companies. At present, the government does not consider this a violation of a person's right to privacy. A cell phone is a small transmitter that sends and receives signals to a cellular tower. A single tower can reveal the general direction of a phone at the time a call was made. If several towers are in an area, the exact location of a phone can be determined. The FBI recently caught a band of bank robbers by tracing the location of their cell phones at the time of the robberies.

From the information given above, it can validly concluded that

(A) if a person uses a cell phone, then the government can usually determine the person's location.

(B) if a criminal does not use a cell phone, then the criminal is not likely to get caught.

(C) if a cell phone company gives the FBI its logs, then the logs will be used to determine location.

(D) if it is possible to determine a criminal's location, then the criminal has used a cell phone.

(E) if a person does not use a cell phone, then the FBI cannot determine the person's location.

8. Most immigrants in the United States were born in Central America. According to a government survey, most of these immigrants work as machine operators or laborers. Many others work in the service, farming, and fishing industries. Very few work in managerial and professional occupations.

From the information given above, it can be validly concluded that at the time of the survey

(A) it is not the case that some managers and professionals were immigrants.

(B) most immigrants were either laborers or machine operators.

(C) none of the farmers and fishermen were immigrants.

(D) most of those not employed as laborers were immigrants.

(E) none of the managers and professionals were immigrants.

9. Recently, U.S. Customs and Border Protection officers in Laredo, Texas, intercepted two shipments of illegal drugs at the Laredo port of entry. At the World Trade Bridge, they encountered a tractor-trailer driven by a Mexican citizen who presented 12 skids of tile for inspection. Using an imaging system and a canine, the officers discovered that the skids also contained 773 bundles of marijuana. In a separate incident at the

Lincoln-Juarez International Bridge, officers inspected a pick-up truck driven by a Mexican citizen. An X-ray scan and a canine revealed that the truck contained 40 pounds of cocaine. In both cases, officers seized the vehicles and the drugs and referred the case to the Immigration and Customs Enforcement special agents for further investigation.

From the information given above, it CANNOT be validly concluded that

(A) a drug smuggler may hide drugs inside skids in a tractor-trailer.

(B) law enforcement officers refer some cases to special agents in immigration.

(C) law enforcement officers in Texas may use X-ray scans to detect drugs.

(D) most drugs are smuggled into the United States in trucks driven by Mexican citizens.

(E) law enforcement officers in Texas may use canines to help them detect drugs in vehicles.

10. Recently, Border Patrol Agents in Phoenix discovered 60 illegal immigrants in a drop house, which is temporary housing. In addition to the 60 illegal immigrants in the drop house, authorities discovered 2 smugglers who were U.S. citizens and 10 children ages 5 to 11. While most of the immigrants were from El Salvador, some were from Honduras and Guatemala. The smugglers were arrested. The illegal immigrants were taken into custody, and the children were returned to relatives in their native countries.

From the information given above, it CANNOT be validly concluded that

(A) some of the illegal immigrants were from Guatemala.

(B) none of the children was from El Salvador.

(C) all of the adult immigrants were taken into custody.

(D) none of the smugglers was an illegal immigrant.

(E) none of the children was arrested.

11. In a certain city, it is illegal for a person to operate a horse-drawn carriage without a permit. To receive a permit, an individual must complete an application at city hall. Upon receipt of the application, the chief of police and city council members will investigate the individual to ensure that he or she does not have a criminal record, is in good financial standing, is of good moral character, and has equipment that is in good working order. The individual must also plan to operate the horse-drawn carriage in an area of the city that will not obstruct the flow of traffic. Melanie K. has a permit to operate a horse-drawn carriage in the city.

From the information given above, it CANNOT be validly concluded that Melanie K.

(A) has a carriage in good working order.

(B) does not have a criminal record.

(C) knows the chief of police.

(D) does not obstruct the flow of traffic.

(E) completed an application.

12. Ricardo V. was convicted of a felony and is serving a twelve-year prison sentence. When he is released, he will likely be on parole. Ricardo V. cannot vote while he is in prison. Whether he will regain this right when he is released from prison and on parole depends upon the state in which he lives. In California, he may only vote upon completion of parole. In Indiana and Illinois, he may vote as soon as he is released from prison, regardless of whether or not he is on parole.

From the information given above, it can validly concluded that

(A) if Ricardo V. cannot vote while on parole, then he lives in California.

(B) if Ricardo V. can vote while on parole, then he does not live in California.

(C) if Ricardo V. can vote while on parole, then he lives in Indiana or Illinois.

(D) if Ricardo V. can vote when he is released from prison, then he is not on parole.

(E) if Ricardo V. cannot vote when he is released, then he is on parole.

13. Border Patrol Agents suspected that some workers in a candy factory were illegal immigrants from Mexico, Cuba, and Honduras. While the owner of the factory believed all workers were legal, upon investigation, Border Patrol Agents discovered that only some of the women from Mexico were legal, and none of the men from Cuba were legal. Half of the immigrants from Honduras were illegal. Of those who were legal immigrants, some were under the age of 16 and did not have working papers.

From the information given above, it can validly concluded that

(A) some of the female employees from Mexico were working illegally.

(B) none of the men from Mexico was working illegally.

(C) some of the illegal employees from Honduras were under 16.

(D) all of the female employees from Honduras were working legally.

(E) some of the male employees from Cuba were working legally.

14. Some individuals have multiple citizenships. This means that they are legal citizens in more than one country. While some countries allow multiple citizenships, others take measures to prevent it. China, Denmark, Japan, and Singapore require individuals to relinquish, or give up, citizenship if they voluntarily seek citizenship in another country. Elle A. is a citizen of Denmark who wants to become a citizen of the United States.

From the information given above, it can validly concluded that

(A) if Elle A. is not a citizen of Denmark, she is not a citizen of the United States.

(B) if Elle A. is a citizen of Denmark, she is also a citizen of China.

(C) if Elle A. is a citizen of Denmark, she may also become a citizen in Singapore.

(D) if Elle A. becomes a U.S. citizen, she will remain a citizen of Denmark.

(E) if Elle A. becomes a U.S. citizen, she will have to give up her citizenship in Denmark.

15. Ronald N. is a former Federal employee who was entitled to benefits under the Federal Employment Compensation Act because of a job-related injury. When an eligible Federal employee has such an injury, the benefit is determined by this test: If the beneficiary is married or has dependents, benefits are three quarters of the person's salary at the time of the injury; otherwise, benefits are set at two thirds of the salary. Ronald N.'s benefits were two thirds of his salary when he was injured.

From the information given above, it can be validly concluded that, when Ronald N. was injured, he

(A) was not married and had no dependents.

(B) was married with dependents.

(C) had never been married.

(D) was either married or had dependents.

(E) had dependents but was not married.

16. In a certain state, homicide is an act resulting in the death of an individual. Homicide may be either criminal or noncriminal. These situations are considered homicide: justifiable use of force, assisting in suicide, manslaughter, and killing an unborn child by injuring its mother. Murder is more serious than homicide because there is an intent to kill. However, the killing of an individual while committing other serious crimes may also be considered murder. These crimes include arson, burglary, kidnapping, carjacking, and terrorism. Nicholas L. has been convicted of murder in this state.

From the information given above, it can validly concluded that Nicholas L.

(A) would have been convicted of homicide in another state.

(B) was assisting in the suicide of a terminally ill person.

(C) may have committed a killing that was noncriminal.

(D) was committing burglary at the time of the killing.

(E) may have killed while committing another serious crime.

SPANISH LANGUAGE PROFICIENCY

Part I

Directions: Read the sentence and then choose the most appropriate synonym for the underlined word.

1. Los agentes tuvieron que esforzarse mucho para no <u>malograr</u> la operación.
   - (A) lograr
   - (B) estropear
   - (C) concluir
   - (D) completar
   - (E) magullar

2. Entre el <u>buzón</u> había un paquete sospechoso.
   - (A) correo
   - (B) autobús
   - (C) buzo
   - (D) bolsillo
   - (E) buceo

3. Espera mientras <u>zafo</u> estos nudos rápidamente.
   - (A) ajusto
   - (B) afirmo
   - (C) desordeno
   - (D) ato
   - (E) deshago

4. Felizmente, nos <u>concedieron</u> cinco días de plazo.
   - (A) prohibieron
   - (B) otorgaron
   - (C) ordenaron
   - (D) impidieron
   - (E) mandaron

5. Echar esa sustancia en el río puede ser muy <u>nocivo</u> para los habitantes.
   - (A) beneficioso
   - (B) perjudicial
   - (C) inocuo
   - (D) sustancial
   - (E) arroyo

6. Aquella broma me pareció muy <u>sosa</u>.
   - (A) graciosa
   - (B) inquietante
   - (C) chistosa
   - (D) de mal gusto
   - (E) insulsa

7. Pueden reconocer a la persona por la <u>gorra</u> que lleva puesto.
   - (A) gorro
   - (B) camisa
   - (C) chaleco
   - (D) gorda
   - (E) gorrión

8. ¿Conoces a los <u>hacendados</u> de esta región?
   - (A) terratenientes
   - (B) ganados
   - (C) cosechas
   - (D) habitantes
   - (E) ciudadanos

9. Creemos que la señora <u>finge</u> estar enferma.
   - (A) pretende
   - (B) simula
   - (C) dedo
   - (D) finura
   - (E) esfinge

10. ¿Han visto una <u>pareja</u> de extraños por este camino?

(A) parezca

(B) paraje

(C) oreja

(D) par

(E) parte

11. En el campamento encontramos unas <u>brasas</u> y varios implementos.

(A) toldas

(B) carbón

(C) botas

(D) linternas

(E) brazos

12. El <u>yeso</u> de los muros estaba pelado y sucio.

(A) hierro

(B) ladrillo

(C) piedra

(D) cal

(E) calcomanía

13. Ese individuo es bien conocido como un <u>matón</u>.

(A) asesino

(B) moretón

(C) pendenciero

(D) sopetón

(E) cachetón

14. Cuando el hombre me vio, se fue corriendo como una <u>flecha</u>.

(A) dardo

(B) afrecho

(C) flechar

(D) arco

(E) veloz

15. Cuando vieron a los agentes, los sospechosos se <u>escabulleron</u>.

(A) cansaron

(B) esfumaron

(C) miraron

(D) inclinaron

(E) subieron

16. Ayer les <u>devolvimos</u> las sumas sobrantes.

(A) mantuvimos

(B) reintegrar

(C) devoramos

(D) guardamos

(E) devengamos

17. Aquellas jóvenes resultaron muy <u>respondonas</u>.

(A) respuestas

(B) respetuosas

(C) deferentes

(D) calladas

(E) contestonas

18. No hay ningún personal <u>novato</u> en esta misión.

(A) curtido

(B) noveno

(C) inexperto

(D) ducho

(E) hábil

19. El hombre cargaba una especie de lanza con un <u>gancho</u> en la punta.

(A) rancho

(B) garfio

(C) ancho

(D) grato

(E) chancho

20. Ella se queja de cierto <u>malestar</u>.

(A) molestia

(B) maleza

(C) maldad

(D) malentendido

(E) comodidad

Part II

Section I

Directions: Read each sentence carefully. Select the appropriate word or phrase to fill each blank space.

1. La señora y la niña _____ ___.
   - (A) está / cansados
   - (B) están / cansada
   - (C) está / cansada
   - (D) están / cansados
   - (E) están / cansadas

2. Tomás y yo _____ mañana a las ocho _____ noche.
   - (A) Llegaremos / de la
   - (B) Llegará, para la
   - (C) Llegaré, a la
   - (D) Llegaremos / de el
   - (E) Llegan / del

3. Lupe, estos papeles son para _____ porque _____ pediste.
   - (A) usted / los
   - (B) tú / les
   - (C) contigo / las
   - (D) te / lo
   - (E) ti / los

4. Este vehículo es el _____ veloz que _____ aquí.
   - (A) muy / habemos
   - (B) mucho / han
   - (C) poco / ha
   - (D) tan / haber
   - (E) menos / hay

5. Tengo que llevar mis botas _____ _____ para que lo arregle.
   - (A) a lo / zapatador
   - (B) a la / zapatista
   - (C) al / zapatero
   - (D) a las / zapatón
   - (E) a el / zapateador

6. Siempre salimos de _____ casas _____ lunes a las siete.
   - (A) sus / las
   - (B) nuestra / la
   - (C) mi / el
   - (D) nuestras / los
   - (E) su / unos

7. Las niñas llegaron con _____ manos _____.
   - (A) las / vacías
   - (B) las /vacíos
   - (C) los / vacía
   - (D) las / vacíos
   - (E) los / vacía

Section II

Directions: Read each sentence carefully. Select the one sentence that is correct.

1. (A) Este individuo no tiene ningún elemento sospechoso en su persona.

   (B) Este individuo tiene en persona ningún elemento sospechoso.

   (C) Esta individuo tiene no elemento sospechoso en personal.

   (D) Esta persona no tiene alguno elemento individuo en persona.

2. (A) Estaba en el campo, él sintió repente enfermo.

   (B) Estando en el campo, se sintió repentinamente enfermo.

   (C) Cuando estando en el campo, sintió repentino enfermo.

   (D) Estaba en el campo, repentinamente se sintiendo enfermo.

3. (A) Ya es hora para cumplir la misión encomendada que salimos.

   (B) Ya es hora de salgamos para cumplir la misión encomendada.

   (C) Ya es hora de que cumplir salimos para la encomendada misión.

   (D) Ya es hora de que salgamos para cumplir la misión encomendada.

4. (A) La humanidad entera depende del agua para sobrevivir.

   (B) El entero humanidad depende del agua para supervivir.

   (C) Para sobrevivir, toda la humanidad depende.

   (D) Todo el humanidad dependiendo del agua para sobrevivir.

5. (A) Es preciso que terminamos estos labores antes del sol caer mañana.

   (B) Es preciso que terminemos estas labores antes de la caída del sol mañana.

   (C) Terminamos precisas estas labores antes que cayendo la sol noche.

   (D) Cuando caer el sol preciso, terminamos estas labores antes que es la noche.

6. (A) No hubieron personas suficientas de verano aquella tarde para reunir las provisiones necesarias.

   (B) No hubo personas suficientes aquella tarde de verano para reunir las provisiones necesarias.

   (C) No había suficiente persona aquella verano tarde para reuniendo las provisiones necesarias.

   (D) No eran personas suficientos aquel verano tarde para reunieron los provisiones necesarios.

7. (A) Necesitamos de informar al capitán entonces él dé las órdenes del caso.

   (B) Es necesario a informen el capitán para él poder dar las órdenes del caso.

   (C) Es necesario informar al capitán para que dé las órdenes del caso .

   (D) Es necesario informe a el capitán por que el caso da las órdenes.

Section III

Directions: Read each sentence carefully. Select the correct word or phrase to replace the underlined portions of the sentence. In those cases in which the sentence needs no correction, select answer choice (E).

1. Esa era la persona <u>que el</u> nombre yo no recordaba.
   - (A) cuya
   - (B) de ella
   - (C) cuyo
   - (D) suyo
   - (E) No es necesario hacer ninguna corrección.

2. No quiero en <u>absoluto</u> que nadie hable de este asunto.
   - (A) nada
   - (B) absolutamente
   - (C) jamás
   - (D) absoluta
   - (E) No es necesario hacer ninguna corrección.

3. Podremos salir a terminar el trabajo esta tarde aunque <u>llovizne</u>.
   - (A) lloviendo
   - (B) cayendo lluvia
   - (C) lluvia
   - (D) llovieron
   - (E) No es necesario hacer ninguna corrección.

4. ¿Tenemos los equipos necesarios para <u>recordar</u> la conversación telefónica?
   - (A) graben
   - (B) recordemos
   - (C) grabar
   - (D) grabemos
   - (E) No es necesario hacer ninguna corrección.

5. Algunos <u>son</u> demasiado cansados para seguir andando hoy.
   - (A) es
   - (B) estamos
   - (C) somos
   - (D) estando
   - (E) No es necesario hacer ninguna corrección.

6. ¿Ya <u>le</u> preguntaron a las personas de dónde vienen y cómo se llaman?
   - (A) les
   - (B) nos
   - (C) la
   - (D) las
   - (E) No es necesario hacer ninguna corrección.

7. En este recorrido hemos visitado <u>varias</u> países.
   - (A) vario
   - (B) muchas
   - (C) varios
   - (D) ningún
   - (E) No es necesario hacer ninguna corrección.

ARTIFICIAL LANGUAGE

The Vocabulary Lists

The words on the following lists are the same; they are merely arranged differently, as they would be in a bilingual dictionary. In the first list, you can look up words in English to find their equivalent word in the Artificial Language. In the second list, you can look up words in the Artificial Language to find their equivalent word in English. During the actual test, you will have the vocabulary lists with you for consultation at all times. Nonetheless, you should note that the words given below are not the same as those given in the actual test. Therefore, it is best not to try to memorize them before taking the actual test.

Word List Arranged Alphabetically by the English Word				Word List Arranged Alphabetically by the Artificial Language Word			
English	Artificial Language	English	Artificial Language	Artificial Language	English	Artificial Language	English
a, an	bex	skillful	janle	almanlek	government	kaplek	man
alien	huslek	that	velle	arker	to drive	kometlek	friend
and	loa	the	wir	avelek	enemy	lexker	to station
boy	ekaplek	this	volle	bex	a, an	liaker	to injure
country	failek	to be	synker	bonker	to guard	loa	and
difficult	glasle	to border	regker	browlek	river	mor	friend
enemy	avelek	to cross	chonker	chonker	to cross	pirker	to escape
friend	kometlek	to drive	arker	colle	legal	quea	of
from	mor	to escape	pirker	daqlek	jeep	regker	to border
government	almanlek	to guard	bonker	degker	to shoot	synker	to be
he, him	yev	to have	tulker	ekaplek	boy	tatker	to spy
jeep	daqlek	to identify	kalenker	failek	country	trenedlek	paper
legal	colle	to injure	liaker	frigker	to work	tulker	to have
loyal	inle	to inspect	zelker	glasle	difficult	velle	that
man	kaplek	to shoot	degker	huslek	alien	volle	this
of	quea	to spy	tatker	inle	loyal	wir	the
paper	trenedlek	to station	lexker	janle	skillful	yev	he, him
river	browlek	to work	frigker	kalenker	to identify	zelker	to inspect

Grammatical Rules for the Artificial Language

The grammatical rules given here are similar, but not identical, to those used in the ALT. Some of the suffixes (word endings) and prefixes (additions to the beginning of a word) used in the actual test differ from those used in the practice test.

During the actual test, you will have access to the rules at all times. Consequently, it is important that you understand these rules, but it is not necessary that you memorize them. In fact, memorizing them will hinder rather than help you, since there are differences between the rules in the version of the Artificial Language that appears here and the one that appears in the actual test.

You should note that the next part of this section contains a glossary of grammatical terms to assist you if you are not thoroughly familiar with the meaning of these grammatical terms.

Rule 1: To form the feminine singular form of a noun, a pronoun, an adjective, or an article, add the suffix nef to the masculine singular form. Only nouns, pronouns, adjectives, and articles take feminine endings in the Artificial Language. When gender is not specified, the masculine form is used.

Example: If a male eagle is a verlek, then a female eagle is a verleknef. If an ambitious man is a tosle man, an ambitious woman is a toslenef woman.

Rule 2: To form the plural of nouns, pronouns, adjectives, and articles, add the suffix oz to the correct singular form.

Example: If one male eagle is a verlek, several male eagles are verlekoz. If an ambitious woman is a toslenef woman, several ambitious women are toslenefoz women.

Rule 3: Adjectives modifying nouns and pronouns with feminine and/or plural endings must have endings that agree with the words they modify. In addition, an article (*a/an* and *the*) preceding a noun must also agree with the noun in gender and number.

Example: If an active male eagle is a sojle verlek, an active female eagle is a sojlenef verleknef and several active female eagles are sojlenefoz verleknefoz. If this male eagle is volle verlek, these female eagles are vollenefoz verleknefoz. If the male eagle is wir verlek, the female eagle is wirnef verleknef and the female eagles are wirnefoz verleknefoz. If a male eagle is bex verlek, several male eagles are bexoz verlekoz.

Rule 4: The stem of a verb is obtained by omitting the suffix ker from the infinitive form of the verb.

Example: The stem of the verb tirker is tir.

Rule 5: All subjects and their verbs must agree in number; that is, singular subjects require singular verbs and plural subjects require plural verbs. (See Rules 6 and 7.)

Rule 6: To form the present tense of a verb, add the suffix em to the stem for the singular or the suffix im to the stem for the plural.

Example: If to bark is nalker, then nalem is the present tense for the singular (the dog barks) and nalim is the present tense for the plural (the dogs bark).

Rule 7: To form the past tense of a verb, first add the suffix zot to the stem, and then add the suffix em if the verb is singular or the suffix im if it is plural.

Example: If to bark is nalker, then nalzotem is the past tense for the singular (the dog barked) and nalzotim is the past tense for the plural (the dogs barked).

Rule 8: To form the past participle of a verb, add the suffix to to the stem of the verb. It can be used to form compound tenses with the verb to have, as a predicate with the verb to be, or as an adjective.

In the last two cases, it takes masculine, feminine, singular, and plural forms in agreement with the noun to which it refers.

Example of use in a compound tense with the verb to have:

If to bark is nalker and to have is tulker, then tulem nalto is the *present perfect* for the singular (the dog has barked) and tulim nalto is the *present perfect* for the plural (the dogs have barked). Similarly, tulzotem nalto is the *past perfect* for the singular (the dog had barked) and tulzotim nalto is the *past perfect* for the plural (the dogs had barked).

Example of the use as a predicate with the verb to be:

If to adopt is rapker and to be is synker, then a boy was adopted is a ekaplek synzotem rapto and many girls were adopted is ekapleknefoz synzotim raptonefoz.

Example of use as an adjective:

If to delight is kasker then a delighted boy is a kasto ekaplek and many delighted girls are kastonefoz ekapleknefoz.

Rule 9: To form a noun from a verb, add the suffix lek to the stem of the verb.

Example: If longker is to write, then a writer is a longlek.

Rule 10: To form an adjective from a noun, substitute the suffix le for the suffix lek.

Example: If pellek is beauty, then a beautiful male eagle is a pelle verlek and a beautiful female eagle is a pellenef verleknef. (Note the feminine suffix nef.)

Rule 11: To form an adverb from an adjective, add the suffix ki to the masculine form of the adjective. (Note that adverbs do not change their form to agree in gender or number with the word they modify.)

Example: If pelle is beautiful, then beautifully is pelleki.

Rule 12: To form the possessive of a noun or pronoun, add the suffix ae to the noun or pronoun after any plural or feminine suffixes.

Example: If a boglek is a dog, then a dog's collar is a boglekae collar. If he is yev, then his book is yevae book. If she is yevnef, then her book is yevnefae book.

Rule 13: To make a word negative, add the prefix fer to the correct affirmative form.

Example: If an active male eagle is a sojle verlek, an inactive male eagle is a fersojle verlek. If the dog barks is boglek nalem, then the dog does not bark is boglek fernalem.

Glossary of Grammatical Terms

This glossary will be available to you during the actual test, but it is recommended that you study the glossary before taking the test. The glossary contains basic grammatical concepts that apply to English, Spanish, and the Artificial Language. The glossary contains fairly extensive and comprehensive explanations of each grammatical concept. **The explanations in the actual test are not comprehensive. Consequently, it is particularly important that you study these explanations very carefully.**

Article: An article is a word that precedes a noun and determines whether it is a definite or indefinite noun; for instance <u>the</u> book, <u>an</u> object.

Adjective: An adjective is a word used to modify a noun or pronoun (for example, <u>intelligent</u> women). Generally, an adjective serves to answer questions such as <u>which</u>, <u>what kind of</u>, and <u>how many</u>. For example, "<u>This</u> book" would be the adjectival answer to the question "which book?" "a <u>beautiful</u>
                    1   2
book" would be the adjectival answer to the question "what kind of book?" and "<u>several</u> days"
                                                                                                3
would be the adjectival answer to the question "how many days?"

In English, adjectives have only one form, regardless of the type of noun they modify. More specifically, whether a noun is feminine or masculine, singular or plural, the adjective used to modify it remains the same; for example, the adjective <u>strong</u> is exactly the same when it refers to one man, one woman, or many men. By contrast, in both Spanish and the Artificial Language, the ending of the adjective is different if the adjective is modifying a singular masculine noun, a singular feminine noun, a plural masculine noun, or a plural feminine noun.

Adverb: An adverb is a word used to modify a verb. For example, the sentence "It was produced" could be modified to express <u>where</u> it was produced by saying "It was produced <u>locally</u>."

Generally, an adverb is used to answer the questions <u>where</u> (as in the example above), <u>when</u> (as for example, "he comes <u>frequently</u>"), or <u>how</u> (as for example, "she thinks <u>logically</u>"). Adverbs sometimes are used to modify an adjective or another adverb. For example, in the sentence "She has a <u>really</u> beautiful mind," the adverb <u>really</u> modifies the adjective <u>beautiful</u>. In the sentence "She thinks <u>very</u> logically," the adverb <u>very</u> modifies the adverb <u>logically</u>. In the Artificial Language, the only adverbs used are those that modify verbs. In the Spanish language, as well as in the English language, adverbs are used to modify verbs, adjectives, and other adverbs.

Gender: As a grammatical concept, gender refers to the classification of words according to whether they are masculine, feminine, or neuter.

As stated above, Spanish takes masculine or feminine endings for nouns, adjectives, and articles. The neuter form is used sometimes to express abstraction in a more emphatic manner. The neuter form is <u>NOT</u> used in the Artificial Language. Consequently, it is very important for you to remember that in the Artificial Language <u>all</u> nouns, adjectives, and articles take either a masculine or a feminine ending according to whether the sentence refers to a male or female.

Also, all nouns and adjectives in the Artificial Language were conceived (for the sake of simplicity) to be masculine. Thus, unless the feminine gender is specified in the sentence, the masculine gender is used always.

Infinitive: An infinitive is the general, abstract form of a verb; for example, <u>to look</u>, <u>to think</u>, <u>to remember</u>, <u>to walk</u>. Once the action expressed by the verb is attached to a specific subject (a person, animal, or thing), then we say the verb is "conjugated," or linked to that subject; for example, "he/she thinks," "the dog runs," "the table broke."

In contrast to the way that an infinitive in English is preceded by the word "to" (as in "to think"), in the Artificial Language (and in Spanish), infinitives are defined by their suffix. In the version of the Artificial Language used here, this ending (or suffix) is ker. (In the actual test, the ending will be different.)

Noun: A noun is a word that names a person, place, thing, or abstraction; for example. Lindsay, Chicago, tree, wisdom. A noun can refer to an individual (as in Lindsay, an individual person, or Chicago, an individual place) or to a set (as in "all stones," "all trees," "all cities").

Prefix: A prefix always occurs at the beginning of a word. It can be a single letter or a sequence of letters; for example, amoral, illegal, dysfunctional.

A prefix is the opposite of a suffix, which always occurs at the end of a word, but both serve to change the basic word in some way. For example, polite is the basic word (in this case an adjective) to express the concept of behavior that conforms to accepted social norms, while adding the prefix im and creating the word impolite transforms the word polite into its contradictory concept. You should note that in the Artificial Language a prefix is used to create negative concept (see Rule 13). Such a rule mimics both Spanish and English, in both of which negation is usually expressed by using a negative prefix.

Pronoun: A pronoun is a word used in place of a noun; for example, "she" instead of "Lindsay," "they" instead of "the guards," "it" instead of "the stone," "himself/herself" instead of "the judge."

In both English and Spanish, there is a difference between a pronoun that stands for the subject of an action (as in "She threw the stone," meaning that Lindsay threw the stone), and a pronoun that stands for the object of an action (as in "The stone was thrown at her," meaning that the stone was thrown at Lindsay). By contrast, in the Artificial Language used in this manual, there is no grammatical difference between he and him, both being yev. Remember, however, that in the Artificial Language pronouns take feminine endings when the subject or object of the action is feminine. Accordingly, in the version of the Artificial Language given in this manual, both she (subject) and her (object) would be yevnef (i.e., yev plus the feminine suffix nef).

Suffix: A suffix always occurs at the end of a word. It can be a single letter or a sequence of letters, for example, creamy, readable, nicely. Unlike prefixes, suffixes often change the "part of speech" (i.e., the type of word). For example, in the case of creamy, the suffix y changes the noun cream into the adjective creamy, and in the case of nicely, the suffix ly changes the adjective nice into the adverb nicely.

In addition, suffixes are used to conjugate verbs (for example, to change the present tense into the past tense: you walk, you walked) and to create the plural form of nouns (for example, boy, boys). In Spanish, suffixes are used for the same purposes, but they are used for other purposes too, such as creating plural forms for adjectives and changing the gender of a word.

In the Artificial Language, suffixes are used (1) to change the part of speech (for example, Rule 11 uses a suffix to change an adjective into an adverb), (2) to conjugate verbs (for example, Rules 6 and 7 use suffixes to express present and past tenses), and (3) to create the plural forms of nouns, pronouns, adjectives, and articles (Rule 2). In addition, the Artificial Language mimics Spanish in using a suffix to express gender.

You should study all the rules on suffixes in the Artificial Language, and you should practice using these rules, but you should NOT memorize them because (1) you will have them available to you at all times during the actual test, and (2) in the actual test, some of the suffixes and prefixes are different from the ones used in this practice test.

Verb: A verb is used to express either an action or a state of being. For example, "He <u>prepared</u> dinner" expresses the action of making all preparations for dinner, while "He is a <u>citizen</u>" expresses the state or condition of being a citizen.

A condition or "state of being" can be permanent or transitory. For example, "The agent's horse <u>is a bay mare</u>" expresses a permanent condition for the horse (being a bay mare), while "George <u>is at lunch</u>" expresses a transitory condition for George (being at lunch). The Spanish language, unlike English, has two different verbs to express permanent and transitory conditions, although the Artificial Language is akin to English rather than to Spanish in its use of a single verb to express any state of being.

When a verb is linked to a subject (i.e., "conjugated"), it changes from the abstract infinitive form to a specific form such as a present tense or a past tense. The Artificial Language primarily uses only two tenses: the simple past tense and the simple present tense in the indicative mood (see Rules 6 and 7). (Verbs in the indicative mood express a <u>real</u> action or condition, whereas verbs in the subjunctive mood express <u>hypothetical</u> actions or conditions. The subjunctive mood does not exist in the Artificial Language, but it is very important in Spanish.)

You may find that the past participle is used in the test (see Rule 8). In that case, the present perfect tense (they <u>have crossed</u>) and the past perfect tense (they <u>had crossed</u>) will be used in the Artificial Language.

Be sure to apply the rules as directed in the test material. If no rule governing the past participle is listed in the actual test material, then the past participle is treated as a simple past tense.

Test Questions

Set 1: Questions 1 Through 20

Directions: For each sentence, decide which words have been translated correctly. Use scratch paper to list each <u>numbered</u> word that is correctly translated into the Artificial Language. When you have finished listing the words that are correctly translated in sentences 1 through 20, select your answer according to the following instructions:

Mark:

    (A) if <u>only</u> the word numbered 1 is correctly translated.

    (B) if <u>only</u> the word numbered 2 is correctly translated.

    (C) if <u>only</u> the word numbered 3 is correctly translated.

    (D) if <u>two</u> or <u>more</u> of the numbered words are correctly translated.

    (E) if <u>none</u> of the numbered words is correctly translated.

Be sure to list only the <u>numbered</u> words that are <u>correctly</u> translated.

Study the sample question before going on to the test questions.

Sample Sentence	**Sample Translation**
He identifies the driver.	<u>Volle</u> <u>kalenim</u> wir <u>arlek</u>. 1 2 3

The word numbered 1, *volle,* is incorrect since the translation of *volle* is <u>this</u>. The word *yev* should have been used. The word numbered 2, *kalenim,* is also incorrect because the singular form *kalenem* should have been used. The word numbered 3 is correct and should be written on your note paper. *Arlek* has been correctly formed from the infinitive *arker* (to drive) by applying Rules 4 and 9. So, only the word numbered 3 has been correctly translated. **The correct answer is choice (C).**

Now answer Questions 1 through 20 in the manner indicated. <u>Be sure to record your answers on the separate answer sheet.</u>

Sentence	Translation
Sentence	**Translation**
1. The boy drove the jeep.	Wir ekaplekoz arzotim wir daqlek. 　　　1　　　2　　　3
2. The illegal aliens were enemies of that country.	Wir fercolle huslekoz synzotim avelek que 　　1　　　2　　　　　3 velle failek.
3. The inspectors are loyal.	Wiroz zellekoz synem inleoz. 　1　　2　　3
4. That government is not legal.	Velle almanlek fersynim colle. 　1　　　　2　　3
5. The men and women crossed the river.	Wiroz kaplek loa kapleknef chonzotim wir 　　1　　　　2　　　3 browlek.
6. He was a skillful driver.	Yev syzotem bex janlek arlekoz. 　1　　　　2　　3
7. She identified the enemy's jeep.	Yevnef kalenem wir avelek daqlek. 　1　　2　　　3
8. The boy is a friend.	Wir ekaplek synem bex kometlek. 　1　　2　　　3
9. They crossed the border.	Yev chonzotem wir reglek. 　1　　2　　3
10. The girls were from that country.	Wir kapleknefoz synzotim mor velle 　1　　2 failekoz. 　3
11. The men identified illegal workers.	Wiroz kaplekoz kalenim colleozfer 　1　　2　　3 friglekoz.
12. The illegal alien shot her.	Wir fercolle huslekem degzotem yev. 　1　　2　　3
13. That guard is difficult.	Velle bonlekem synem glasle. 　1　　2　　3
14. The women were from the border station.	Wir kapleknefoz synzotim mor wir reglek 　1　　2　　　3 lexlek.
15. An illegal alien escaped from the guard.	Bex fercolle ferhuslek pirzotim mor wir 　　1　　2 bonker. 　3
16. A friend was injured.	Bexnef kometlek synzotem liato. 　1　　2　　3
17. The guard inspected the alien's papers.	Wir bonlek zelker wir huslekoz 　1　　2　　3 trenedlekoz.
18. The papers were from the government.	Wir trenedlekoz synzot mor wir almanlek. 　1　　2　　3
19. The spies escaped from the country.	Wiroz tatlekae pirzotim mor velle failek. 　1　　2　　　3
20. The loyal guard had shot the enemy.	Wir inle bonker tulim degzotem wir avelek. 　　1　　2　　3

Set 2: Questions 21 Through 30

U.S. inspectors who <u>guard the border</u> must be brave <u>men and women</u>. Illegal aliens are

                           21   22

sometimes <u>spies from enemy countries</u>. They might even try <u>to shoot inspectors</u>. Some aliens

               23   24

are legal, however. They have <u>papers from the government</u>. Inspectors keep the

                           25

<u>country's borders</u> safe from <u>illegal aliens</u> who try <u>to cross the border</u> illegally.

     26   27   28

Keeping America safe is difficult work, but <u>inspectors are loyal</u> men and women who work

                                             29

hard to help their country. Inspectors sometimes <u>work from</u> border stations. Other times, they

                                      30

patrol the border.

21. (A) bonem wir reglek
    (B) bonem wir regli
    (C) bonim wir reglek
    (D) bonzotim wir regker
    (E) bonzotem wir regker

22. (A) kaplekoz loa kapleknefoz
    (B) kaplek loa kapleknef
    (C) ekalek loa ekapleknef
    (D) kaplekoz loaoz kapleknefoz
    (E) kaplekae loa kapleknefae

23. (A) tatlek mor avelek failek
    (B) tatleks mor aveleks faileks
    (C) tatlekoz moroz avelekoz failekoz
    (D) tatleoz mor avelek failekoz
    (E) tatlekoz mor avelekoz failekoz

24. (A) deglek zellekoz
    (B) degker zellekoz
    (C) degker zellek
    (D) degkeroz zellek
    (E) degzotkeroz zellekoz

25. (A) trenedlek mor wir almanlek
    (B) trenedlekoz moroz wiroz almanlek
    (C) trenedlekoz mor wir almanlek
    (D) trenedlekoz moroz wir almanlek
    (E) trenedlekoz mor wir almanlekoz

26. (A) failekoz reglek
    (B) failek reglekoz
    (C) failekae reglek
    (D) failekae reglekoz
    (E) failek reglek

27. (A) fercolleoz huslekoz
    (B) fercolle huslek
    (C) colle ferhuslek
    (D) fercolle ferhuslekoz
    (E) fercolle huslekoz

28. (A) chonzotem wir reglek
    (B) chonker wir reglek
    (C) chonker wir regker
    (D) chonlek wir reglek
    (E) chonker wir reglekoz

29. (A) zelker synim inle
    (B) zelkeroz synem inle
    (C) zellek synem inle
    (D) zellekoz synim inle
    (E) zellekoz synem inle

30. (A) frigzotim quea
    (B) frigem mor
    (C) frigem quea
    (D) frigzotem mor
    (E) frigim mor

Set 3: Questions 31 Through 42

Directions: For this group of questions, select the one answer choice that is the correct translation of the English word or words in parentheses. You should translate the entire sentence in order to determine what form should be used.

31. Wirnef kapleknefoz (were friendly).
    (A) synzotim kometlekki
    (B) synzotem kometlekki
    (C) synim kometlek
    (D) synem kometlekle
    (E) synim kometlekle

32. Wir zellek (shot the spy).
    (A) degker wir tatlek
    (B) degzotem wir tatker
    (C) degzotem wir tatlek
    (D) degem wir tatlek
    (E) deglek wir tatlek

33. (That girl) synem bexnef collenef husleknef.
    (A) Wirnef ekapleknef
    (B) Velle ekapleknef
    (C) Wir ekapleknef
    (D) Vellenef ekapleknef
    (E) Vellenef ekapleknef

34. (The skillful driver) chonzotem wir reglek.
    (A) Wir janle arker
    (B) Wir janle arlek
    (C) Wir janlenef arnef
    (D) Wir janle arerlek
    (E) Wir janlek arerlek

35. Yev synem bex kometlek (from the government).
    (A) mor bex almanlek
    (B) mor wir almanlekle
    (C) mor wir almanzotem
    (D) mor bex almanlekle
    (E) mor wir almanlek

36. Bex fercolle huslek (crossed the river).
    (A) chonim wir ferbrowlek
    (B) chonzotim wir browlek
    (C) chonim wir browle
    (D) chonzotem wir browlek
    (E) chonker wir browlek

37. Wir zellek (worked to identify) wirnef ekapleknef.
    (A) frigzotem kalenker
    (B) frigzotem kalenkernef
    (C) frigker kalenker
    (D) friglek kalenlek
    (E) figzotim kalenker

38. (The alien's papers) synzotim colle.
    (A) Wir huslekoz trenedlekoz
    (B) Wiroz huslekoz trenedlekoz
    (C) Wir huslek trenedlek
    (D) Wirae huslekae trenedlek
    (E) Wir huslekae trenedlekoz

39. (A guard identified) bex huslek mor velle failek.
    (A) Wir bonker kalenker
    (B) Bex bonlek kalenzotim
    (C) Bex bonlek kalenzotem
    (D) Bexem bonlek kalenzotem
    (E) Bex bonker kalenker

40. Velle kaplek synem mor wir (border station).
    (A) regle lexlek
    (B) reglek lexlek
    (C) regle lexle
    (D) regker lexker
    (E) regker lexker

41. Wir tatlek frigzotem (to escape) mor wir bonlek.

(A) pirzotem

(B) pirzotim

(C) pirker

(D) pirto

(E) pirlek

42. Velle ekaplek (was identified).

(A) synim kalenzotim

(B) synim kalenzotem

(C) synem kalento

(D) synem kalenzotem

(E) synzotem kalento

Set 4: Questions 43 Through 50

Directions: For the last group of questions, select the one answer that is the correct form of the underlined expression as it is used in the sentence. At the end of the sentence, you will find instructions in parentheses telling you which form to use. In some sentences, you will be asked to supply the correct form of two or more expressions. In this case, the instructions for these expressions are presented consecutively in the parentheses and are separated by a dash. Be sure to translate the entire sentence before selecting your answer.

43. Wir zellek <u>tulker kalenker</u> wiroz fercolleoz huslekoz. (present perfect singular)

(A) tulim kalenlekki

(B) tulim kalento

(C) tulem kalenzotem

(D) tulem kalento

(E) tulim kalenlek

44. Wirnefoz ekapleknefoz synim <u>inle</u>. (plural feminine adjective)

(A) inlenef

(B) inleoz

(C) inlenefae

(D) inlenefoz

(E) nefinle

45. Volle tatlek <u>liaker</u> velle <u>kometlek</u> kaplek. (past tense—adjective)

(A) liazotem—kometlekki

(B) liaem—kometlek

(C) liazotem—kometle

(D) liaem—kometle

(E) liato—kometo

46. Wir <u>kaplek</u> <u>synker liaker</u>. (feminine singular noun—past participle predicate)

(A) ekaplekoz—synker liato

(B) ekapleknefoz—synem liato

(C) kapleknefoz—synim liato

(D) kapleknef—synzotim liaem

(E) kapleknef—synzotem liato

47. Wir <u>avelek</u> daqlek chonzotem wir <u>regker</u>. (singular possessive adjective—singular noun)

(A) avelaknef—reglenef

(B) aveleae—reglek

(C) aveleoz—regzotem

(D) aveleoz—reglek

(E) aveleae—reglekae

48. <u>Wir</u> <u>colle</u> <u>kaplek</u> synim mor velle failker. (feminine plural adjective—negative feminine plural adjective—feminine plural noun)

(A) Wirnefoz—fercollenefoz—kapleknefoz

(B) Wirnef—fercollenef—kapleknef

(C) Wiroz—colleoz—kaplekoz

(D) Ferwirnefoz—fercolleoz—kapleknefoz

(E) Wirnef—fercollenef—kapeknef

49. Wirnef <u>ekaplek</u> synem <u>kalenker</u>. (feminine singular noun—past participle as predicate)

(A) ekapleknef—kalennef

(B) ekaplek—kalenzotem

(C) ekapleknef—kalenli

(D) ekaplekoz—kalenlek

(E) ekapleknef—kalento

50. Velle bonlek <u>arker</u> wir daqlek <u>janle</u>. (present tense—adverb)

(A) arkim—janleki

(B) arim—janlek

(C) arem—janleki

(D) arto—janle

(E) arzotem—janlek

ANSWER KEY AND EXPLANATIONS

Logical Reasoning

1. B	5. A	8. B	11. C	14. E
2. E	6. E	9. D	12. B	15. A
3. E	7. A	10. B	13. A	16. E
4. D				

1. **The correct answer is choice (B).** If Karen T. was pardoned, she has been forgiven of the crime and the penalty. She has fulfilled her debt to society in relation to this crime. You cannot conclude from the paragraph that she was wrongfully convicted; you can only conclude that she claims she is innocent and was wrongfully convicted, choice (A). The paragraph says only that presidents pardon individuals when they feel that the individuals have fulfilled their debt to society; it does not say that because Karen T. was pardoned, she is innocent of the crime, choice (C). Choices (D) and (E) are also incorrect. It is more likely that a president would parson someone who was wrongfully convicted than let that individual remain in prison, choice (D). Karen T.'s sentence was ten years. It is not likely she would have been released in five years if she were not pardoned, choice (E).

2. **The correct answer is choice (E).** To correctly answer this question, choose the conclusion that *cannot* be made based on the information in the paragraph. The passage does not say or lead you to believe that all Federal employees must undergo random alcohol tests. Only truck drivers must undergo random alcohol tests. The other answer choices are true. You can conclude that some Federal employees must undergo random drug tests, choice (A). You can also conclude that Federal employees suspected of drug use may have to undergo a drug test, choice (B). You can conclude that all trucking companies must test drivers for drugs and alcohol, choices (C) and (D).

3. **The correct answer is choice (E).** The DHS is developing technology that will make it easier for Border Patrol Agents to detect tunnels. The passage leads you to believe that this technology is not yet available, but it will be in the years to come. There is not enough information in the passage to lead you to conclude that the DHS is mainly responsible for detecting tunnels, choice (A). The passage says that tunnels are difficult for Border Patrol Agents to detect, so choice (B) is also incorrect. The passage says that Border Patrol Agents will ride in trucks when using this technology, but it does not say that most agents ride in trucks when patrolling the border, choice (C). The passage does not say how criminals most often smuggle drugs across the border, choice (D).

4. **The correct answer is choice (D).** Since the sheriff's office contacted the Border Patrol Agents, you can conclude that Border Patrol Agents sometimes work with other law enforcement personnel, but you cannot conclude that they work for the sheriff, choice (E). There is not enough information in the passage to lead you to conclude that most illegal immigrants in Florida are from Haiti or the Dominican Republic, choice (A). You

also cannot tell how many immigrants enter the country on vessels, choice (B). While a U.S. citizen smuggled these immigrants into the country, you cannot conclude that U.S. citizens most often smuggle illegal aliens into the country, choice (D).

5. **The correct answer is choice (A).** All police officers in this sector who earn overtime pay patrolling the border must complete a training course. Therefore, if Rita K. is in this program, she has completed this training course. Choice (B) is not correct because Rita K. may be able to earn overtime pay in other ways. Choice (C) is not correct because this program may be offered in other sectors as well. Choice (D) is not correct because Rita K. may choose not to participate in the program. Choice (E) is not correct because police officers in other sectors probably earn overtime pay as well.

6. **The correct answer is choice (E).** The passage says that nearly half of Border Patrol Agents in this sector have been shot at by members of this drug cartel. Therefore, the agents in this sector are very likely to be shot at by members of this drug cartel. The passage does not indicate if agents in other sectors have been killed by members of this cartel, choice (A). It also does not indicate that Emmanuel T. has been shot at or injured, choices (B) and (D); it only states that he works in this sector. Only 2 Border Patrol Agents in this sector have been killed, so choice (C) is incorrect.

7. **The correct answer is choice (A).** According to the information in the passage, if a person uses a cell phone, the government can use the mobile phone company's logs to determine the person's location. Choice (B) is not correct because a criminal may be caught in other ways. Choice (C) is not correct because there may be other reasons the FBI may want to access a cell phone

company's logs. Choice (D) is not correct because a cell phone is not the only way to determine a criminal's location. Choice (E) is also not correct because the FBI may have other means of determining a person's location.

8. **The correct answer is choice (B).** The passage says that most immigrants in the United States were born in Central America and that most of these immigrants work as either machine operators or laborers. Choices (A) and (E) are not correct because the passage says very few of these immigrants work in managerial and professional occupations, but this means that some of them do. Choice (D) is also not correct because most immigrants work as either laborers or machine operators.

9. **The correct answer is choice (D).** To correctly answer this question, choose the answer option that is *not* true. The passage discusses two instances in which law enforcement officers discovered drugs in trucks driven by Mexican citizens. However, you cannot conclude from this passage that most drugs are smuggled into the country in trucks driven by Mexican citizens. You can conclude that a drug smuggler may hide drugs in skids, choice (A) and that law enforcement officers refer some cases to special agents in immigration, choice (B). You can also conclude that law enforcement officers may use X-ray scans and canines to help them detect drugs, choices (C) and (E).

10. **The correct answer is choice (B).** To answer this question, you need to choose the conclusion that *cannot* be made based on the information in the paragraph. There is not enough information in the paragraph to lead you to conclude that none of the children was from El Salvador. Since most of the illegal immigrants were from El Salvador,

it is likely that at least some of the children were from this country. The passage says that some of the illegal immigrants were from Guatemala, so choice (A) is true and therefore not correct. The passage also says that all of the adult immigrants were taken into custody, so choice (C) is also incorrect. The smugglers were U.S. citizens, and the children were returned to relatives in their native countries. Therefore, choices (D) and (E) are incorrect.

11. **The correct answer is choice (C).** To correctly answer this question, you need to choose the statement that *cannot* be concluded from the passage. The passage says that individuals who want to operate a horse-drawn carriage in the city will be investigated by the chief of police and city council members. It does not say that the individuals must know them. Those wishing to operate a horse-drawn carriage must have equipment in good working order, choice (A), and complete an application, choice (E). They must not have a criminal record, choice (B), or obstruct the flow of traffic, choice (D). If Melanie K. has a permit, these conditions must apply to her.

12. **The correct answer is choice (B).** Individuals on parole cannot vote in California. Therefore, if Ricardo V. can vote while he is on parole, he does not live in California. Choice (A) is not correct because there may be other states that do not allow individuals on parole to vote. Choice (C) is also not correct because states other than Indiana and Illinois may allow individuals to vote while they are on parole. Choice (D) is not correct because individuals in Indiana and Illinois are allowed to vote while on parole. Choice (E) is also not correct; there may be other reasons why a person cannot vote when he or she is released from prison.

13. **The correct answer is choice (A).** The passage says that only some of the female employees in the candy factory from Mexico were legal. This means that some of them were working illegally. The passage does not indicate whether the men from Mexico were working legally, choice (B), and it says that some *legal* aliens from Honduras were under the age of 16, choice (C). The passage does not indicate whether the illegal employees from Honduras were male or female, choice (D), and it says that none of the men from Cuba was working legally, choice (E).

14. **The correct answer is choice (E).** The passage says that China, Denmark, Japan, and Singapore require individuals to give up their citizenship if they become citizens in other countries. Therefore, if Elle A. becomes a U.S. citizen, she will have to relinquish her citizenship in Denmark. Choice (A) is incorrect; if Elle A. is not a citizen of Denmark, she may be able to become a citizen of the United States. Choice (B) is also incorrect because Elle A. cannot be a citizen in both Denmark and China. Choice (C) is incorrect because she cannot be a citizen in both Denmark and Singapore. Choice (D) is also incorrect because Elle A. will have to relinquish her citizenship in Denmark if she becomes a U.S. citizen.

15. **The correct answer is choice (A).** The passage says that those who receive three quarters of their salary are married or have dependents. All other workers receive two thirds of their salary. Therefore, if Ronald N. receives two thirds of his salary, he was not married and did not have dependents when he was injured. If he was married with dependents or either married or had dependents at the time of his injury, he would have received three quarters of his salary, choices (B), (D), and (E). There is not enough information in the paragraph to tell if he has ever been married, choice (C).

16. **The correct answer is choice (E).** In this state, the killing of an individual while committing another serious crime may also be considered murder. The passage does not explain the laws in other states, choice (A), and assisting in a suicide is a homicide in this state, choice (B). Only a homicide may be non-criminal, choice (C), and the passage does not say what crime or even if Nicholas L. was committing a crime at the time of the killing, choice (D).

Spanish Language Proficiency

Part I

1. B	5. B	9. B	13. C	17. E
2. A	6. E	10. D	14. A	18. C
3. E	7. A	11. B	15. B	19. B
4. B	8. A	12. D	16. B	20. A

1. **The correct answer is choice (B).** The word *malograr* means to spoil, or fail at something, so the best synonym is *estropear,* "to spoil" or "ruin." Choice (A), *lograr,* "to achieve," is the opposite of *malograr.* Choice (C), "to conclude," and choice (D), "to complete," mean to succeed in a plan rather than to spoil it. The meaning of choice (E), "to bruise," is different from the meaning of *malograr,* although it may sound similar.

2. **The correct answer is choice (A).** The word *buzón* means mailbox, so the term *correo,* "mail," is the closest synonym. Choice (C), "deep-sea diving," and choice (E), "diver," begin with the same syllable as *buzón,* but their meanings are different. Choice (B), "bus," and choice (D), "pocket," may make sense in the sentence, but their meanings are unrelated to the meaning of *buzón.*

3. **The correct answer is choice (E).** The word *zafo* is a form of the verb *zafar,* meaning to unloosen, untie, or let go. Choice (E), *deshago,* is a form of the verb *deshacer,* meaning "to undo." Choice (A), "adjust" or "tighten," and choice (D), "tie," have meanings that are contrary to the idea of loosening or undoing something. Choice (C), "make untidy" or "mess up," is unrelated to the meaning of *zafar.*

4. **The correct answer is choice (B).** The word *concedieron* means to concede or agree to grant something, in this case, a period of time. Choice (A), "forbade," and choice (D), "prevented," mean the opposite of *concedieron.* Choices (C) and (E) both mean "ordered" or "gave an order," so they fit the sentence; however, allowing something and ordering that it be done are not the same thing.

5. **The correct answer is choice (B).** The word *nocivo* refers to something that is harmful. Therefore, choice (B), "damaging," is the best synonym. Choice (A), "beneficial," and choice (B), "harmless," are contrary to the meaning of *nocivo.* Choice (D), "substantial," dates back to the Spanish word *sustancial* but this is not the synonym requested. Choice (E) means a "river or stream," so it has no relation to *nocivo.*

6. **The correct answer is choice (E).** The word *sosa* refers to something that is bland or boring, such as a person or an unsuccessful joke. This meaning matches choice (E), *insulsa,* which means "dull." Choice (A), "amusing," and choice (C), "funny," refer to an unsuccessful joke. Choice (D), "in poor taste," may also refer to an unsuccessful joke, but it does not mean the same as a dull one.

7. **The correct answer is choice (A).** The word *gorra* refers to several types of caps, such as a baseball cap or a bonnet. The masculine

word *gorro* ("cap.") is the same term and is therefore the correct synonym. Choice (B), "shirt," and choice (C), "vest," are also articles of clothing but are unrelated to the meaning of *gorra*. Choice (D), "fat," and choice (E), the bird called the "swallow," begin with the same syllable as the correct answer, but their meanings are unrelated.

8. **The correct answer is choice (A).** The word *hacendados* refers to the <u>owners of ranches</u> or <u>farms;</u> therefore, *terratenientes* ("landowners") is the best synonym. Choice (B), "livestock," and choice (C), "crops," refer to a ranch or farm, but not to the people who own it. Choice (D), "inhabitants," and choice (E), "citizens," do refer to persons, but not necessarily to farmers or landowners.

9. **The correct answer is choice (B).** The word *finge* is a form of the verb *fingir,* meaning to <u>pretend or feign</u>. Therefore, *simula* ("fakes") is the best synonym. Although choice (A) sounds like the English "pretend," it actually means to "attempt" or "try" something. Choice (C), "finger," and choice (D), "refinement" or "politeness," have meanings unrelated to *finge*. Choice (E), "sphinx," contains the word *finge* but the two words are unrelated.

10. **The correct answer is choice (D).** The word *pareja* means a <u>couple</u> and is synonymous with "pair." Choices (A), (B), and (E) all begin with the same syllable as the correct answer, but their meanings are unrelated. Choice (C), "ear," has the same two final syllables as *pareja* but is unrelated.

11. **The correct answer is choice (B).** The term *brasas* refers to <u>coals</u> or <u>embers</u>, which are lit but not flaming. Therefore, *carbón* ("charcoal") is the closest synonym. Choice (A), "tents," choice (C), "boots," and choice (D), "flashlights," are objects that you might find at a campsite, but they are unrelated to

brasas. Choice (E), "arms," is phonetically similar to *brasas,* but its meaning is different.

12. **The correct answer is choice (D).** The word *yeso* refers to the <u>layer of plaster used to coat walls.</u> Therefore, the best synonym is *cal* ("whitewash"), which also refers to the coating on a wall. Choice (A), "iron," sounds similar to *yeso,* but is not a coating. Choice (B), "brick," and choice (D), "stone," are used for walls but do not have the same meaning as *yeso*. Choice (E), "sticker," begins with the same syllable as the correct answer, but its meaning is unrelated.

13. **The correct answer is choice (C).** The word *matón* refers to <u>someone who starts fights and trouble</u>, a <u>bully</u>. Therefore, the best synonym is *pendenciero* ("troublemaker"). Choice (A), "assassin," comes from the same root as *matón,* but the latter is not necessarily a killer. Choice (B), "bruise," and choice (D), "a slap or blow with the hand," may be involved in fighting, but they do not refer to a person. Choice (E), "chubby-cheeked," is unrelated to the meaning of *matón.*

14. **The correct answer is choice (A).** The word *flecha* means an <u>arrow</u> and is used, in this case, to describe speed. Therefore, choice (A), "dart," is the best synonym. Choice (B), "bran," is phonetically similar to *flecha,* but its meaning is unrelated. Choice (C), "to pierce with an arrow," is the action rather than the arrow itself. Choice (D) means "bow" but is not the arrow. Choice (E), "quick," also describes speed, but its meaning is unrelated to *flecha.*

15. **The correct answer is choice (B).** The word *escabulleron* is a form of the verb *esfumarse,* which means to <u>vanish</u> or <u>disappear</u>, so choice (B), "to slip away," is the best synonym. Choice (A), "got tired," choice (C), "looked," choice (D), "leaned," and choice (E), "went up," are not related to the meaning of *escabulleron.*

16. **The correct answer is choice (B).** The word *devolvimos* is a form of the verb *devolver,* which means to <u>return</u> or <u>give something back</u>. Therefore, choice (B), "to refund," is the best synonym. The meanings of choice (A), "maintained," and choice (D), "kept," are contrary of the idea of giving back. Choice (C), "devoured," and choice (E), "accrued" or "earned," have the same initial syllable as *devolvimos,* but their meanings are unrelated.

17. **The correct answer is choice (E).** The word *respondonas* refers to persons who <u>talk back</u>, usually in a disrespectful way. Therefore, choice (E), "sassy," is the best synonym. Choice (A), "restrained," choice (B), ""respectful," choice (C), "quiet," and choice (D), "courteous," have meanings that are contrary to the meaning of *respondonas*.

18. **The correct answer is choice (C).** The word *novato* means a <u>novice</u>, or <u>somebody who lacks experience</u>. Therefore, choice (C), "inexperienced," is the best synonym. Choice (B), "ninth," sounds similar to *noveno* but has a different meaning. Choice (D), "experienced," and choice (E), "skilled," are the opposite of *novato*.

19. **The correct answer is choice (B).** The term *gancho* refers to <u>hooks</u> of various types, including a hanger or a safety pin. Therefore, choice (B), "hook," is the best synonym. Choice (A), "ranch," choice (C), "wide," and choice (E), "pig," end on the same two syllables as *gancho,* but their meanings are unrelated to the meaning of *gancho*.

20. **The correct answer is choice (A).** The word *malestar* means <u>discomfort</u> that is either physical or emotional. Therefore, choice (A), "nuisance or pain," is the best synonym. Choice (D), "misunderstanding," and choice (B), "weeds," begin with the same syllable as *malestar,* but their meanings are different. Choice (C), "badness" or "wickedness," has the same root as *malestar* but a different meaning. Choice (E), "comfort," means the opposite of *malestar*.

Part II

Section I

1. E	**3.** E	**5.** C	**6.** D	**7.** A
2. A	**4.** E			

1. **The correct answer is choice (E).** This sentence has a compound subject; therefore, it must have a plural verb, *están,* and a plural feminine adjective, *cansadas.* Choices (A) and (C) use the singular verb. Choices (B) and (C) use the singular adjective. Choice (D) uses a masculine adjective.

2. **The correct answer is choice (A).** *Llegaremos* is the proper future verb form for the plural subject, and *de* is the preposition that combines with an article to indicate a general time of day. Choices (B), (C), and (E) use incorrect forms of the verb and incorrect prepositions. Choice (D) uses an incorrect combination of preposition and article.

3. **The correct answer is choice (E).** The personal pronoun *ti* ("you") is the correct familiar form to use after *para* and the indirect object pronoun *los* agrees with the plural noun *papeles.* Choice (A) uses the formal pronoun *usted,* which does not match the familiar verb form *pediste.* Choices (B), (C), and (D) use incorrect pronouns.

4. **The correct answer is choice (E).** The word *menos* placed between an article and an adjective correctly forms a comparison ("the least"), and *hay* is the proper form of the verb *haber* meaning "to be." Choices (A), (B), (C), and (D) form the comparison incorrectly and use an improper form of *haber.*

5. **The correct answer is choice (C).** The word *al* is a contraction of the preposition *a* and the masculine article *el.* The suffix *-ero* is the correct ending for *zapato* ("shoe") to indicate one who makes or fixes shoes. Choices (A), (B), (D), and (E) use the preposition and article incorrectly and also add a wrong suffix to *zapato.*

6. **The correct answer is choice (D).** The possessive *nuestras* agrees with the noun *casas* in gender and number, and the article *los* agrees with the noun *lunes.* In choices (A), (B), (C), and (E) either the possessive pronoun or the article, or both, do not match the noun they modify.

7. **The correct answer is choice (A).** The noun *manos* ("hands") is feminine plural although it ends in *-o.* Therefore, it takes the article *las* and a feminine adjective, *vacías.* Choices (B) and (D) have a masculine adjective. Choice (C) has a masculine article. Choice (E) has a masculine article and a single article.

Section II

1. A	3. D	5. B	6. B	7. C
2. B	4. A			

1. **The correct answer is choice (A).** The sentence has the proper structure and contains no errors. Choices (B), (C), and (D) contain several errors, including incorrect use of negatives, omission of the possessive pronoun, and misplaced clauses.

2. **The correct answer is choice (B).** The sentence has the proper structure and contains no errors. Choices (A), (C), and (D) contain various errors, including illogical structures, incorrect verb forms, and improper adverbs.

3. **The correct answer is choice (D).** The sentence has the proper structure and contains no errors. Choices (A), (B), and (C) contain various errors, including illogical structures, misplaced clauses, and incorrect verb forms.

4. **The correct answer is choice (A).** The sentence has the proper structure and contains no errors. Choices (B) and (D) contain various errors, including illogical structures, incorrect verb forms, and incorrect word choices. Choice (C) is not a complete thought.

5. **The correct answer is choice (B).** The sentence has the proper structure and contains no errors. Choices (A), (C), and (D) contain various errors, including illogical structures, incorrect verb forms, and incorrect ways of indicating "sunset."

6. **The correct answer is choice (B).** The sentence has the proper structure and contains no errors. Choices (A), (C), and (D) contain various errors, including illogical structures, misplaced clauses, improper noun gender, and incorrect forms of the verb *haber*.

7. **The correct answer is choice (C).** The sentence has the proper structure and contains no errors. Choices (A), (B), and (D) contain various errors, including illogical structures, improper usage of the personal *a*, incorrect verbs, and incorrect prepositions.

Section III

1. A	**3.** E	**5.** B	**6.** A	**7.** C
2. E	**4.** C			

1. **The correct answer is choice (A).** *Cuya* is the correct possessive pronoun that agrees with the object possessed (*nombre*). In choice (B), the pronoun agrees with the possessor (*persona*) instead. Choices (C) and (D) use incorrect possessives.

2. **The correct answer is choice (E).** The expression *no... en absoluto* correctly indicates a definite and resolute negative. Choices (A), (B), (C), and (D) use incorrect expressions to denote the negative.

3. **The correct answer is choice (E).** The subjunctive form of the verb *lloviznar* is *llovizne;* therefore, choice (E) is appropriate for a phrase that expresses possibility. Choices (A) and (B) are both gerunds. Choice (C) is a noun, and choice (D) uses an indicative form of the verb.

4. **The correct answer is choice (C).** This is the correct infinitive verb (*grabar*), which means "to record." Choices (A) and (D) use incorrect forms of the verb. Choice (B) uses the false cognate *recordar* ("to remember").

5. **The correct answer is choice (B).** The correct form of the verb *estar* is *estamos,* which refers to the speaker and others and indicates a temporary condition. Choices (A) and (C) use forms of the verb *ser* and thus denote a permanent condition. Choice (D) is the gerund form of *estar*.

6. **The correct answer is choice (A).** Here, the indirect object pronoun *les* agrees in gender and number with the noun *personas*. The other choices use incorrect pronouns.

7. **The correct answer is choice (C).** The adjective *varios* agrees in gender and number with the masculine plural noun *países*. Choice (A) uses a nonexistent adjective. Choice (B) uses a feminine adjective. Choice (D) uses an illogical negative adjective.

answers diagnostic test

Artificial Language

1. C	11. A	21. C	31. A	41. C
2. B	12. B	22. A	32. C	42. E
3. D	13. D	23. E	33. D	43. D
4. D	14. B	24. B	34. B	44. D
5. C	15. E	25. C	35. E	45. C
6. A	16. D	26. D	36. D	46. E
7. A	17. A	27. A	37. A	47. B
8. D	18. C	28. B	38. E	48. A
9. C	19. D	29. D	39. C	49. E
10. E	20. C	30. E	40. A	50. C

1. **The correct answer is choice (C).** Only the word numbered 3 is correctly translated. The correct translation of the word *boy,* the word numbered 1, is *ekaplek.* The artificial language word in this sentence, *ekaplekoz,* is the translation of the word *boys.* To translate the word numbered 2, *drove,* begin with the translation of *to drive,* which is *arker.* According to Rule 4, the stem of a verb is created by dropping the *ker.* Then, according to Rule 7, to create the past tense of a verb, add the suffix *zot* to the stem, and then add *em* if the verb is singular. Therefore, the correct translation of *drove* is *arzotem.*

2. **The correct answer is choice (B).** Only the word numbered 2 is correctly translated in this sentence. To create the translation of the word *illegal,* add the prefix *fer* to *colle,* the translation of the word *legal.* Then add the suffix *oz* because the adjective modifies a plural noun (Rule 2). The word numbered 3 is also translated incorrectly. To create the translation of the word *enemies,* begin with *avelek,* the translation of the word *enemy.* To make a noun plural (Rule 2), add the suffix *oz* to the singular form. The correct translation of *enemies* is *avelekoz.*

3. **The correct answer is choice (D).** In this sentence, the words numbered 1 and 2 are translated correctly, but the word numbered 3 is not. *Synem* is the translation of the word *is.* To create the translation of the word *are,* begin with *synker,* the translation of *to be.* Drop the *ker* to form the verb stem (Rule 4). Add *im* to make the verb plural. The correct translation is *synim.*

4. **The correct answer is choice (D).** In this sentence, the words numbered 1 and 3 are translated correctly, but the word numbered 2 is not. *Fersynim* is the translation of the words *are not.* The suffix *im* is plural. To create the translation of *is not,* add the prefix *fer* to *synem,* the translation of the word *is.* The correct translation is *fersynem.*

5. **The correct answer is choice (C).** Only the word numbered 3 is correctly translated in this sentence. *Kaplek* is the translation of the word *man* and *kapleknef* is the translation of the word *woman.* To make the words plural, add the suffix *oz* (Rule 2). The correct translation of *men* is *kaplekoz,* and the correct translation of *women* is *kapleknefoz.*

6. **The correct answer is choice (A).** Only the word numbered 1 is correctly translated in this sentence. The word *skillful* is not correctly translated. The translation of *skillful* is *janle*. There is no reason to drop the *le* and add *lek*. The word numbered 3 in this sentence is *arlekoz*. This is the translation of the word *drivers*. To make this word singular—*driver*—drop the suffix *oz*.

7. **The correct answer is choice (A).** Only the word numbered 1 is correctly translated in this sentence. To create the translation of the word *identified*, begin with the translation of *kalenker*, the translation of *to identify*. Drop the *ker* to form the verb root (Rule 4). According to Rule 7, to make the word past tense, add the suffix *zot*. Then, since the word is singular, add the suffix *em*. The correct translation of the word *identified* is *kalenzotem*. The word *enemy's* is also incorrectly translated. The translation of *enemy* is *avelek*. To make this word possessive, add the suffix *ae* (Rule 12). The correct translation is *avelekae*.

8. **The correct answer is choice (D).** All of the words in this sentence are correctly translated.

9. **The correct answer is choice (C).** Only the word numbered 3 is correctly translated in this sentence. The correct translation of the word *they* is *yevoz*. In the artificial language, *they* is the plural of *he/him*. To create the translation of the word *crossed*, begin with *chonker*, the translation of the words *to cross*. Drop the *ker* to form the verb stem. According to Rule 7, to form the past tense of the verb, add *zot* to the verb stem. Because the word is plural, add the suffix *im*. The correct translation is *chonzotim*.

10. **The correct answer is choice (E).** None of the words in this sentence is correctly translated. *Wir* is the correct translation of the word *the*. However, in this sentence it should have the suffix *nef* because it modifies *girls*, which is feminine (Rule 3). Then add the suffix *oz* because the noun *girls* is plural (Rule 2). The correct translation is *wirnefoz*. *Kapleknefoz* is the translation of the word *women*. The translation of the word *girls* is *ekapleknefoz*. *Failekoz* is the translation of the word *countries*. The translation of *country* is *failek*.

11. **The correct answer is choice (A).** Only the word numbered 1 is correctly translated in this sentence. To create the translation of the word *identified*, begin with the translation of *to identify*, which is *kalenker*. Drop the *ker* (Rule 4), and add the suffixes *zot* and *im* since the word is plural and singular. The correct translation is *kalenzotim*. The translation of the word *legal* is *colle*. To create the translation of the word *illegal,* add the prefix *fer*. Then add the suffix *oz* because it modifies a plural noun (Rule 2). The correct translation of *illegal* is *fercolleoz*.

12. **The correct answer is choice (B).** Only the word numbered 2 is correctly translated. The correct translation of *alien* is *huslek*. The translation of *her* is *yevnef*.

13. **The correct answer is choice (D).** In this sentence, the words numbered 1 and 3 are correctly translated, but the word numbered 2 is not. To create the translation of the word *guard*, begin with *bonker*, the translation of *to guard*. Drop the *ker* to create the verb stem (Rule 4). According to Rule 9, to form a noun from a verb, add the suffix *lek* to the stem of the verb. Therefore, the correct translation is *bonlek*.

14. **The correct answer is choice (B).** Only the word numbered 2 is correctly translated. While *wir* is the correct translation of the article *the,* because it modifies *women*, it needs the suffix *nef* (Rule 3). To create the translation of the word *border*, begin with *regker*, the translation of *to border*. Drop the

ker (Rule 4). To form a noun from a verb (Rule 9), add the suffix *lek* to the stem of the verb. In this sentence, *border* is an adjective modifying *station*. According to Rule 10, to form an adjective from a noun, substitute the suffix *le* for the suffix *lek*. The correct translation is *regle*.

15. **The correct answer is choice (E).** None of the words in this sentence is correctly translated. The correct translation of the word *alien* is *huslek*. There is no need to add the prefix *fer*. To create the translation of the word *escaped,* begin with *pirker*, the translation of *to escape*. Drop the *ker* to create the verb stem (Rule 4). To create a past tense verb, add the suffix *zot*. Then add the suffix *em* because the verb is singular (Rule 7). The correct translation is *pirzotem*. To create the translation of the word *border*, begin with *regker*, the translation of *to border*. Drop the *ker* to create the verb stem (Rule 4). According to Rule 9, to form a noun from a verb, add the suffix *lek* to the stem of the verb. Therefore, the correct translation is *bonlek*.

16. **The correct answer is choice (D).** The words numbered 2 and 3 are correctly translated in this sentence. *Bexnef* is not the correct translation of *a* in this sentence because we do not know if the friend is male or female. According to Rule 1, when gender is not specified, the masculine form is used. Therefore, the correct translation of *a* is *bex*.

17. **The correct answer is choice (A).** Only the word numbered 1 is correctly translated in this sentence. To create the translation of the word *inspected,* begin with *zelker*, the translation of *to inspect*. Drop the *ker* to create the verb stem (Rule 4). According to Rule 7, to form the past tense of a verb, add the suffix *zot*. Since the verb is singular, add the suffix *em*. The correct translation

is *zelzotem*. To create the translation of the word *alien's*, add the suffix *ae* (Rule 12) to *huslek,* the translation of *alien*. The correct translation is *huslekae*.

18. **The correct answer is choice (C).** Only the word numbered 3 is correctly translated in this sentence. The translation of *the* is *wir,* but in this sentence *the* modifies *papers*, which is plural. According to Rule 3, adjectives modifying plural nouns must have endings that agree with the word they modify. Therefore, the correct translation is *wiroz*. The correct translation of the word *were* is *synem*.

19. **The correct answer is choice (D).** Only the word numbered 2 is not correctly translated. To create the translation of the word *spies*, begin with *tatker,* the translation of *to spy*. Drop the *ker* to create the verb stem. According to Rule 9, to form a noun from a verb, add the suffix *lek* to the stem of the verb. The correct translation of the word *spy* is *tatlek*. To make this plural, add the suffix *oz*. The correct translation of *spies* is *tatlekoz*. The correct translation of the word *country* is *failek*.

20. **The correct answer is choice (C).** Only the word numbered 3 is correctly translated. To create the word *guard,* begin with *bonker,* the translation of *to guard*. Drop the *ker* to create the verb stem. According to Rule 9, to form a noun from a verb, add the suffix *lek* to the verb stem. The correct translation is *bonlek*. The term "had shot" is past perfect for the singular. According to Rule 8, the suffix *to* should be added to the verb stem, and we need the compound tense with the verb *to have*. The correct translation is *tulzotem degto*.

21. **The correct answer is choice (C).** To create the word *guard,* begin with *bonker,* the translation of *to guard*. Drop the *ker* to create the verb stem (Rule 4). To create a

present-tense verb (Rule 6), add the suffix *im* because the verb is plural. The correct translation is *bonim*. The translation of *the* is *wir*. To create the translation of the noun *border*, begin with *regker*, the translation of *to border*. Drop the *ker* to create the verb stem. According to Rule 9, to form a verb from a noun, add the suffix *lek*. The correct translation is *reglek*.

22. **The correct answer is choice (A).** To create the word *men*, begin with *kaplek*, the translation of *man*. To make a noun plural, add the suffix *oz* (Rule 2). The correct translation of *men* is *kaplekoz*. The translation of the word *and* is *loa*. To create the translation of the word *women*, begin with *kaplek*, the translation of *man*. Add the suffix *nef* to make it feminine and add the suffix *oz* to make it plural. The correct translation of the word *women* is *kapleknefoz*.

23. **The correct answer is choice (E).** To create the word *spy*, begin with *tatker*, the translation of *to spy*. Drop the *ker* to create the verb stem (Rule 4). To make a verb a noun, add the suffix *lek* (Rule 9). To make the noun plural, add the suffix *oz* (Rule 2). The correct translation is *tatlekoz*. The translation of *from* is *mor*. The translation of the word *enemy* is *avelek*. To make this plural, add the suffix *oz* (Rule 2). The translation of the word *country* is *failek*. To make the translation plural, add the suffix *oz* (Rule 2). The correct translation is *failekoz*.

24. **The correct answer is choice (B).** The translation of *to shoot* is *degker*. To create the word *inspectors,* begin with *zelker*, the translation of *to inspect*. Drop the *ker* to create the verb stem (Rule 4). To make a verb a noun, add *lek* (Rule 9). To make the noun plural, add *oz* (Rule 2). The correct translation is *zellekoz*.

25. **The correct answer is choice (C).** The translation of paper is *trenedlek*. To make

this plural, add the suffix *oz* (Rule 2). The correct translation is *trenedlekoz*. The translation of *from* is *mor*, and the translation of *the* is *wir*. The translation of *government* is *almanlek*.

26. **The correct answer is choice (D).** The translation of *country* is *failek*. To make this possessive, add the suffix *ae* (Rule 12). The correct translation is *failekae*. To create the noun *border*, begin with *regker*, the translation of *to border*. Drop the *ker* to create the verb stem (Rule 4). To make the verb a noun, add the suffix *lek* (Rule 9). To make the noun plural, add the suffix *oz*. The correct translation is *reglekoz*.

27. **The correct answer is choice (A).** The translation of the word *legal* is *colle*. To create the translation of the word *illegal,* add the prefix *fer*. Because *illegal* modifies *aliens*, and *aliens* is plural, add the suffix *oz* (Rule 2). The correct translation is *fercolleoz*. The translation of the word *alien* is *huslek*. To make this plural, add the suffix *oz* (Rule 2). The correct translation is *huslekoz*.

28. **The correct answer is choice (B).** The translation of *to cross* is *chonker*, and the translation of *the* is *wir*. To create the noun *border*, begin with *regker*, the translation of *to border*. Drop the *ker* (Rule 4) to create the verb stem. Add *lek* to make the verb a noun (Rule 9). The correct translation is *reglek*.

29. **The correct answer is choice (D).** The translation of *to inspect* is *zelker*. To make the verb a noun, drop the *ker* (Rule 4), and add *lek* (Rule 9). To make the noun plural, add *oz* (Rule 2). The correct translation is *zellekoz*. The translation of the word *are* is *synim*, and the translation of *loyal* is *inle*.

30. **The correct answer is choice (E).** To create the translation of the present tense verb *work*, begin with *frigker*, the translation of *to work*. Drop the *ker* to create the verb stem

(Rule 4). To form the present tense of the verb, add *im* because the verb is plural. The translation of *from* is *mor*.

31. **The correct answer is choice (A).** The complete sentence translates as, "The women were friendly." The translation of *were* is *synzotim*. To create this translation, begin with *synker*, the translation of *to be*. Drop the *ker* (Rule 4). To make the verb past tense, add *zot*. Because the verb is plural, add *im* (Rule 7). To create the translation of *friendly*, begin with *kometlek*, the translation of *friend*. According to Rule 11, to form an adverb from an adjective, add the suffix *ki* to the masculine form of the adjective. Therefore, the correct translation is *kometlekki*.

32. **The correct answer is choice (C).** The complete sentence translates as, "The inspector shot the spy." To create the translation of the word *shot*, begin with *degker*, the translation of *to shoot*. Drop the *ker* (Rule 4). Add *zot* to make the verb past tense, and *em* because it is singular (Rule 7). The correct translation is *degzotem*. The translation of *the* is *wir*. To create the noun *spy*, begin with *tatker*, the translation of *to spy*. Drop the *ker* (Rule 4). According to Rule 9, to form a noun from a verb, add the suffix *lek* to the stem of the verb. The correct translation is *tatlek*.

33. **The correct answer is choice (D).** The complete sentence translates as, "That girl is a legal alien." The translation of the word *that* is *velle*. Because the subject of the sentence is feminine, add the suffix *nef* (Rule 3). The correct translation is *vellenef*. To create the translation of the word *girl*, begin with *ekaplek*, the translation of *boy*. Add the suffix *nef* to make it feminine. The correct translation is *ekapleknef*.

34. **The correct answer is choice (B).** The complete sentence translates as, "The skillful driver crossed the border." The translation of *the* is *wir*, and the translation of *skillful* is *janle*. To create the word *driver*, begin with *arker*, the translation of *to drive*. Drop the *ker* (Rule 4). To make the verb stem a noun, add *lek* (Rule 9). The correct translation is *arlek*.

35. **The correct answer is choice (E).** The complete sentence translates as, "He is a friend from the government." The translation of *from* is *mor*, and the translation of *the* is *wir*. The translation of *government* is *almanlek*.

36. **The correct answer is choice (D).** The complete sentence translates as, "An illegal alien crossed the river." To create the translation of *crossed*, begin with *chonker*, the translation of *to cross*. Drop the *ker* (Rule 4). To make the verb past tense, add *zot*. Then add *em* because the verb is singular (Rule 7). The correct translation is *chonzotem*. The translation of *the* is *wir*, and the translation of *river* is *browlek*.

37. **The correct answer is choice (A).** The complete sentence translates as, "The inspector worked to identify the girl." To create the translation of *worked*, begin with *frigker*, the translation of *to work*. Drop the *ker* (Rule 4). To make the verb past tense, add *zot*. Because the verb is singular, add *em* (Rule 7). The correct translation is *frigzotem*. The translation of the infinitive *to identify* is *kalenker*.

38. **The correct answer is choice (E).** The complete sentence translates as, "The alien's papers are legal." The translation of *the* is *wir*. To create the translation of *alien's*, begin with *huslek*, the Artificial Language word for *alien*. According to Rule 12, to form the possessive of a noun, add the suffix *ae*. The correct translation is *huslekae*. The translation of paper is *trenedlek*. To make this plural, add the suffiz *oz* (Rule 2). The correct translation is *trenedlekoz*.

39. **The correct answer is choice (C).** The entire sentence translates as, "A guard identified an alien from that country." The translation of *a* is *bex*. To create the noun *guard*, begin with *bonker*, the translation of the infinitive *to guard*. Drop the *ker* (Rule 4). Add *lek* to make the verb a noun (Rule 9). The correct translation is *bonlek*. To create the translation of the word *identified*, begin with *kalenker*, the translation of *to identify*. Drop the *ker* to create the stem of the verb (Rule 4). To make the verb past tense, add *zot*. Because the verb is singular, add *em* (Rule 7). The correct translation is *kalenzotem*.

40. **The correct answer is choice (A).** The complete sentence translates as, "That man is from the border station." To create the adjective *border*, begin with the infinitive *regker*, the translation of *to border*. Drop the *ker* to create the verb stem (Rule 4). According to Rule 9, to form a noun from a verb, add the suffix *lek*. Rule 10 states that to form an adjective from a noun, substitute the suffix *le* for *lek*. Therefore, the correct translation is *regle*. To create the translation of the noun *station*, begin with *lexker*, the translation of *to station*. Drop the *ker* (Rule 4). According to Rule 9, to form a noun from a verb, add *lek*. The correct translation is *lexlek*.

41. **The correct answer is choice (C).** The complete sentence translates as, "The spy worked to escape from the guard." The translation of *to escape* is *pirker*.

42. **The correct answer is choice (E).** The entire sentence translates as, "The boy was identified." To create the translation of *was*, begin with *synker*, the translation of *to be*. Drop the *ker* (Rule 4). To make the verb past tense, add *zot*. Because it is singular, add the suffix *em* (Rule 7). The correct translation is *synzotem*. Since *was* is part of the past participle *was identified*, follow Rule 8. This rule states that to form the past participle of

a verb, add the suffix to the stem of the verb. Therefore, the correct translation is *kalento*.

43. **The correct answer is choice (D).** The complete sentence translates as "The inspector has identified the illegal aliens." To create the present perfect singular of *tulker (to identify)* follow Rule 9. Drop the *ker* in *tulker*, and add *em* because the verb is singular. The correct translation is *tulem*. Drop the *ker* from *kalenker* and add the suffix *to*. The correct translation is *kalento*.

44. **The correct answer is choice (D).** The entire sentence translates as, "The girls are loyal." To create the feminine plural of *inle (loyal)*, add *nef* (Rule 1) and *oz* (Rule 2).

45. **The correct answer is choice (C).** The entire sentence translates as, "This spy injured that friendly man." To create the past tense of *liaker (to injure)*, drop the *ker* (Rule 4). Then add *zot* and *em* because the verb is singular (Rule 7). The correct translation is *liazotem*. To create the adjective *friend (kometlek)*, drop the *lek* and add *le* (Rule 10). The correct translation is *kometle*.

46. **The correct answer is choice (E).** The complete sentence translates as, "The woman was injured." To create the translation of *woman*, add the suffix *nef* to *kaplek* (Rule 1). The correct translation is *kapleknef*. Follow Rule 8 to create the past participle predicate of *synker liaker*. The translation of *was* is *synzotem*. Drop the *ker* from *liaker* and add *to*. The correct translation is *liato*.

47. **The correct answer is choice (B).** The complete sentence translates as, "The enemy's jeep crossed the border." To create the singular possessive adjective *enemy's* from *enemy (avelek)*, drop the *lek* and add *le* (Rule 10). Then add *ae* to make the adjective possessive (Rule 12). To create a noun from *regker (border)*, drop the *ker* (Rule 4). Then,

add *lek* (Rule 9). The correct translation is *reglek*.

48. **The correct answer is choice (A).** The entire sentence translates as "The illegal women are from that country." To create the feminine plural adjective form of *wir (the)*, add *nef* (Rule 1) and *oz* (Rule 2). The correct translation is *wirnefoz*. To create the negative feminine plural of *colle*, add the prefix *fer* (Rule 13). Then add *nef* (Rule 1) and *oz* (Rule 2). The correct translation is *fercollenefoz*. To create the feminine plural noun *women*, add *nef* to *kaplek* (Rule 1). Then add *oz* (Rule 2). The correct translation is *kapleknefoz*.

49. **The correct answer is choice (E).** The complete sentence translates as, "The girl was identified." To create the feminine singular noun *girl*, add *nef* (Rule 1) to *ekaplek*, which means *boy*. The correct translation is *ekapleknef*. To create the past participle as predicate from *kalenker*, which means *to identify*, drop the *ker* (Rule 4). Then add the suffix *to* (Rule 8). The correct translation is *kalento*.

50. **The correct answer is choice (C).** The entire sentence translates as, "That guard drives the jeep skillfully." To create the present tense of *arker*, drop the *ker*. According to Rule 6, to create the present tense of the verb, add *em* because it is singular. The correct translation is *arem*. To create the adverb *skillfully*, begin with *janle*, the translation of *skillful*. Follow Rule 11 and add *ki* to the masculine form of the adjective. The correct translation is *janleki*.

PART III

PREPARING FOR THE BORDER PATROL EXAM

The Logical Reasoning Test

chapter 4

OVERVIEW

- **Preparing for the Logical Reasoning questions: reading the paragraph**
- **Preparing for the Logical Reasoning questions: reading the question**
- **Tips for taking the Logical Reasoning Test**
- **Summing it up**

Every day, Border Patrol Agents face difficult situations that require them to use logic and decision-making skills. The Logical Reasoning Test assesses your ability to solve complex problems. Officials use this test to evaluate applicants to determine who has the best chance of succeeding at the academically rigorous U.S. Border Patrol Academy. They also use this test to predict which candidates are best suited for a career as a Border Patrol Agent.

PREPARING FOR THE LOGICAL REASONING QUESTIONS: READING THE PARAGRAPH

Before you take the Logical Reasoning Test, be aware that there is no penalty for guessing. This means that you should respond to every question, even if you are unsure of the correct answer. However, instead of blindly guessing, try to eliminate answer choices that you know are incorrect. This increases your chances of choosing the correct answer. Do not assume that there is a pattern to the correct answer choice letters. You may end up with several As or Bs in a row. Do not eliminate an answer choice based on the letter of the previous answer choice you picked.

The questions on the Logical Reasoning Test are based on paragraphs, also called passages, which relate to Border Patrol or law enforcement. Accept everything that you read in these paragraphs as fact. A paragraph might contain a factual error—it might give a detail that you know is untrue. Border Patrol officials are not testing your factual knowledge. They are only testing your ability to reason based on what you have read. Therefore, assume that what you are reading is true and base your answer only on this information.

When you read a paragraph, determine the type of information it provides. A paragraph might give you details about a situation or an event, an individual, a group of people, or a category or categories. Note whether the information is positive or negative. Most information in the paragraphs on this test is positive, such as "All of the book club members enjoy reading." However, negative information, such as "Several members have not read *Gulliver's Travels*," is just as important as positive information. Be sure to recognize the type of information provided by the paragraph.

Examine the author's choice of words carefully. Some statements contain key words or phrases such as "all," "every," "not," "none," "some," "most," "a few," "almost all," "many," and "if… then." These words tell you something about the relationships between various subjects, individuals, groups, or categories.

"All" and "Every" Statements

Statements containing the words "all" or "every" often explain how two persons or ideas are related. Usually, everything in the first group is also in the second group. Read this statement:

"All of the illegal aliens were from El Salvador."

In this sentence, the first group is "illegal aliens" and the second group is "people from El Salvador." The first group is included in the second group, but there is not enough information to conclude that the second group can be included in the first group. Therefore, the statement, "All people from El Salvador are illegal aliens" is invalid, or incorrect.

Suppose a clerk tells you that, "All of the movies on this shelf are romantic comedies." In this statement, the first group is "movies on the shelf" and the second group is "romantic comedies." From this statement, you cannot assume that all the romantic comedies in the store are on this shelf. This is an invalid or incorrect conclusion. Other romantic comedies may be located on other shelves in the store.

Read the following list of examples of "all" and "every" statements. Each example contains a valid statement given in a paragraph followed by an invalid statement.

Given statement: All the trumpet players are students.

Therefore, invalid: All students are trumpet players.

Given statement: Every teacher is an employee of the school district.

Therefore, invalid: Every employee of the school district is a teacher.

Given statement: All the librarians are women.

Therefore, invalid: All women are librarians.

Given these "all" and "every" statements, you can conclude that some of members of the second group are part of the first group. The following examples show which statements you can validly conclude from the given statements.

Given statement: All the trumpet players are students.

Therefore, valid: Some students are trumpet players.

Given statement: Every teacher is an employee of the school district.

Therefore, valid: Some employees of the school district are teachers.

Given statement: All the librarians are women.

Therefore, valid: Some women are librarians.

"Not" or "None" Statements

Statements that contain the words "not" or "none" are also important. These statements tell you that the first group has no relationship with the second group. For example, if you say, "New Border Patrol Agents are not assigned to the northern border," you can also say that, "None of the Border Patrol Agents assigned to the northern border are new agents." Other important phrases to look for include "it is not that case that" and "not all of." Take note of words containing the prefixes "dis-," "un-,"and "non-."

"Some" Statements

Sometimes a statement will provide information about only part of a group. The word "some" provides information about a small part of a larger group. For example, the statement, "Some students attended the pep rally" refers to a small part of all students. This statement does not provide enough information to make a judgment about what the other students might have done. You cannot confidently argue that the rest of the students did not attend the pep rally. The only thing you can say with certainty is that at least some of the students did attend the pep rally. Statements that refer to only a portion of a larger group may also contain the phrases "most," "a few," or "almost all."

"If . . . Then" Statements

Certain statements provide information about how events are related. They explain that one event happened because of another event. These statements use the words "if" and "then." A simple example is, "If Maureen wakes up late, then she will miss her bus." You might see a statement like this on the test: "If a candidate fails to master Spanish, then that candidate cannot work for Border Patrol." This if . . . then example shows a clear link between events. These statements may also show a connection between events that have already happened. An example of this would be "If the battery has died, then the laptop will not turn on." Using an if . . . then statement is only one way to show this relationship between events and situations. Phrases such as "whenever," "every time," and "each time" also indicate this sort of relationship. For example, "Every time I go to the grocery store, I see my next-door neighbor."

You cannot reverse the order of these statements and maintain the validity of the sentence. For example, in the statement "If a person works for the mayor's office, then that person is an employee of the county," "a person works for the mayor's office" is the first statement and "that person is an employee of the county" is the second statement. Switching the order of these statements makes the sentence invalid. "If a person is an employee of the county, then that person works for the mayor's office" is an invalid statement. You cannot validly conclude that anyone who works for the county is an employee of the mayor's office. A county employee could work for the department of transportation, children and youth, or the office of community development.

TIP

Correct answer choices often use the word "some." For example, if a paragraph says that most illegal immigrants in a certain city are from Honduras, but a few are from Belize, a correct answer might state, "Some illegal immigrants in this city are from Belize."

NOTE

Some of the answer options on the Logical Reasoning Test will negate "if . . . then" statements and put them in the wrong order. For example, if a paragraph says, "All Border Patrol Agents receive special training," an incorrect answer option might say "If a person receives special training, the person is a Border Patrol Agent."

However, you can reverse the two statements and retain the validity of the sentence if you negate both statements. When you negate a statement, you make it negative. For example, you can validly conclude that "If a person is not an employee of the county, then that person does not work for the mayor's office." Remember, you must reverse the order of the two statements before negating them. Leaving them in their original positions makes the sentence invalid.

Look for the following phrases, words, and prefixes on the Logical Reasoning Test:

- Negative words and prefixes that provide information about the relationships between groups, individuals, or events, such as "not," "never," and "seldom" and the prefixes "non-," "un-," or "dis-."

- Positive words that tell you about a large group, including "all," "most," and "always."

- If . . . then statements that explain relationships between events and situations. Remember that you cannot maintain the validity of the sentence if you switch the order of the two statements without negating them.

PREPARING FOR THE LOGICAL REASONING QUESTIONS: READING THE QUESTION

The Logical Reasoning Test contains two types of lead-in questions that ask you to complete a sentence by choosing the proper response option. The first type is a positive lead-in question, which states: "From the information given above, it can validly be concluded that . . . ." Four invalid conclusions and one valid conclusion follow positive lead-in questions. It is your responsibility to choose the only valid conclusion.

The following is an example of a positive lead-in question.

Example 1

Border Patrol Agents pull over a driver for speeding near the Texas-Mexico border. The driver is a U.S. citizen from El Paso. Believing that the driver is intoxicated, the agents conduct a field sobriety test, which the driver fails. After pulling up his record, the agents discover that this is his second drunk-driving offense. In Texas, a driver's license is suspended for 90 days for the first offense. After the second and third offenses, the driver's license is suspended for 180 days. A driver must serve a mandatory jail sentence following the third offense, and the police will confiscate the driver's vehicle.

From the information given above, it can be validly concluded that, if convicted, the driver will

    (A) serve a mandatory jail sentence.

    (B) lose his license for 90 days.

    (C) have his vehicle confiscated.

    (D) lose his license for 180 days.

    (E) receive probation.

This is the driver's second offense. If convicted, he could lose his license for 180 days. The driver does not face mandatory jail time or risk having his vehicle confiscated at this point. Nothing in the paragraph indicates that the drive will receive probation. **The correct answer is choice (D).**

The second type is a negative lead-in question, which states: "From the information given above, it CANNOT validly be concluded that . . . ." Four valid conclusions and one invalid conclusion follow negative lead-in conclusions. After reading the paragraph, you must choose the only invalid conclusion.

The following is an example of a negative lead-in question.

Example 2

"Project 28" was a plan to test a virtual fence along the United States-Mexico Border. The virtual fence consisted of a series of towers that used radar, sensors, and cameras to detect motion. Border Patrol Agents at Border Patrol Command Posts were alerted whenever motion was detected on the border. A virtual fence has several advantages over a physical fence along the U.S. border. Illegal immigrants crossing the border can easily damage a physical fence, and the cost to continually repair a fence is staggering. In some cases, the physical fence does not work. Immigrants find ways to climb the fence and build ramps to drive over it. Environmental groups are strongly opposed to physical fencing because it restricts animals' access to their habitats. "Project 28" was not a success, however. The equipment frequently failed and agents were unable to detect movement. The project was recently halted and money allotted to the project was redirected elsewhere.

From the information given above, it CANNOT validly be concluded that the virtual fence

(A) used a series of towers with sensors to detect motion across the border.

(B) was better for the environment than a physical fence.

(C) was more successful than a physical fence in stopping illegal border crossings.

(D) did not work as well as people hoped that it would.

(E) did not allow illegal immigrants to build ramps and drive over it.

To answer this type of question, you need to choose the answer option that states an incorrect conclusion. This is why it is important to carefully read the question before choosing an answer. In the sample question above, four answer options give correct conclusions. The conclusion in choice (A) is correct, so this is not the right answer. The virtual fence did use a series of towers with sensors to detect motion across the border. Choice (B) is also true and therefore incorrect. The paragraph explains that environmental groups did not like the idea of a physical fence because it limited animals' access to their habitats. This is not true of a virtual fence. Choice (C) is the correct answer. The virtual fence was not successful, and there is no way to tell if it was better than a physical fence in stopping border crossings. Choices (D) and (E) are also true and therefore incorrect. **The correct answer is choice (C).**

Some questions include additional information that can help you eliminate clearly wrong answers. For example, the question "From the information given above, it can validly be concluded that interns at the Border Patrol Academy…" allows you to eliminate answers that do not refer to interns at the Border Patrol Academy. Sometimes reading the question before the paragraph allows you to determine what information you should be looking for as you read. Be sure that you understand what the question is asking before you attempt to choose the correct response option.

TIPS FOR TAKING THE LOGICAL REASONING TEST

Remember the following tips when taking the Logical Reasoning Test.

- Base your answers only on the information provided in the paragraph. Do not worry whether this information is correct or incorrect. Assume that it is correct and use it to choose your answer.

- Pay attention to the use of positive and negative words.

- Note the use of positive and negative lead-in questions.

- Pay attention to sentences that contain the words "all," "none," and "some."

- Do not base your answer choices on the pattern of letters selected.

- After completing the practice exercise, read the answer explanations carefully. These explanations can help you understand your mistakes.

EXERCISES: LOGICAL REASONING

Directions: In Questions 1 through 16, some questions will ask you to select the only answer that can be validly concluded from the paragraph. These questions include a paragraph followed by five answer choices. Preceding the five answer choices will be the phrase "From the information given above, it can be validly concluded that…" In other questions, you may be asked to select the only answer that **cannot** be validly concluded from the paragraph. These questions include a paragraph followed by five answer choices. Preceding the five answer choices will be the phrase "From the information given above, it **CANNOT** be validly concluded that…"

You must use only the information provided in the paragraph, without using any outside information whatsoever.

1. Two Border Patrol Agents respond to a distress call concerning a group of illegal aliens stranded in a ravine. When the agents arrive, they find a group of 4 men and 3 women. One of the men has a broken leg, and 2 of the women are dehydrated. One of the men speaks English. All of the illegal aliens are from Belize. None of the illegal aliens could provide identification.

   From the information given above, it can validly be concluded that

   (A) none of the illegal aliens is related.

   (B) the man who speaks English is from Belize.

   (C) the man who broke his leg also speaks English.

   (D) the man who speaks English has identification.

   (E) the woman who was not dehydrated was not from Belize.

2. Rachel W. is a new Border Patrol Agent waiting for her assignment. The Border Patrol divides the continental United States into nineteen sectors. The northern sectors cover the states of Washington, Idaho, Montana, North Dakota, Michigan, New York, Vermont, and Maine. The southern sectors cover California, Arizona, New Mexico, Texas, Louisiana, Mississippi, Alabama, and Florida. Rachel is originally from New Hampshire and hopes to receive an assignment that is close to home. As a rule, Border Patrol assigns new agents to southern sectors, but it will make exceptions on a case-by-case basis.

   From the information given above, it can validly be concluded that

   (A) Rachel will receive an assignment in Vermont.

   (B) Rachel will receive an assignment in Mississippi.

   (C) Rachel will ask the Border Patrol to make an exception.

   (D) the Border Patrol usually assigns new agents to sectors close to their families.

   (E) the Border Patrol usually assigns experienced agents to the northern sectors.

3. In Pennsylvania, persons arrested for driving under the influence (DUI) for the first time receive 6 months probation and must pay a fine of $300 if their blood-alcohol concentration is 0.08–0.099. If their blood-alcohol concentration is 0.110–0.159, they receive a jail sentence of 2 days to 6 months, have their license suspended for 12 months, and must pay a fine of $500–$5,000. If their blood-alcohol concentration is 0.16 or higher, they receive a jail sentence of 3 days to 6 months, have their license suspended for 12 months, and must pay a fine of $1,000–$5,000. Catherine B. received a DUI for the first time. Her blood-alcohol concentration was 0.120.

From the information given above, it can validly be concluded that

(A) if Catherine B. receives a fine of $1,000, then she lives in Pennsylvania.

(B) if Catherine B. lives in Pennsylvania, then she will go to jail for 2 days to 6 months.

(C) if Catherine B. does not live in Pennsylvania, then she will not go to jail for 2 days to 6 months.

(D) if Catherine B. lives in Pennsylvania, then she will not have her license suspended.

(E) if Catherine B. does not live in Pennsylvania, then she will not have to pay a fine.

4. Recently, Border Patrol Agents received leads from informants about possible illegal activity taking place in the parking lot of an apartment complex. When they arrived at the complex, they drove through the parking lot, looking for individuals and vehicles matching their leads. They examined several suspicious vehicles, including many unregistered vehicles. All of the unregistered vehicles and some of the registered vehicles had been reported stolen. Some of the unregistered vehicles also contained illegal weapons. No arrests have been made in connection with this incident.

From the information given above, it can validly be concluded that

(A) some of the vehicles that contained illegal weapons were registered.

(B) all of the vehicles that did not contain illegal weapons were registered.

(C) all of the registered vehicles had been reported stolen.

(D) all of the vehicles that did not contain illegal weapons were unregistered.

(E) none of the unregistered vehicles was reported stolen.

5. The U.S. Department of Agriculture (USDA) restricts certain items from being brought into the United States. All travelers entering the United States are required to declare meats, fruits, vegetables, plants, seeds, animals, and animal products. They must declare these items if they are carried in checked baggage, carry-on luggage, or in a vehicle. Upon inspection, U.S. Customs and Border Protection (CBP) specialists will determine if these items may be brought into the country. If CBP agriculture specialists find items not declared by passengers, they confiscate and dispose of the items. A passenger not declaring an item may face a fine of up to $1,000 if the item is discovered. Mimi V. is travelling from Costa Rica to visit her son in Miami, Florida. She has food from Costa Rica in her carry-on bag.

From the information given above, it CANNOT be validly concluded that

(A) Mimi V. must declare the food in her carry-on bag.

(B) Mimi V. may be fined if she does not declare the food.

(C) inspectors may not allow Mimi V. to take the food into the United States.

(D) Mimi V. will be fined for trying to take the food into the country.

(E) inspectors may not find the food if Mimi V. does not declare it.

6. Law enforcement officials receive a tip about a man selling drugs from his apartment. The informant tells the police that she lives on the same floor as this man. After obtaining a search warrant, the police investigate the man's apartment. The police find marijuana, ecstasy, and cocaine. They place the man under arrest and charge him with possession with the intent to sell. Officers confiscate all the drugs as evidence.

From the information given above, it CAN-NOT be validly concluded that

(A) the informant lives in the same building as the drug dealer.

(B) the police had the right to search the drug dealer's home.

(C) the informant may also face charges regarding the drugs.

(D) the police removed the drugs from the apartment.

(E) the informant told the police about the drug dealer.

7. Michael J. is an illegal alien who works for a large farm in California. Michael J. was injured on the job because the equipment provided by the employer was outdated and unsafe. The company he works for refuses to pay for his medical expenses, and they fire Michael J. when he can no longer perform his job. Michael contacts a lawyer and discovers that illegal aliens working on farms are entitled to worker's compensation benefits under California law.

From the information given above, it can be validly concluded that Michael J.

(A) is a Mexican citizen.

(B) will sue the company.

(C) will likely be rehired.

(D) must return to his native country.

(E) will likely receive compensation.

8. To join the U.S. Border Patrol Tactical Unit (BORTAC), Border Patrol Agents must meet certain requirements. They must have a minimum of three years of service with the Border Patrol, pass the Border Patrol Physical Efficiency exam with a score of 90 percent, and pass an oral interview conducted by current BORTAC members. Ricardo Y. is a Border Patrol Agent who wants to join BORTAC.

From the information given above, it can be validly concluded that

(A) if Ricardo Y. has only one year of experience, then he will not be able to join BORTAC.

(B) if Ricardo Y. receives a test score of 90 percent, then he will be able to join BORTAC.

(C) if Ricardo Y. cannot join BORTAC, then he did not pass the oral interview.

(D) if Ricardo Y. cannot join BORTAC, then he does not have enough experience.

(E) if Ricardo Y. has worked as a Border Patrol Agent, then he will be able to join BORTAC.

9. France participates in the Visa Waiver Program (VWP), which allows foreign nationals to enter the United States without applying for a visa. A foreign national must meet certain requirements to enter the country without applying for a visa. The person cannot remain in the United States for more than 90 days, cannot work or study while in the country, and must have a machine-readable passport. The foreign national must also not have a criminal record, which prevents them from participating in the program. Gianfranco is from France and has entered the United States with the VWP program.

From the information given above, it CANNOT be validly concluded that Gianfranco

(A) has a machine-readable passport.

(B) will stay in the country for 90 days.

(C) does not have a criminal record.

(D) will not work or study in the country.

(E) is a foreign national from France.

10. Some 4.4 million Mexican immigrants were living in the United States in 2000. Although most of these immigrants worked in production, transportation, and material-moving occupations, not all of them did. For example, some worked in sales and office occupations. Very few worked in management positions.

From the information given above, it can be validly concluded that in 2000, in the United States,

(A) most Mexican immigrants worked in either sales or office occupations.

(B) it is not the case that some of the Mexican immigrants were managers.

(C) none of the salespeople were Mexican immigrants.

(D) most of those not employed in management positions were Mexican immigrants.

(E) some of the salespersons were Mexican immigrants.

ANSWER KEY AND EXPLANATIONS

1. B	**3.** B	**5.** D	**7.** E	**9.** B
2. E	**4.** B	**6.** C	**8.** A	**10.** E

1. **The correct answer is choice (B).** The paragraph states that all of the immigrants are from Belize. This would include the man who speaks English. Given the information in the paragraph, you cannot validly conclude that the illegal aliens are related or that the man who speaks English is also the one who broke his leg, so choices (A) and (C) are incorrect. The sixth sentence tells you that none of the illegal aliens has identification, so choice (D) is incorrect. Since all of the illegal aliens are from Belize, choice (E) is also incorrect.

2. **The correct answer is choice (E).** The paragraph explains that the Border Patrol usually assigns new agents to the southern sectors. From this statement, you can validly conclude that the Border Patrol usually assigns experienced agents to the northern sectors. There is not enough information in the paragraph to determine if Rachel will be assigned to a sector in Vermont or Mississippi, choices (A) and (B). There is also nothing in the paragraph to indicate that Rachel will ask the Border Patrol to make an exception and assign her to a sector close to home, choice (C). From reading the paragraph, you cannot conclude that the Border Patrol assigns new agents to sectors that are near their families, choice (D).

3. **The correct answer is choice (B).** Catherine B. had a blood-alcohol concentration of 0.120. The paragraph explains that in Pennsylvania, the punishment for this crime includes a jail sentence of 2 days to 6 months. You cannot conclude that if Catherine B. receives a fine of $1,000 she lives in Pennsylvania or if she does not live in Pennsylvania that she will not have to pay a fine, choices (A) and (E), because other states may give the same fine. You also cannot conclude that she will not go to jail for 2 days to 6 months if she lives in a state other than Pennsylvania, choice (C), because other states may give the same jail sentence. Choice (D) is incorrect because the passage states that her license will be suspended for 12 months.

4. **The correct answer is choice (B).** The paragraph says that some of the unregistered vehicles contained illegal weapons. Therefore, all of the vehicles that did not contain illegal weapons were registered. This statement also makes choices (A) and (D) incorrect. The passage says that only some of the registered vehicles were reported stolen, so choice (C) is also incorrect. All of the unregistered vehicles were reported stolen, so choice (E) is incorrect.

5. **The correct answer is choice (D).** To correctly answer this question, choose the answer option that makes an incorrect statement based on the information in the paragraph. The paragraph says that food (meat, fruit, vegetables, seeds, and animal products) must be declared, so choice (A) is true and therefore incorrect. Choice (B) is also true; Mimi V. may be fined if she does not declare the food. Choice (C) is correct, too; inspectors may not allow Mimi V. to take the food into the United States even if she does declare it. Choice (D) is the correct answer because it is not true. Mimi will not be fined for trying to take the food into the country; she will only be fined if she does not declare the food. Choice (E) is also true

and therefore incorrect. Inspectors might not find the food if Mimi chooses not to declare it.

6. **The correct answer is choice (C).** To correctly answer this question, choose the answer option that makes an incorrect statement based on the information in the paragraph. Choice (A) is true and therefore incorrect; the paragraph says that the informant lives on the same floor as the drug dealer. Choice (B) is also true; police had a search warrant, so they had the right to search the apartment. Choice (C) is not true and therefore correct. Nothing in the paragraph leads you to believe that the informant will also face charges. Choices (D) and (E) are also true; police removed the drugs from the apartment, and the informant tipped off police about the drug dealer.

7. **The correct answer is choice (E).** The paragraph explains that Michael was injured by equipment provided by the employer that was outdated and unsafe. This tells you that Michael's injury was the employer's fault, so Michael will likely receive compensation. Nothing in the paragraph indicates that Michael is from Mexico or that he will sue the company, choices (A) and (B). There is no information in the paragraph that tells you if the company will rehire Michael or if Michael must return to his native country, choices (C) and (D).

8. **The correct answer is choice (A).** The paragraph says that Ricardo Y. has only been with the Border Patrol for one year and that Border Patrol Agents need three years of experience to join BORTAC. Therefore, Ricardo Y. cannot join. Choice (B) is incorrect because in addition to scoring 90 on the test, Ricardo Y. must meet the experience requirement and pass an oral interview to join BORTAC. The same logic applies to choices (C) and (D); there are several rea-

sons why Ricardo may not be able to join BORTAC. Choice (E) does not indicate how long Ricardo has worked as a Border Patrol Agent, so this answer choice is also incorrect.

9. **The correct answer is choice (B).** Based on the information in the paragraph, you cannot conclude that Gianfranco will stay in the country for 90 days—he may stay up to 90 days, but there is not enough information to indicate how long he will stay. The other answer choices give requirements of the VWP program, so they are true and therefore incorrect.

10. **The correct answer is choice (E).** The passage says that some Mexican immigrants worked in sales and office occupations. Choice (A) is incorrect because most Mexican immigrants worked in production, transportation, and material-moving occupations. Choice (B) is also incorrect because the passage says very few worked in management—this means that some did work in this occupation. Choice (C) is incorrect because some immigrants worked in sales. Choice (D) is incorrect because the passage only gives information about Mexican immigrants. It does not say how many people who were not Mexican immigrants worked in occupations other than management.

SUMMING IT UP

- The Logical Reasoning Test determines your ability to solve complex problems on the job.

- Border Patrol officials use the Logical Reasoning Test to determine which applicants have the best chance of succeeding at the Border Patrol Academy.

- The Logical Reasoning Test questions are based on paragraphs. Base your answers only on what you read in the paragraph.

- Be aware of both positive and negative words in the paragraph.

- Look for words that indicate relationships between people, events, and categories.

- Read each answer choice carefully before choosing an answer.

Spanish Language Proficiency Test

chapter 5

OVERVIEW

- Preparing for Spanish Language Proficiency vocabulary questions
- Preparing for Spanish Language Proficiency grammar questions
- Tips for taking the Spanish Language Proficiency Test
- Summing it up

The majority of those crossing the border into the United States speak only Spanish. For this reason, the U.S. Border Patrol requires its agents to become fluent in Spanish. Being able to speak, comprehend, write, and read Spanish helps Border Patrol Agents communicate effectively with both legal and illegal immigrants and Mexican law-enforcement officials.

Many candidates come to the Border Patrol with a good working knowledge of the Spanish language. While some are native Spanish speakers, others learned Spanish in high school or college. Candidates who are fluent in Spanish should take the Spanish Language Proficiency Test. Those who are not should take the Artificial Language Test (ALT), which measures a candidate's ability to learn Spanish. These candidates will learn the Spanish language at the U.S. Border Patrol Academy.

The Spanish Language Proficiency Test has two parts. Part I tests your knowledge of Spanish vocabulary by asking you to choose an appropriate synonym for an underlined word. Part II has three sections testing your knowledge of grammar. In Section I, you will select the answer choice that correctly fills in a blank. In Section II, each answer choice will show a sentence, and you have to choose the sentence that is grammatically correct. To answer the questions in Section III, you will select the answer choice that correctly replaces incorrect words or phrases in a sentence.

Follow these tips to help you study for the Spanish Language Proficiency Test:

- **Study with a friend.** Studying with a partner allows you to check your pronunciation and grammar by reading aloud.

- **Memorize vocabulary.** Set aside extra time to memorize vocabulary words. Create lists of vocabulary words and practice them every day. Although you cannot possibly study every word on the exam, a large vocabulary will allow you to make an educated guess about words you do not know.

- **Practice with a native speaker.** Ask a friend who is a native speaker to help you study. If you do not know any native speakers, try listening to a CD or MP3 of a native speaker. This will help you learn pronunciation and intonation.

- **Take breaks.** Do not try to cram your studying into one long session. Break your study time into smaller sessions. Take breaks between study sessions to give your mind time to process the information you have read.

Remember, if you are not proficient in Spanish, you should take the ALT. Candidates who do not know Spanish will spend an additional forty days at the Border Patrol Academy participating in an intense Spanish program.

PREPARING FOR SPANISH LANGUAGE PROFICIENCY VOCABULARY QUESTIONS

The best way to prepare for the vocabulary portion of the test is to memorize vocabulary words. For each question on Part I of the Spanish Language Proficiency Test, you will read a sentence with an underlined word. Then you will select the answer choice that gives an appropriate synonym for the underlined word. The more vocabulary words you memorize, the more likely you are to recognize the words on this part of the exam.

If you do not recognize the underlined word, use context clues to help you figure out the correct answer. Use the other words in the sentence to determine the meaning of the underlined word. This will allow you to eliminate obviously incorrect answers and increase your chances of choosing the correct answer.

Also try to determine the underlined word's part of speech. Figure out if the word is a noun, verb, pronoun, or preposition. If you know that you are looking for a noun, you can eliminate answer choices that contain verbs or prepositions. When selecting an answer, make sure that your choice also agrees with the sentence in form, number, and gender.

Complete the following practice exercise. If you have difficulty with this exercise, you may need to spend more time studying the Spanish vocabulary.

EXERCISES: SPANISH LANGUAGE PROFICIENCY VOCABULARY

Part I

Directions: Read the sentence and then choose the most appropriate synonym for the underlined word.

1. Encontramos una enramada cerca del rio.
   (A) remar
   (B) árboles
   (C) enojada
   (D) enredada
   (E) cobertizo

2. Es preciso serenarse para no causar más problemas.
   (A) acalorar
   (B) serenata
   (C) apaciguar
   (D) cantar
   (E) calentar

3. Dos mujeres y un hombre iban a lomo de mula.
   (A) espalda
   (B) costado
   (C) lame
   (D) lobo
   (E) lado

4. De pronto oímos a alguien sollozando en la noche.
   (A) llorando
   (B) callando
   (C) sollozo
   (D) riendo
   (E) soltando

5. Veamos cuán rápidamente se trepa por ese camino.
   (A) tropa
   (B) escalona
   (C) atrapa
   (D) raspa
   (E) escala

6. Esa noche, todo terminó en bronca.
   (A) riña
   (B) ronca
   (C) bronco
   (D) tertulia
   (E) velada

7. No sabemos por qué se ha demorado tanto el envío.
   (A) envidia
   (B) recibo
   (C) flete
   (D) envenenamiento
   (E) remesa

8. Unos agentes llegaron con noticias del occidente.
   (A) accidente
   (B) informe
   (C) oeste
   (D) incidente
   (E) oficial

ANSWER KEY AND EXPLANATIONS

Part I

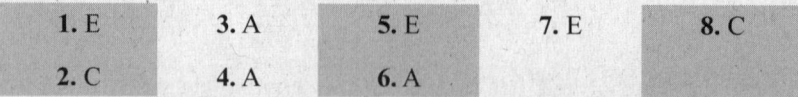

1. E	**3.** A	**5.** E	**7.** E	**8.** C
2. C	**4.** A	**6.** A		

1. **The correct answer is choice (E).** The word *enramada* refers to a small <u>hut or shelter</u> made of branches, so the term *cobertizo,* "shed," is the best synonym. Choice (A), "to row," is phonetically similar to the target word but it has a different meaning. Choice (B), "trees," has to do with branches, but it is not a hut. Choice (C),"angry," and choice (D), "tangled," are adjectives with meanings that are unrelated to a shed.

2. **The correct answer is choice (C).** The word *serenarse* means <u>to calm down</u>; therefore, *apaciguar,* "to soothe" or "to pacify" is the best synonym. Choice (A), "to become heated," and choice (E), "to warm," are contrary to the meaning of *serenarse.* Choice (B), "serenade," is a noun from the same root as the target word but with a different meaning. Choice (D), "to sing," is not related to the meaning of *serenarse.*

3. **The correct answer is choice (A).** The expression *a lomo de* means <u>to ride on an animal's back</u>. Therefore, *espalda,* "back," is the best synonym. Choices (B) and (E) both mean "side," so they would refer to the wrong part of the mule. Choice (C), "licks," and choice (D), "wolf," have nothing to do with the meaning of *lomo.*

4. **The correct answer is choice (A).** The word *sollozando* is a form of the verb *sollozar* that means <u>to sob</u>. Therefore, *llorando,* "crying," is the best synonym. Choice (B), "being quiet," and choice (D), "laughing," mean the opposite of "sobbing." Choice (C), a "sob," is not a verb. Choice (E), "letting go," is not related to the meaning of *sollozando.*

5. **The correct answer is choice (E).** The word *trepa* is a form of the verb *trepar,* which means <u>to scale with difficulty, using hands and feet</u>. Therefore, *escala,* "climbs," is the closest synonym. Choice (A), "troop," is a noun and unrelated to *trepar.* Choice (B), "puts in terraced or staggered form," comes from the same root as the correct answer, but its meaning is different. Choice (C), "traps," and choice (D), "scrapes," have meanings that are unrelated to *trepar.*

6. **The correct answer is choice (A).** The word *bronca* refers to a <u>quarrel</u>, so *riña,* "fight," is the best synonym. Choice (B), "hoarse," sounds similar to *bronca* but is unrelated. Choice (C), "hoarse," sounds as if it were the masculine form of *bronca,* but its meaning is also unrelated. Choice (D), a "gathering," and choice (E), an "evening party," both have a peaceful connotation and, therefore, have the opposite meaning of *bronca.*

7. **The correct answer is choice (E).** The word *envío* means a <u>consignment</u> or a <u>shipment</u>. Therefore, *remesa,* "remittance," is the best synonym. Choice (A), "envy," and choice (D), "poisoning," begin with the same syllable as the target word but have different meanings. Choice (B), "receipt," and choice (C), "freight," may be related to the idea of sending something, but they do not refer to the shipment itself.

8. **The correct answer is choice (C).** The term *occidente* means <u>west</u>. Therefore, the best synonym is *oeste,* "west." Choice (A), "accident," and choice (D), "incident," both have the same ending as the target word but have different meanings. Choice (B), "report," and choice (E), "official," are entirely unrelated to the meaning of *occidente.*

PREPARING FOR SPANISH LANGUAGE PROFICIENCY GRAMMAR QUESTIONS

Part II of the Spanish Language Proficiency Test has three sections, each with a different type of grammar question. Keep these tips in mind when studying for the grammar on the Spanish Language Proficiency Test:

- All nouns in Spanish are either masculine or feminine. Nouns ending in -o or a consonant are generally masculine. Nouns ending in -e can be masculine or feminine. Feminine articles such as *la (the)* or *una (a or an)* precede feminine nouns. When memorizing vocabulary, memorize the article that goes with each noun. This will make it easier to recognize irregular nouns.

- Pronouns take the place of nouns in a sentence. You may come across a variety of pronouns on the test, including subject pronouns, direct object pronouns, indirect object pronouns, and prepositional pronouns. Familiarize yourself with the prepositions and their various forms before taking the test.

- Verbs express an action or a state of being. When taking the Spanish Language Proficiency Test, make sure that the verbs agree with nouns or pronouns in tense and form. Memorize several commonly used irregular verb forms before taking the test.

- Adjectives modify nouns. An adjective must agree with the noun it is modifying in number and gender.

Section I of Part II contains sentences, each with a blank. You will select the answer choice with the word(s) that best completes the sentence. You will choose from five answer choices labeled (A) through (E). Remember to select an answer that agrees with the sentence in verb form, gender, and number. Also be sure to select an answer that uses the same tense. You can easily eliminate inappropriate words by examining each choice carefully before choosing an answer.

Section II tests your knowledge of sentence structure, verb forms, verb tenses, and prepositions. For this section, you will read four sentences labeled A through D and choose the grammatically correct sentence. As you read each sentence, make sure that you can identify important elements such as the subject, verb, and direct object. If one of these components is missing, you might have an incomplete sentence. Next, make sure that all elements agree in terms of form, tense, number, and gender. Also be aware of incorrect word usage. This will help you eliminate incorrect answer choices.

In Section III of Part II, you will decide if a sentence uses an italicized word or phrase correctly. This is tricky because a word or phrase can have an appropriate meaning and still be incorrect. Make sure the word or phrase fits the grammatical structure of the sentence. If the italicized portion of the sentence is incorrect, then you must select an appropriate replacement from four answer choices that are labeled (A) through (D). Remember to choose an answer that is not only appropriate in meaning, but also matches the tense and structure of the sentence. Occasionally, you will come across a question where no correction is necessary. In this case, select answer choice (E): No es necesario hacer ninguna corrección, which means "It is not necessary to make any correction."

Try the following practice exercise. If you have trouble with this exercise, review the grammatical rules of the Spanish language before taking the Spanish Language Proficiency Test.

NOTE

The eight-week Spanish language training program at the U.S. Border Patrol Academy is task-based. This means that it focuses on language related to the tasks a Border Patrol Agent performs. Expect to learn law-enforcement-specific language in this training program.

EXERCISES: SPANISH LANGUAGE PROFICIENCY GRAMMAR

Part II

Section I

Directions: Read each sentence carefully. Select the appropriate word or phrase to fill each blank space.

1. _____ zapatos son demasiado grandes para_____ .
   - **(A)** Estos / ti
   - **(B)** Este / tu
   - **(C)** Estar / contigo
   - **(D)** Están / te
   - **(E)** Esta / tuyo

2. Vamos a _____ jardín de _____ universidad.
   - **(A)** estudio / las
   - **(B)** estudiamos / la
   - **(C)** estudias / el
   - **(D)** estudiar / la
   - **(E)** estudiando / el

3. _____ compañeros los serán primeros que _____ ir.
   - **(A)** Mis / querrán
   - **(B)** Míos / quererán
   - **(C)** Yo / querán
   - **(D)** Me / quieren
   - **(E)** Mes / querer

Section II

Directions: Read each sentence carefully. Select the one sentence that is correct.

1. **(A)** La pesada remolque de diez y séis llantas transportaba una grande caja y muchos enseres.
   (B) El pesado remolque de dieciséis llantas transportaba una caja grande y muchos enseres.
   (C) El pesado diezyseis llantas remolque transportaba enseres una caja grande.
   (D) La pesada remolque de diez-y-seis llantas y muchos enseres transportaba una grande caja.

2. **(A)** El fin de semana pasado estuví para la casa del campo de mi amigo parientes.
   (B) La fin de semana pasada fui en la casa del campo de unos parientes de mi amigo.
   (C) El fin de semana pasado estuve en la casa de campo de unos parientes de mi amigo.
   (D) Fin de semana pasado unos parientes estar a la campo casa de mi amigo.

3. **(A)** Estamos de acuerdo con que haya una reforma, pero esta debe realizarse cuidadosamente.

   (B) Estamos de acuerdo que ayer una reforma, pero este debe se realiza cuidadosa.

   (C) Estamos de acuerdo que habemos una reforma, pero estas deben realizar cuidadomente.

   (D) Realizamos de acuerdo que una reforma, pero esta se debe cuidadosamente.

Section III

Directions: Read each sentence carefully. Select the correct word or phrase to replace the underlined portions of the sentence. In those cases in which the sentence needs no correction, select answer choice (E).

1. ¡Pronto, <u>sale</u> a ver esto!

   (A) salir

   (B) sala

   (C) sal

   (D) salto

   (E) No es necesario hacer ninguna corrección

2. Mis compañeros ni saben que fui allá <u>ninguno</u> les importa.

   (A) ni

   (B) nadie

   (C) no

   (D) nunca

   (E) No es necesario hacer ninguna corrección.

3. ¿<u>Cualesquiera</u> son los lugares que debemos inspeccionar hoy?

   (A) Quiénes

   (B) Cuáles

   (C) Cuál

   (D) Cualquiera

   (E) No es necesario hacer ninguna corrección.

ANSWER KEY AND EXPLANATIONS

Part II

Section I

| 1. A | 2. D | 3. A |

1. **The correct answer is choice (A).** *Estos* is the demonstrative pronoun that matches the noun *zapatos;* and *ti* is the correct prepositional pronoun. Choices (B) and (E) use incorrect demonstratives and incorrect prepositional pronouns. Choices (C) and (D) use forms of the verb *estar* instead of the demonstrative *este*, as well as incorrect prepositional pronouns.

2. **The correct answer is choice (D).** The infinitive *estudiar* is the correct form to complete the compound future verb; the article *los* agrees in gender and number with the noun *jardín*; and the article *la* agrees in gender and number with the noun *universidad.* Choices (A), (B), (C), and (E) use incorrect forms of the verb and articles that do not match the noun they accompany.

3. **The correct answer is choice (A).** *Mis* is the appropriate possessive article for *compañeros;* and *querrán* is the correct future form of the verb *querer.* Choices (B), (C), (D), and (E) use incorrect or nonexistent possessives and incorrect verb forms.

Section II

| 1. B | 2. C | 3. A |

1. **The correct answer is choice (B).** This sentence has the proper structure and does not contain errors. Choices (A) and (D) contain various errors, including nonagreement of articles and adjectives with nouns, incorrect terms for expressing the number "sixteen," and illogical structures. Choice (C) has several errors, including misplaced clauses and an incorrect term for expressing the number "sixteen."

2. **The correct answer is choice (C).** This sentence has the proper structure and is without errors. Choices (A) and (D) have several errors, including missing or misused articles, improper verb forms, misplaced clauses, and incorrect prepositions. Choice (B) has an improper article, incorrect verb, and incorrect prepositions.

3. **The correct answer is choice (A).** This sentence has the proper structure and is without errors. Choices (B) and (C) have several errors, including use of the wrong term for the verb *haya*, an incorrect pronoun, an improper use of the reflexive verb *realizarse,* and an incorrect form of an adverb. Choice (D) has misplaced clauses and is not a complete sentence.

Section III

| 1. C | 2. A | 3. B |

1. **The correct answer is choice (C).** This is the appropriate imperative form of the verb *salir*, "to go or come out." Choice (A) is the infinitive. Choice (B) is the imperative of the verb *salar* ("to put salt on something"). Choice (D) is not a verb.

2. **The correct answer is choice (A).** This completes the negative expression *ni . . . ni*. Choices (B), (C), and (D) are also negatives, but they are used incorrectly.

3. **The correct answer is choice (B).** This is correct because *cuáles* is the correct plural pronoun to use as a subject for the plural noun *lugares*. Choices (A) and (D) use pronouns that refer to persons rather than things. Choice (C) does not match the noun *lugares* in number.

answers exercises

TIPS FOR TAKING THE SPANISH LANGUAGE PROFICIENCY TEST

- Memorize as much vocabulary as possible before taking the test. Although you cannot memorize every word that appears on the test, having a large vocabulary will help you make an educated guess about unfamiliar words.

- When answering a grammar question, make sure that the parts of the sentence agree in form, tense, number, and gender.

- Answer the easy questions first and come back to the more difficult questions later.

- Remember, the Border Patrol determines your score based on the number of questions you answer correctly. There is no penalty for guessing, so you should answer every question on the test. If you are unsure of the correct answer, eliminate all of the obviously incorrect answer choices before making a selection.

- If you finish before time is up, go back and check your work.

SUMMING IT UP

- Candidates who are proficient in Spanish should take the Spanish Language Proficiency Test. If you are unsure of your proficiency, take the Artificial Language Test (ALT). Candidates who do not know Spanish will spend an additional forty days at the U.S. Border Patrol Academy taking an intense Spanish language course.

- The Spanish Language Proficiency Test has two parts; the first part asks questions about vocabulary and the second asks various questions about grammar. Part II has three sections that ask questions about sentence structure, agreement, verb forms, and word usage. All questions are multiple choice.

- Review vocabulary lists and grammatical rules well in advance of the test. Study in small time segments so you can better digest what you have read.

The Artificial Language Test (ALT)

OVERVIEW

- Vocabulary Lists
- Grammatical rules for the Artificial Language
- Glossary of grammatical terms
- How to use the Artificial Language
- Types of questions on the Artificial Language Test
- Summing it up

When you take the Border Patrol Test, you will take *either* the Spanish Language Proficiency Test or the Artificial Language Test (ALT). If you do not yet know the Spanish language, or if you do not know it well, you will take the ALT. This test is challenging, to say the least. It is like learning a new language. Many of the grammatical rules on this test are similar to those in the Spanish language. The Border Patrol uses the ALT to predict your ability to master the Spanish language at the U.S. Border Patrol Academy.

You will be given the following reference materials to use during the test:

- Vocabulary Lists
- Grammatical Rules for the Artificial Language
- Glossary of Grammatical Terms

They have been reprinted for you here in the Practice Exercise. You can also access them online at the U.S. Customs and Border Protection Web site (www.cbp.gov).

VOCABULARY LISTS

The Vocabulary Lists give you the Artificial Language words that will be used on the test. You could just memorize these lists; it is possible to do this. The number of words on these lists is much smaller than the number of words in the English or Spanish language. But there is no guarantee that the Vocabulary Lists you will use here are *exactly* like the ones you will be given on the test. However, it is likely that they will be very similar.

Nevertheless, doing well on the ALT is not as easy as memorizing the Vocabulary Lists. To answer many of the test questions, you will have to change the grammatical form of the words on the Vocabulary Lists. For example, according to the Vocabulary Lists, the Artificial Language word *chonker* means "to cross." A test question might ask you to choose the correct translation of *crossed,* which is not on the Vocabulary Lists. You have to use the Grammatical Rules for the

Artificial Language to create the translation of the past-tense verb *crossed* from the translation of the infinitive *to cross.*

If you look at the Vocabulary Lists at the end of this chapter, you will see that these "lists" are actually one list with two major columns. The first column is titled "Word List Arranged Alphabetically by the English Word." This column lists the English words in alphabetical order. Across from each English word is its Artificial Language translation. For example, across from the word *difficult* is *glasle,* its Artificial Language translation.

The second major column is titled "Word List Arranged Alphabetically by the Artificial Language Word." This column lists the words in the opposite order—the Artificial Language word is first, fol-lowed by its English translation. In this column, *glasle* is followed by its English translation, *difficult.*

Why the two columns? The columns make it easier for you to answer the test questions. Sometimes, it might be faster to use the first column, but other times, it might be easier to first find the Artificial Language word.

GRAMMATICAL RULES FOR THE ARTIFICIAL LANGUAGE

The Grammatical Rules for the Artificial Language is a list of guidelines explaining how to do the following:

- Form the feminine singular of a noun, a pronoun, an adjective, or an article
- Form the plural of nouns, pronouns, adjectives, and articles
- Add feminine and plural endings to adjectives and articles to make them agree with the nouns they modify
- Form the verb stem (which is used to create forms of the verb other than the infinitive)
- Add suffixes to make subjects and verbs agree in number
- Form the present tense of a verb
- Form the past tense of a verb
- Form the past participle of a verb
- Form a noun from a verb
- Form an adjective from a noun
- Form an adverb from an adjective
- Form the possessive of a noun or a pronoun
- Add a prefix to make a word negative

While some aspects of the Artificial Language may be different on the actual test than in the ref-erence materials at the end of this chapter, the grammatical rules will be the same. For example, according to the Grammatical Rules for the Artificial Language, to create the plural of the word *country,* add the suffix *oz* to *failek,* the Artificial Language word for *country.* The word *countries* in the Artificial Language is *failekoz.* While the suffix you are told to use to make words plural may be different on the actual test, the rule will be same—you will add a short suffix to a word. Therefore, it is important that you study these rules until you are comfortable using them. This will make the test much easier for you.

GLOSSARY OF GRAMMATICAL TERMS

The Glossary of Grammatical Terms lists the English parts of speech. While you can use this glossary during the test, you should study it—even memorize it—ahead of time. Some questions on the ALT will ask you to form a part of speech, such as an adverb. If you do not know what an adverb is, answering this question will be difficult.

This glossary also explains how the Artificial Language is similar to the Spanish language. For example, the Spanish language uses masculine or feminine endings for nouns, adjectives, and articles. The Artificial Language also uses these endings.

The following parts of speech are discussed in the Glossary of Grammatical Terms:

- Article
- Adjective
- Adverb
- Infinitive
- Noun
- Pronoun
- Verb

Also discussed are gender, prefixes, and suffixes.

TIP

Only one prefix is used in the Artificial Language—*fer,* a prefix meaning *not.* It is frequently used with *colle,* the Artificial Language word for *legal. Fercolle* means *illegal.*

HOW TO USE THE ARTIFICIAL LANGUAGE

Translating English words into the Artificial Language takes practice. Begin by studying the examples in this section. They will teach you how to use the reference materials to create sentences in the Artificial Language. Then, use the Vocabulary Lists to create some simple sentences using the listed words. Remember that you may only use the words on these lists or some form of these words to create sentences. Follow the Grammatical Rules for the Artificial Language to create the translations.

Example 1

The man drove a jeep.

From the Vocabulary Lists, you can see that the translation of *the* is *wir,* and the translation of *man* is *kaplek.* To create the translation of the past-tense verb *drove,* begin with *arker,* the translation of *to drive.* According to Rule 4, to create the verb stem, drop the *ker.* The verb stem is *ar.* To make the verb past tense, follow Rule 7. Add *zot* to the verb stem. The verb is singular (because *man* is singular), so add *em.* The translation of *drove* in this sentence is *arzotem.* Go back to the Vocabulary Lists. The translation of *a* is *bex,* and the translation of *jeep* is *daqlek.* The complete sentence translates as, *"Wir kaplek arzotem bex daqlek."*

Example 2

> That alien is legal.

From the Vocabulary Lists, you can see that the translation of *that* is *velle*. The subject of the sentence is neither feminine nor plural, so you do not have to add a suffix. The translation of *alien* is *huslek*. To create the translation of *is,* begin with *synker,* the translation of *to be*. According to Rule 4, drop the *ker* to create the verb stem. Then follow Rule 6 because the verb is in the present tense. Since *is* is singular, add the suffix *em*. The correct translation is *synem*. According to the Vocabulary Lists, the translation of *legal* is *colle*. The complete sentence translates as, *"Velle huslek synem colle."*

Example 3

> A spy was identified.

On the Vocabulary Lists, you will see that the translation of *a/an* is *bex*. To create the translation of the noun *spy*, begin with *tatker,* the translation of the infinitive *to spy*. Drop the *ker* to create the verb stem (Rule 4). Then follow Rule 9 to form a noun from a verb. According to this rule, add the suffix *lek* to the verb stem. The translation of *spy* in this sentence is *tatlek*. To create the verb *was*, use the translation of the infinitive *to be*, which is *synker*. Drop the *ker* to create the verb stem. Then follow Rule 7, which explains how to create the past tense of a verb. Add the suffix *zot* to *syn,* the verb stem. Then add the suffix *em* because the verb is singular. The correct translation of *was* is *synzotem*. In this sentence, *identified* is a past participle. Follow Rule 8 to create the past participle. Add the suffix *to* to the verb stem, which is *kalen*. The correct translation of the past participle *identified* is *kalento*. The complete sentence translates as, *"Bex tatlek synzotem kalento."*

Example 4

> The illegal aliens injured the inspectors.

According to the Vocabulary Lists, the translation of *the* is *wir*. In this sentence, *the* modifies *aliens,* which is plural. According to Rule 3, adjectives modifying nouns with plural endings must have endings that agree with the words they modify. Therefore, *wir* should have the suffix *oz*. The translation of the word *legal* is *colle*. Follow Rule 13 to make the word negative. According to this rule, you need to add the prefix *fer*. The translation of *illegal* is *fercolle*. However, in this sentence *illegal* modifies the plural noun *aliens*, so you need to add the suffix *oz*. The corrected translation is *fercolleoz*.

The translation of *alien* is *huslek*. To make the translation plural, add the suffix *oz*. To create the past-tense verb *injured,* begin with *liaker,* the translation of the infinitive *to injure*. Drop the *ker* to create the verb stem (Rule 4). Follow Rule 7 to make the verb past tense. According to this rule, add the suffix *zot* and then the suffix *im* because the verb is plural. The correct translation of *injured* in this sentence is *liazotim*.

The next word in the sentence is *the*. The translation of *the* is *wir,* and since it modifies the plural noun *inspectors*, add the suffix *oz*. The correct translation is *wiroz*. To create the plural noun *inspectors,* begin with *zelker,* the translation of the infinitive *to inspect*. Drop the *ker* to create the verb stem (Rule 4). According to Rule 9, to form a noun from a verb, add the suffix *lek*. Then add the suffix *oz* to make the noun plural. The correct translation of *inspectors* is *zellekoz*. The complete sentence translates as, "*Wiroz fercolleoz huslekoz liazotim wiroz zellekoz.*"

Example 5

The guard inspected the woman's papers.

This sentence is more difficult to translate—but not impossible, so hang in there. From the Vocabulary Lists, you know that the translation of *the* is *wir*. To create the translation of the noun *guard*, begin with *bonker*, the translation of the infinitive *to guard*. According to Rule 4, drop the *ker* to create the verb stem. Then follow Rule 9 to form a noun from a verb. This rule says to add *lek* to the verb stem. The correct translation of *guard* is *bonlek*.

To create the past-tense verb *inspected*, begin with *zelker*, the translation of the infinitive *to inspect*. According to Rule 4, drop the *ker* to create the verb stem. Follow Rule 7 to create the past tense of a verb. According to this rule, add *zot* to the verb stem, and then add *em* because the verb is singular (because *guard* is singular). The correct translation of *inspected* in this sentence is *zelzotem*.

The next word in this sentence is *the*. According to the Vocabulary Lists, the translation of *the* is *wir*. In this sentence, *the* modifies the feminine noun *woman*, so according to Rule 3, add the suffix *nef*. The correct translation is *wirnef*.

To create the translation of *woman*, add *nef*, the feminine suffix, to *kaplek*, the translation of *man*. The translation of *woman* is *kapleknef*. To make this translation possessive, follow Rule 12, and add the suffix *ae*. The correct translation of *woman's* is *kapleknefae*.

The translation of the word *paper* is *trenedlek*. To make this plural, add the suffix *oz* (Rule 2). The entire sentence translates as: *Wir bonlek zelzotem wirnef kapleknefae trenedlekoz.*

TYPES OF QUESTIONS ON THE ARTIFICIAL LANGUAGE TEST

The Artificial Language Test has four sets of questions. Each set contains a different type of question. There are 50 questions on the entire test.

- Set 1 (questions 1–20)—To answer these questions, you have to decide which words in a sentence have been correctly translated into the Artificial Language.
- Set 2 (questions 21–30)—For these questions, you have to select the answer choice that correctly translates an underlined word or group of words.
- Set 3 (questions 31–42)—To answer the questions in this set, you must select the correct translation of words in parentheses.
- Set 4 (questions 43–50)—For these questions, you must select the correct Artificial Language grammatical form of underlined words in a sentence.

TIP

EXERCISES: ARTIFICIAL LANGUAGE

Set 1: Questions 1 Through 20

To answer the first set of questions on the Artificial Language Test, you must decide which words in a sentence have been correctly translated from English into the Artificial Language. The English sentence appears in the left column, and its Artificial Language translation is in the right column. Three words in the translation are underlined and numbered. The sentences in this set of questions look like this.

Example 1

Sentence	Translation
That woman is legal.	Vellenef kapleknef synem colle.
	1 2 3

The directions on the test tell you to use scratch paper to list each numbered word that is correctly translated into the Artificial Language. The directions tell you to do this for Questions 1 through 20. Then, select your answer following these instructions:

Mark:

- **(A)** if <u>only</u> the word numbered 1 is correctly translated.
- **(B)** if <u>only</u> the word numbered 2 is correctly translated.
- **(C)** if <u>only</u> the word numbered 3 is correctly translated.
- **(D)** if <u>two</u> or <u>more</u> of the numbered words are correctly translated.
- **(E)** if <u>none</u> of the numbered words is correctly translated.

Note that these directions ask you to identify the words that are *correctly* translated, and not those that are *incorrectly* translated. The three words in the sentence above are correctly translated. **The correct answer is choice (D).**

Now, try answering these questions.

Sentence	Translation
1. The illegal aliens crossed the border.	Wir fercolleoz huslekoz chonzotem 1 2 3 wir reglek.
2. That girl is a friend.	Vollenef ekaplekoz synem bex kometlek. 1 2 3
3. The man inspected the papers.	Wir kaplek zelzotem wir trenedlek. 1 2 3
4. Guards skillfully drive jeeps.	Bonlekoz janleki arim daqleknef. 1 2 3
5. A spy was injured.	Bex tatlek synzotim liaker. 1 2 3

ANSWER KEY AND EXPLANATIONS

Set 1

| 1. B | 2. C | 3. A | 4. D | 5. A |

1. **The correct answer is choice (B).** In this sentence, only the word numbered 2 is correctly translated. While *wir* is the correct translation of *the,* according to Rule 3, adjectives modifying nouns with plural endings must have endings that agree with the words they modify. *Aliens* is plural, so *the* should also have a plural ending. The correct translation of *the* in this sentence is *wiroz. Chonzotem,* or *crossed,* is incorrect because it has a singular ending. The correct translation is *chonzotim.*

2. **The correct answer is choice (C).** Only the word numbered 3 is correctly translated. *Volle* is the translation of *this. Velle* is the translation of *that.* Because *that* modifies a feminine noun, it should have a feminine ending. The correct translation is *vellenef. Ekaplekoz,* the word numbered 2, is the translation of *boys.* To create the translation of *girl,* add *nef,* the feminine suffix, to *ekaplek,* the translation of *boy.* The correct translation of girl is *ekapleknef.*

3. **The correct answer is choice (A).** Only the word numbered 1 is correctly translated. In this sentence, *wir,* the translation of *the,*

modifies *papers,* so it should have the suffix *oz.* The correct translation is *wiroz. Trenedlek* is the translation of *paper.* To make this word plural, the suffix *oz* must be added. The correct translation is *trenedlekoz.*

4. **The correct answer is choice (D).** The words numbered 1 and 2 are correctly translated. The correct translation of *jeeps* is *daqlekoz.*

5. **The correct answer is choice (A).** Only the word numbered 1 is correctly translated in this sentence. *Synzotim* is the translation of *were.* According to Rule 6, a singular verb has a singular ending. Therefore, the translation of *was* is *synzotem. Liaker,* the word numbered 3, is the translation of *to injure.* To create the past-tense verb *injured,* drop the *ker* at the end of *liaker.* According to Rule 4, this creates the verb stem. Then, according to Rule 7, to form the past tense of a verb, add the suffix *zot.* Because the verb is singular, add the suffix *em.* The correct translation is *liazotem.*

EXERCISES: ARTIFICIAL LANGUAGE

Set 2: Questions 21 Through 30

This set of questions asks you to read a short paragraph. Some of the words in the paragraph are underlined and have a number underneath. Below the paragraph is a set of five possible translations for each underlined word or words. You need to select the answer choice that gives the correct translation. Look at this example:

Example 1

The <u>men and women</u> who guard the border are loyal. They must deal with both friends and
           1

<u>enemies</u>.
  2

    1. **(A)** kaplek loa kapleknef
       (B) ekaplek loa ekapleknef
       (C) kaplekoz loa ekapleknefoz
       (D) kaplekoz loa kapleknefoz
       (E) kaplek loa kepleknefoz

To answer this question, choose the correct translation of *men and women*. To create the Artificial Language word *men*, begin with *kaplek*, the word for *man*. According to Rule 2, add the suffix *oz* to make the word plural. The correct translation of *men* is *kaplekoz*. *Loa* is the correct translation of the conjunction *and*. To create the translation of the word *women*, began with *kaplek*, the translation of *men*. According to Rule 1, add *nef* to make it feminine. Then, according to Rule 2, add *oz* to make it plural. The correct translation is *kapleknefoz*. **The correct answer is choice (D).**

Example 2

    2. **(A)** avelekoz
       (B) avelek
       (C) aveleknef
       (D) avele
       (E) avelekker

To answer this second example, choose the correct translation of *enemies*. The translation of *enemy* is *avelek*. To make this plural—*enemies*—add *oz*. The correct translation is *avelekoz*. **The correct answer is choice (A).**

Read this paragraph and answer the questions that follow.

Border Patrol Agents <u>work</u> very hard.
　　　　　　　　　　　1

They <u>inspect papers</u> from the government.
　　　　2

They patrol the border on foot and also <u>drive jeeps</u>. Their work is often
　　3

dangerous. Some illegal aliens <u>are spies</u>
　　　　　　　　　　　　　　　4

from other countries. Border Patrol Agents must keep these criminals from crossing the <u>border</u> and entering the
　　　　　　　　　5

country.

1. **(A)** frigem
   (B) frigzotim
   (C) frigim
   (D) frigker
   (E) frigzotem

2. **(A)** zelim trenedlekoz
   (B) zelimoz trandedlekoz
   (C) zelem trenedlekoz
   (D) zelker trenedlek
   (E) zelker trenedlekoz

3. **(A)** arzotem daqlekae
   (B) arem daqlekoz
   (C) arzotim daqlek
   (D) arimoz daqlekoz
   (E) arim daqlekoz

4. **(A)** synzotim tatlekoz
   (B) synem tatlek
   (C) synim tatlekoz
   (D) synim tatlek
   (E) synzotem tatlekoz

5. **(A)** reglek
   (B) regto
   (C) regker
   (D) regzotem
   (E) reglekoz

ANSWER KEY AND EXPLANATIONS

Set 2

1. C	2. A	3. E	4. C	5. A

1. **The correct answer is choice (C).** To create the present-tense verb *work,* use *frigker,* the translation of the infinitive *to work* on the Vocabulary Lists. Create the verb stem by dropping the *ker* (Rule 4). According to Rule 6, to form the present tense of a verb, add the suffix *im* if the verb is plural. This correct translation is *frigim.*

2. **The correct answer is choice (A).** To create the present-tense verb *inspect,* use *zelker,* the translation of the infinitive *to inspect* on the Vocabulary Lists. Drop the *ker* to create the verb stem (Rule 4). Add *im* because the verb is plural (Rule 6). The correct translation of *inspect* in this sentence is *zelim.* According to the Vocabulary Lists, the translation of *paper* is *trenedlek.* To make this plural, add the suffix *oz* (Rule 2). The correct translation of *papers* is *trenedlekoz.*

3. **The correct answer is choice (E).** To create the present-tense verb *drive,* use the translation of the infinitive *to drive,* which is *arker.* Drop the *ker* to create the verb stem (Rule 4). Because the verb is plural, add the suffix *im* (Rule 6). The translation of *drive* in this sentence is *arim.* The translation of *jeep* on the Vocabulary Lists is *daqlek.* To make this plural, add the suffix *oz.* The translation of *jeeps* is *daqlekoz.*

4. **The correct answer is choice (C).** To create the plural, present-tense verb *are,* begin with *synker,* the translation of the infinitive *to be.* Drop the *ker* to create the verb stem (Rule 4). Follow Rule 6: To create a present-tense plural verb, add the suffix *im.* The correct translation is *synim.* To create the noun *spies,* use *tatker,* the translation of the infinitive *to spy* on the Vocabulary Lists. Drop the *ker* to create the verb stem (Rule 4). According to Rule 9, to form a noun from a verb, add the suffix *lek.* To make this noun plural, add the suffix *oz* (Rule 2). The correct translation is *tatlekoz.*

5. **The correct answer is choice (A).** To create the noun *border,* use *regker,* the translation of the infinitive *to border* on the Vocabulary Lists. Drop the *ker* to create the verb stem (Rule 4). According to Rule 9, to form a noun from a verb, add the suffix *lek.* The correct translation is *reglek.*

EXERCISES: ARTIFICIAL LANGUAGE

Set 3: Questions 31 Through 42

The questions in this set are written in the Artificial Language with a group of words in English in parentheses. You must choose the answer choice that gives the correct Artificial Language translation of the words in parentheses. These questions look like this:

Example 1

Velle ekaplek synem bex (illegal alien).

- **(A)** colle huslek
- **(B)** fercollenef husleknef
- **(C)** fercolle huslek
- **(D)** fercolleoz huslekoz
- **(E)** fercolle huslekoz

This sentence translates as, "That boy is an illegal alien." The translation of the word *legal* on the Vocabulary Lists is *colle*. According to Rule 13, to make a word negative, add the prefix *fer*. The translation of *illegal* in this sentence is *fercolle*. The translation of *alien* on the Vocabulary Lists is *huslek*. **The correct answer is choice (C).**

Always translate the entire sentence before choosing an answer. Doing so makes it much easier to choose the correct answer. Now, try answering these questions.

1. (The inspectors) chonzotim wir browlek.
   - **(A)** Wir zelek
   - **(B)** Wir zelekoz
   - **(C)** Wir zelker
   - **(D)** Wiroz zelkeroz
   - **(E)** Wiroz zellekoz

2. Vellenef ekapleknef (is from) bex avele failek.
   - **(A)** synzotem quea
   - **(B)** synem mor
   - **(C)** synzotim mor
   - **(D)** synim mor
   - **(E)** synker quea

3. (The skillful guard) kalezotem wir tatlek.
   - **(A)** Wir janle bonlek
   - **(B)** Wir janle bonle
   - **(C)** Wir janleoz bonlekoz
   - **(D)** Wir janlelek bonlek
   - **(E)** Wir janle bonker

4. Wir (alien's government) synem colle.
   - **(A)** huslekae almanlekae
   - **(B)** huslekoz almanlek
   - **(C)** huslekoz almanlekoz
   - **(D)** huslekae almanlek
   - **(E)** huslek almanlek

5. Volle kaplek (is not injured).
   - **(A)** fersynem liazotem
   - **(B)** fersynem liaem
   - **(C)** synim ferliaker
   - **(D)** synem ferliaker
   - **(E)** fersynim liazotim

ANSWER KEY AND EXPLANATIONS

Set 3

| 1. E | 2. B | 3. A | 4. D | 5. A |

1. **The correct answer is choice (E).** The translation of *the* is *wir*. In this sentence, *it* modifies a plural noun, so the suffix *oz* must be added (Rule 2). The correct translation is *wiroz*. To create the plural noun *inspectors*, drop the *ker* from the ending of *zelker*, the translation of the infinitive *to inspect*. According to Rule 9, to form a noun from a verb, add the suffix *lek*. To make the noun plural, add the suffix *oz*. The correct translation is *zellekoz*. The complete sentence translates as, "The inspectors crossed the river."

2. **The correct answer is choice (B).** To create the translation of *is,* begin with *synker*, the translation of *to be*. Drop the *ker* (Rule 4). Add the suffix *em* because the verb is singular (Rule 6). According to the Vocabulary Lists, the translation of *from* is *mor*. The complete sentence translates as, "That girl is from an enemy country."

3. **The correct answer is choice (A).** The translation of *the* is *wir*, and the translation of *skillful* is *janle*. To create the noun *guard*, use the translation of the infinitive *to guard*, which is *bonker*. Drop the *ker* (Rule 4). To form a noun from a verb, add the suffix *lek* (Rule 9). The correct translation is *bonlek*. The complete sentence translates as, "The skillful guard identified the spy."

4. **The correct answer is choice (D).** The translation of *alien* is *huslek*. According to Rule 12, to make a noun possessive, add *ae*. The correct translation of *alien's* is *huslekae*. The translation of *government* is *almanlek*. The complete sentence translates as, "The alien's government is legal."

5. **The correct answer is choice (A).** To create the translation of *is,* begin with *synker*, the translation of *to be*. Drop the *ker* and add *em* because the verb is singular (Rules 4 and 6). To make the verb negative, add the prefix *fer*. The correct translation is *fersynem*. Note that if the question had asked for the translation of *uninjured*, the *fer* prefix would be attached to the translation of *injured*. To create the past-tense verb *injured*, use *liaker*, the translation of *to injure*. Drop the *ker* to create the verb stem. To make the verb past tense, add the suffix *zot*. Then add the suffix *em* because the verb is singular (Rule 7). The correct translation is *liazotem*. The complete sentence translates as, "This man is not injured."

EXERCISES: ARTIFICIAL LANGUAGE

Set 4: Questions 43 Through 50

For the last group of questions on the Artificial Language Test (ALT), you must choose the correct form of the underlined translation in the sentence. The form the translation should be in is in parentheses after the sentence. The underlined translations in these questions are usually from the Vocabulary Lists but are not in the correct grammatical form. For example, a question might look like this:

Example 1

Wiroz huslekoz <u>tulker chonker</u> wir reglek. (present perfect plural verb)

    (A) tulem chonzotem

    (B) tulker chonto

    (C) tunim chonzotim

    (D) tulim chonto

    (E) tulim chonker

Begin by translating the whole sentence. It means, "The aliens have crossed the border." You can see an example of a present perfect verb in the explanation under Rule 8. *Tulim* is the correct translation of *have* (plural). To create the present perfect *crossed*, drop the *ker* from *chonker*. Then, according to Rule 8, add *to*. The correct translation is *tulim chonto*. **The correct answer is choice (D).**

Look at the examples in the discussion under Rule 8 to find the correct perfect tense. The description under this rule is more specific than the information in the Glossary of Grammatical Terms.

Some questions in this set will ask you to choose the correct grammatical form for more than one word or group of related words. When this is the case, the instructions—the forms the translations should be in—are separated by a dash, as in the following question.

Example 2

Wirnef <u>kaplek</u> <u>kalenker</u> wir tatlek. (feminine singular noun—past tense)

    (A) kapleknef—kalenzotem

    (B) kalpeknefoz—kalenzotim

    (C) kapleknef—kalento

    (D) ekapeknef—kalento

    (E) kapekoz—kalenzotem

The translation of the complete sentence is, "The woman identified the spy." *Kaplek* is the translation of *man*. To make this *woman*—a feminine singular noun—add the suffix *nef* (Rule 1). The correct translation is *kapleknef*. To create the past tense of *kalenker, to identify,* drop the *ker* (Rule 4). Add the suffix *zot* and then the suffix *em* because the verb is singular (Rule 7). The correct translation is *kalenzotem*. **The correct answer is choice (A).**

Now, try answering these questions:

1. <u>Velle</u> <u>kaplek</u> trenedlekoz fersynzotem colle. (singular adjective—singular possessive noun)

   (A) Velle ekaplekae

   (B) Velle kaplekae

   (C) Velleoz kaplekoz

   (D) Velle kaplekoz

   (E) Velle ekaplek

2. <u>Wir</u> <u>colle</u> <u>huslek</u> daqlek synim mor velle failek. (feminine plural adjective—negative feminine plural adjective—possessive feminine plural noun)

   (A) wirnefoz—fercollenefoz—husleknefozae

   (B) ferwirnefoz—fercollenefoz—husleknefoz

   (C) wirnef—fercollenef—husleknefozae

   (D) wiroz—fercolleoz—huslekoz

   (E) wirnefoz—collenefoz—huslekozae

3. Wirnef <u>tatker</u> synzotem <u>kalenker</u>. (feminine singular noun—past participle as predicate)

   (A) tatkernef—kalento

   (B) tatleknef—kalenzotem

   (C) tatkernef—kalenzotem

   (D) tatlenef—kalenzotim

   (E) tatleknef—kalento

ANSWER KEY AND EXPLANATIONS

Set 4

1. B   **2.** A   **3.** E

1. **The correct answer is choice (B).** The translation of the entire sentence is, "That man's papers were not legal." The singular adjective *that* is *velle*. *Kaplek* is the translation of *man*. To make this possessive, add the suffix *ae* (Rule 12). The correct translation is *kaplekae*.

2. **The correct answer is choice (A).** The translation of the entire sentence is, "The illegal aliens' jeep is from that country." The English language translation of *the* is *wir*. To make this feminine, add the suffix *nef* (Rule 1). To make it plural, add the suffix *oz* (Rule 2). The correct translation is *wirnefoz*. *Colle* is the translation of the adjective *legal*. To make it negative, add the prefix *fer* (Rule 13). To make it feminine, add the suffix *nef*, and to make it plural, add the suffix *oz*. The correct translation is *fercollenefoz*. *Huslek* is the translation of *alien*. To make this feminine, add the suffix *nef*, and to make it plural, add the suffix *oz*. To make it possessive, add the suffix *ae* (Rule 12). The correct translation is *husleknefozae*.

3. **The correct answer is choice (E).** The translation of the entire sentence is, "The spy was identified." *Tatker* is the translation of the infinitive *to spy*. To make this a noun, drop the *ker* (Rule 4) and add l*ek* (Rule 9). To make the noun feminine, add the suffix *nef* (Rule 1). The correct translation is *tatleknef*. To create the past participle of *kalenker*, *to identify*, drop the *ker* (Rule 4). Then add the suffix *to* (Rule 8). The correct translation is *kalento*.

EXERCISES: ARTIFICIAL LANGUAGE TEST

The Vocabulary Lists

The words on the following lists are the same; they are merely arranged differently, as they would be in a bilingual dictionary. In the first list, you can look up words in English to find their equivalent word in the Artificial Language. In the second list, you can look up words in the Artificial Language to find their equivalent word in English. During the actual test, you will have the vocabulary lists with you for consultation at all times. Nonetheless, you should note that the words given below are not the same as those given in the actual test. Therefore, it is best not to try to memorize them before taking the actual test.

Word List Arranged Alphabetically by the English Word				Word List Arranged Alphabetically by the Artificial Language Word			
English	Artificial Language	English	Artificial Language	Artificial Language	English	Artificial Language	English
a, an	bex	skillful	janle	almanlek	government	kaplek	man
alien	huslek	that	velle	arker	to drive	kometlek	friend
and	loa	the	wir	avelek	enemy	lexker	to station
boy	ekaplek	this	volle	bex	a, an	liaker	to injure
country	failek	to be	synker	bonker	to guard	loa	and
difficult	glasle	to border	regker	browlek	river	mor	friend
enemy	avelek	to cross	chonker	chonker	to cross	pirker	to escape
friend	kometlek	to drive	arker	colle	legal	quea	of
from	mor	to escape	pirker	daqlek	jeep	regker	to border
government	almanlek	to guard	bonker	degker	to shoot	synker	to be
he, him	yev	to have	tulker	ekaplek	boy	tatker	to spy
jeep	daqlek	to identify	kalenker	failek	country	trenedlek	paper
legal	colle	to injure	liaker	frigker	to work	tulker	to have
loyal	inle	to inspect	zelker	glasle	difficult	velle	that
man	kaplek	to shoot	degker	huslek	alien	volle	this
of	quea	to spy	tatker	inle	loyal	wir	the
paper	trenedlek	to station	lexker	janle	skillful	yev	he, him
river	browlek	to work	frigker	kalenker	to identify	zelker	to inspect

Grammatical Rules for the Artificial Language

The grammatical rules given here are similar, but not identical, to those used in the ALT. Some of the suffixes (word endings) and prefixes (additions to the beginning of a word) used in the actual test differ from those used in the practice test.

During the actual test, you will have access to the rules at all times. Consequently, it is important that you understand these rules, but it is not necessary that you memorize them. In fact, memorizing them will hinder rather than help you, since there are differences between the rules in the version of the Artificial Language that appears here and the one that appears in the actual test.

You should note that the next part of this section contains a glossary of grammatical terms to assist you if you are not thoroughly familiar with the meaning of these grammatical terms.

<u>Rule 1</u>: To form the feminine singular form of a noun, a pronoun, an adjective, or an article, add the suffix <u>nef</u> to the masculine singular form. Only nouns, pronouns, adjectives, and articles take feminine endings in the Artificial Language. When gender is not specified, the masculine form is used.

Example: If a <u>male eagle</u> is a <u>verlek</u>, then a <u>female eagle</u> is a <u>verleknef</u>. If an <u>ambitious</u> man is a <u>tosle</u> man, an ambitious woman is a <u>toslenef</u> woman.

<u>Rule 2</u>: To form the plural of nouns, pronouns, adjectives, and articles, add the suffix <u>oz</u> to the correct singular form.

Example: If one <u>male eagle</u> is a <u>verlek</u>, several <u>male eagles</u> are <u>verlekoz</u>. If an <u>ambitious</u> woman is a <u>toslenef</u> woman, several <u>ambitious</u> women are <u>toslenefoz</u> women.

<u>Rule 3</u>: Adjectives modifying nouns and pronouns with feminine and/or plural endings must have endings that agree with the words they modify. In addition, an article (*a/an* and *the*) preceding a noun must also agree with the noun in gender and number.

Example: If an <u>active male eagle</u> is a <u>sojle verlek</u>, an <u>active female eagle</u> is a <u>sojlenef verleknef</u> and several <u>active female eagles</u> are <u>sojlenefoz verleknefoz</u>. If <u>this male eagle</u> is <u>volle verlek</u>, <u>these female eagles</u> are <u>vollenefoz verleknefoz</u>. If <u>the male eagle</u> is <u>wir verlek</u>, <u>the female eagle</u> is <u>wirnef verleknef</u> and <u>the female eagles</u> are <u>wirnefoz verleknefoz</u>. If <u>a male eagle</u> is <u>bex verlek</u>, <u>several male eagles</u> are <u>bexoz verlekoz</u>.

<u>Rule 4</u>: The stem of a verb is obtained by omitting the suffix <u>ker</u> from the infinitive form of the verb.

Example: The stem of the verb <u>tirker</u> is <u>tir</u>.

<u>Rule 5</u>: All subjects and their verbs must agree in number; that is, singular subjects require singular verbs and plural subjects require plural verbs. (See Rules 6 and 7.)

<u>Rule 6</u>: To form the present tense of a verb, add the suffix <u>em</u> to the stem for the singular or the suffix <u>im</u> to the stem for the plural.

Example: If <u>to bark</u> is <u>nalker</u>, then <u>nalem</u> is the present tense for the singular (the dog <u>barks</u>) and <u>nalim</u> is the present tense for the plural (the dogs <u>bark</u>).

<u>Rule 7</u>: To form the past tense of a verb, first add the suffix <u>zot</u> to the stem, and then add the suffix <u>em</u> if the verb is singular or the suffix <u>im</u> if it is plural.

Example: If <u>to bark</u> is <u>nalker</u>, then <u>nalzotem</u> is the past tense for the singular (the dog <u>barked</u>) and <u>nalzotim</u> is the past tense for the plural (the dogs <u>barked</u>).

<u>Rule 8</u>: To form the past participle of a verb, add the suffix <u>to</u> to the stem of the verb. It can be used to form compound tenses with the verb <u>to have</u>, as a predicate with the verb <u>to be</u>, or as an adjective.

In the last two cases, it takes masculine, feminine, singular, and plural forms in agreement with the noun to which it refers.

Example of use in a compound tense with the verb to have:

If to bark is nalker and to have is tulker, then tulem nalto is the *present perfect* for the singular (the dog has barked) and tulim nalto is the *present perfect* for the plural (the dogs have barked). Similarly, tulzotem nalto is the *past perfect* for the singular (the dog had barked) and tulzotim nalto is the *past perfect* for the plural (the dogs had barked).

Example of the use as a predicate with the verb to be:

If to adopt is rapker and to be is synker, then a boy was adopted is a ekaplek zynzotem rapto and many girls were adopted is ekapleknefoz synzotim raptonefoz.

Example of use as an adjective:

If to delight is kasker then a delighted boy is a kasto ekaplek and many delighted girls are kastonefoz ekapleknefoz.

Rule 9: To form a noun from a verb, add the suffix lek to the stem of the verb.

Example: If longker is to write, then a writer is a longlek.

Rule 10: To form an adjective from a noun, substitute the suffix le for the suffix lek.

Example: If pellek is beauty, then a beautiful male eagle is a pelle verlek and a beautiful
          female eagle is a pellenef verleknef. (Note the feminine suffix nef.)

Rule 11: To form an adverb from an adjective, add the suffix ki to the masculine form of the adjective. (Note that adverbs do not change their form to agree in gender or number with the word they modify.)

Example: If pelle is beautiful, then beautifully is pelleki.

Rule 12: To form the possessive of a noun or pronoun, add the suffix ae to the noun or pronoun after any plural or feminine suffixes.

Example: If a boglek is a dog, then a dog's collar is a boglekae collar. If he is yev, then his
          book is yevae book. If she is yevnef, then her book is yevnefae book.

Rule 13: To make a word negative, add the prefix fer to the correct affirmative form.

Example: If an active male eagle is a sojle verlek, an inactive male eagle is a fersojle verlek.
          If the dog barks is boglek nalem, then the dog does not bark is boglek fernalem.

Glossary of Grammatical Terms

This glossary will be available to you during the actual test, but it is recommended that you study the glossary before taking the test. The glossary contains basic grammatical concepts that apply to English, Spanish, and the Artificial Language. The glossary contains fairly extensive and comprehensive explanations of each grammatical concept. **The explanations in the actual test are not comprehensive. Consequently, it is particularly important that you study these explanations very carefully.**

Article: An article is a word that precedes a noun and determines whether it is a definite or indefinite noun; for instance <u>the</u> book, <u>an</u> object.

Adjective: An adjective is a word used to modify a noun or pronoun (for example, <u>intelligent</u> women). Generally, an adjective serves to answer questions such as <u>which</u>, <u>what kind of</u>, and <u>how many</u>. For example,

"<u>This</u> book" would be the adjectival answer to the question "which book?" "a <u>beautiful</u> book"
1   2

would be the adjectival answer to the question "what kind of book?" and "<u>several</u> days" would be
3

the adjectival answer to the question "how many days?"

In English, adjectives have only one form, regardless of the type of noun they modify. More specifically, whether a noun is feminine or masculine, singular or plural, the adjective used to modify it remains the same; for example, the adjective <u>strong</u> is exactly the same when it refers to one man, one woman, or many men. By contrast, in both Spanish and the Artificial Language, the ending of the adjective is different if the adjective is modifying a singular masculine noun, a singular feminine noun, a plural masculine noun, or a plural feminine noun.

Adverb: An adverb is a word used to modify a verb. For example, the sentence "It was produced" could be modified to express <u>where</u> it was produced by saying "It was produced <u>locally</u>."

Generally, an adverb is used to answer the questions <u>where</u> (as in the example above), <u>when</u> (as for example, "he comes <u>frequently</u>"), or <u>how</u> (as for example, "she thinks <u>logically</u>"). Adverbs sometimes are used to modify an adjective or another adverb. For example, in the sentence "She has a <u>really</u> beautiful mind," the adverb <u>really</u> modifies the adjective <u>beautiful</u>. In the sentence "She thinks <u>very</u> logically," the adverb <u>very</u> modifies the adverb <u>logically</u>. In the Artificial Language, the only adverbs used are those that modify verbs. In the Spanish language, as well as in the English language, adverbs are used to modify verbs, adjectives, and other adverbs.

Gender: As a grammatical concept, gender refers to the classification of words according to whether they are masculine, feminine, or neuter.

As stated above, Spanish takes masculine or feminine endings for nouns, adjectives, and articles. The neuter form is used sometimes to express abstraction in a more emphatic manner. The neuter form is <u>NOT</u> used in the Artificial Language. Consequently, it is very important for you to remember that in the Artificial Language <u>all</u> nouns, adjectives, and articles take either a masculine or a feminine ending according to whether the sentence refers to a male or female.

Also, all nouns and adjectives in the Artificial Language were conceived (for the sake of simplicity) to be masculine. Thus, unless the feminine gender is specified in the sentence, the masculine gender is used always.

Infinitive: An infinitive is the general, abstract form of a verb; for example, <u>to look</u>, <u>to think</u>, <u>to remember</u>, <u>to walk</u>. Once the action expressed by the verb is attached to a specific subject (a person, animal, or thing), then we say the verb is "conjugated," or linked to that subject; for example, "he/she thinks," "the dog runs." "the table broke."

In contrast to the way that an infinitive in English is preceded by the word "to" (as in "to think"), in the Artificial Language (and in Spanish), infinitives are defined by their suffix. In the version of the Artificial Language used here, this ending (or suffix) is <u>ker</u>. (In the actual test, the ending will be different.)

Noun: A noun is a word that names a person, place, thing, or abstraction; for example. <u>Lindsay</u>, <u>Chicago</u>, <u>tree</u>, <u>wisdom</u>. A noun can refer to an individual (as in <u>Lindsay</u>, an individual person, or <u>Chicago</u>, an individual place) or to a set (as in "<u>all stones</u>," "<u>all trees</u>," "<u>all cities</u>").

Prefix: A prefix always occurs at the beginning of a word. It can be a single letter or a sequence of letters; for example, <u>a</u>moral, <u>il</u>legal, <u>dys</u>functional.

A prefix is the opposite of a suffix, which always occurs at the end of a word, but both serve to change the basic word in some way. For example, <u>polite</u> is the basic word (in this case an adjective) to express the concept of behavior that conforms to accepted social norms, while adding the prefix <u>im</u> and creating the word <u>impolite</u> transforms the word <u>polite</u> into its contradictory concept. You should note that in the Artificial Language a prefix is used to create negative concept (see Rule 13). Such a rule mimics both Spanish and English, in both of which negation is usually expressed by using a negative prefix.

Pronoun: A pronoun is a word used in place of a noun; for example, "she" instead of "Lindsay," "they" instead of "the guards," "it" instead of "the stone," "himself/herself" instead of "the judge."

In both English and Spanish, there is a difference between a pronoun that stands for the subject of an action (as in "<u>She</u> threw the stone," meaning that <u>Lindsay</u> threw the stone), and a pronoun that stands for the object of an action (as in "The stone was thrown at <u>her</u>," meaning that the stone was thrown at Lindsay). By contrast, in the Artificial Language used in this manual, there is no grammatical difference between <u>he</u> and <u>him</u>, both being <u>yev</u>. Remember, however, that in the Artificial Language pronouns take feminine endings when the subject or object of the action is feminine. Accordingly, in the version of the Artificial Language given in this manual, both <u>she</u> (subject) and <u>her</u> (object) would be <u>yevnef</u> (i.e., <u>yev</u> plus the feminine suffix <u>nef</u>).

Suffix: A suffix always occurs at the end of a word. It can be a single letter or a sequence of letters, for example, cream<u>y</u>, read<u>able</u>, nice<u>ly</u>. Unlike prefixes, suffixes often change the "part of speech" (i.e., the type of word). For example, in the case of creamy, the suffix <u>y</u> changes the noun <u>cream</u> into the adjective <u>creamy</u>, and in the case of <u>nicely</u>, the suffix <u>ly</u> changes the adjective <u>nice</u> into the adverb <u>nicely</u>.

In addition, suffixes are used to conjugate verbs (for example, to change the present tense into the past tense: you walk, you walk<u>ed</u>) and to create the plural form of nouns (for example, boy, boy<u>s</u>). In Spanish, suffixes are used for the same purposes, but they are used for other purposes too, such as creating plural forms for adjectives and changing the gender of a word.

In the Artificial Language, suffixes are used (1) to change the part of speech (for example, Rule 11 uses a suffix to change an adjective into an adverb), (2) to conjugate verbs (for example, Rules 6 and 7 use suffixes to express present and past tenses), and (3) to create the plural forms of nouns, pronouns, adjectives, and articles (Rule 2). In addition, the Artificial Language mimics Spanish in using a suffix to express gender.

You should study all the rules on suffixes in the Artificial Language, and you should practice using these rules, but you should NOT memorize them because (1) you will have them available to you at all times during the actual test, and (2) in the actual test, some of the suffixes and prefixes are different from the ones used in this practice test.

Verb: A verb is used to express either an action or a state of being. For example, "He <u>prepared</u> dinner" expresses the action of making all preparations for dinner, while "He is a <u>citizen</u>" expresses the state or condition of being a citizen.

A condition or "state of being" can be permanent or transitory. For example, "The agent's horse <u>is a bay mare</u>" expresses a permanent condition for the horse (being a bay mare), while "George <u>is at lunch</u>" expresses a transitory condition for George (being at lunch). The Spanish language, unlike English, has two different verbs to express permanent and transitory conditions, although the Artificial Language is akin to English rather than to Spanish in its use of a single verb to express any state of being.

When a verb is linked to a subject (i.e., "conjugated"), it changes from the abstract infinitive form to a specific form such as a present tense or a past tense. The Artificial Language primarily uses only two tenses: the simple past tense and the simple present tense in the indicative mood (see Rules 6 and 7). (Verbs in the indicative mood express a <u>real</u> action or condition, whereas verbs in the subjunctive mood express <u>hypothetical</u> actions or conditions. The subjunctive mood does not exist in the Artificial Language, but it is very important in Spanish.)

You may find that the past participle is used in the test (see Rule 8). In that case, the present perfect tense (they <u>have crossed</u>) and the past perfect tense (they <u>had crossed</u>) will be used in the Artificial Language.

Be sure to apply the rules as directed in the test material. If no rule governing the past participle is listed in the actual test material, then the past participle is treated as a simple past tense.

exercises

Practice Questions

Set 1: Questions 1 Through 4

Directions: For each sentence, decide which words have been translated correctly. Use scratch paper to list each <u>numbered</u> word that is correctly translated into the Artificial Language. When you have finished listing the words that are correctly translated in sentences 1 through 4, select your answer according to the following instructions:

Mark:

    (A) if <u>only</u> the word numbered 1 is correctly translated.

    (B) if <u>only</u> the word numbered 2 is correctly translated.

    (C) if <u>only</u> the word numbered 3 is correctly translated.

    (D) if <u>two</u> or <u>more</u> of the numbered words are correctly translated.

    (E) if <u>none</u> of the numbered words is correctly translated.

Be sure to list only the <u>numbered</u> words that are <u>correctly</u> translated.

Sentence	**Translation**
1. That girl is a friend.	Velle ekaplek synem bex kometlek. 1 2 3
2. The loyal inspector skillfully drove the jeep.	Wir inle zelker janleki arem wir daqlek. 1 2 3
3. The guard shot the spy.	Wir bonlek degem wir tatle. 1 2 3
4. That government has to identify enemies.	Velle almanlek tulim kalenzotim avelekoz. 1 2 3

Set 2: Questions 5 Through 8

Directions: For each question in this group, select the one of five suggested choices that correctly translates the underlined word or group of words into the Artificial Language.

Border Patrol Agents must stop illegal aliens who try <u>to cross the border</u>. Some of
                                                            5

<u>these aliens</u> are spies and enemies. Some even <u>shoot and injure</u> Border Patrol Agents.
  6   7

These loyal agents work for <u>the government</u>.
                              8

5. **(A)** chonzotim wir bonlek   6. **(A)** volle husklek

    (B) chonker wir bonlek   **(B)** velleoz huslek

    (C) chonker wir bonker   **(C)** volle huslekoz

    (D) chonker wiroz bonkeroz   **(D)** volleoz huslekoz

    (E) chonzotem wir bonker   **(E)** yevoz huslek

7. (A) degem loa liaem
   (B) degzotim loa liazotim
   (C) degker loa liaker
   (D) deglek loa lialek
   (E) degim loa liaim

8. (A) wir almanlek
   (B) wirnef almanlek
   (C) wir almanlekoz
   (D) wiroz almanlekoz
   (E) wirnef almanlek

Set 3: Questions 9 Through 12

Directions: For this group of questions, select the one response option that is the correct translation of the English word or words in parentheses. You should translate the entire sentence in order to determine what form should be used.

9. Wirnefoz kapleknefoz (work legally).
   (A) frigem colleki
   (B) frigim colleki
   (C) frigim colle
   (D) frigzotim colle
   (E) frigzotim colleki

10. Yevoz synim more wir (border station).
    (A) reglek lexle
    (B) reglek lexlek
    (C) regle lexle
    (D) regker lexlek
    (E) regle lexlek

11. Yevnef arzotem velle (spy's jeep).
    (A) tatlekoz daqlekoz
    (B) tatlekoz daglek
    (C) tatlekae daqlek
    (D) tatkerae daqlek
    (E) tatlekae daqlekae

12. Wiroz ekaplekoz (are not) fercolleoz huslekoz.
    (A) fersynem
    (B) synimfer
    (C) fersynzotim
    (D) fersynim
    (E) synemfer

Set 4: Questions 13 Through 15

Directions: For the last group of questions, select the one answer that is the correct form of the underlined expression as it is used in the sentence. At the end of the sentence, you will find instructions in parentheses telling you which form to use. In some sentences, you will be asked to supply the correct form of two or more expressions. In this case, the instructions for these expressions are presented consecutively in the parentheses and are separated by a dash. Be sure to translate the entire sentence before selecting your answer.

13. Velleoz synim <u>glase</u> <u>zelker</u>. (plural adjective—plural noun)
    - **(A)** ferglasle—zellekoz
    - **(B)** glasleoz—zellekoz
    - **(C)** glasle—zellekoz
    - **(D)** glasle—zelzotim
    - **(E)** glasleki—zelzotim

14. Wirnefoz <u>kaplek</u> synzotim tatlekoz loa <u>yev</u> liazotim bex bonlek. (feminine plural noun—feminine plural pronoun)
    - **(A)** kaplekoz—yevoz
    - **(B)** kapleknef—yevnef
    - **(C)** kapleknefae—yevnefae
    - **(D)** kapleknef—yevoz
    - **(E)** kapleknefoz—yevnefoz

15. Wiroz <u>liaker</u> kaplekoz synim <u>avelek</u> mor velle failek. (plural past participle adjective—plural noun)
    - **(A)** liazotimoz—avelekoz
    - **(B)** liato—avelek
    - **(C)** liatooz—avelekoz
    - **(D)** liato—avelekoz
    - **(E)** liazotem—avelekoz

ANSWER KEY AND EXPLANATIONS

1. D	**4.** A	**7.** E	**10.** E	**13.** B
2. B	**5.** B	**8.** A	**11.** C	**14.** E
3. A	**6.** D	**9.** B	**12.** D	**15.** C

1. **The correct answer is choice (D).** The words numbered 1 and 3 are correctly translated. *Ekaplek* is the translation of *boy*. To create the translation of *girl*, add the suffix *nef* (Rule 1). The correct translation is *ekapleknef*.

2. **The correct answer is choice (B).** Only the word numbered 2 is correctly translated. *Zelker* is the translation of *to inspect*. To create the translation of *inspector*, drop the *ker* (Rule 4) and add *lek* (Rule 9). To create the translation of the past-tense verb *drove*, begin with *arker*, the translation of the infinitive *to drive*. Drop the *ker* (Rule 4). Add the suffix *zot* and the suffix *em* because the verb is singular (Rule 7). The correct translation is *arzotem*.

3. **The correct answer is choice (A).** Only the word numbered 1 is correct. To create the past-tense verb *shot*, drop the *ker* from *degker*, the translation of *to shoot*. Add the suffix *zot* and then the suffix *em* because the verb is singular (Rule 7). The correct translation is *degzotem*. To create the noun *spy*, drop the *ker* from *tatker* (Rule 4) and add the suffix *lek* (Rule 9). The correct translation is *tatlek*.

4. **The correct answer is choice (A).** Only the word numbered 1 is correct. *Tulim* is the translation of *have*; *tulem* is the translation of *has*. The translation of the infinitive *to identify* is *kalenker*.

5. **The correct answer is choice (B).** The translation of the infinitive *to cross* is *chonker*, and the translation of *the* is *wir*. To create the translation of the noun *border*, drop the

ker from *bonker* (Rule 4) and add *lek* (Rule 9). The correct translation is *bonlek*.

6. **The correct answer is choice (D).** The translation of *this* is *volle*. To make this plural (*these*), add *oz*. The correct translation is *volleoz*. The translation of *alien* is *huslek*. To make it plural, add the suffix *oz* (Rule 2). The correct translation is *huslekoz*.

7. **The correct answer is (E).** To create the plural present-tense verb *shoot*, drop the *ker* from *degker*, the translation of *to shoot*. Add *im* because the verb is plural (6). The translation of *and* is *loa*. Follow the same procedure to create the plural present-tense verb *injure*. The correct translation is *liaim*.

8. **The correct answer is choice (A).** The translation of *the* is *wir*, and the translation of *government* is *almanlek*.

9. **The correct answer is choice (B).** The translation of *to work* is *frigker*. To create the present-tense verb *work*, drop the *ker* (Rule 4) and add *im* because the verb is plural (Rule 7). The correct translation is *frigim*. The translation of *legal* is *colle*. According to Rule 11, to form an adverb from an adjective, add the suffix *ki*. The correct translation is *colleki*. The translation of the entire sentence is, "The women work legally."

10. **The correct answer is choice (E).** The translation of the noun *border* is *reglek*. According to Rule 10, to form an adjective from a noun, drop the *lek* and add *le*. The correct translation is *regle*. To create the translation of the noun *station*, drop the *ker*

from *lexker,* the translation of *to station.* Add the suffix *lek* (Rule 9). The correct translation is *lexlek.* The translation of the entire sentence is, "They are from the border station."

11. **The correct answer is choice (C).** To create the noun *spy,* drop the *ker* from *tatker,* the translation of *to spy.* Add the suffix *lek* (Rule 9). To make the noun possessive, add the suffix *ae* (Rule 12). The correct translation is *tatlekae.* The translation of *jeep* is *daqlek.* The complete sentence translation is, "She drove that spy's jeep."

12. **The correct answer is choice (D).** To create the translation of *are,* drop the *ker* from *synker,* the translation of *to be.* Because the verb is plural, add the suffix *im.* To make the word negative, add the prefix *fer* (Rule 13). The correct translation is *fersynim.* The complete sentence translation is, "The boys are not illegal aliens."

13. **The correct answer is choice (B).** The translation of the complete sentence is, "Those are difficult inspectors." The translation of *difficult* is *glasle.* To make this plural, add the suffix *oz* (Rule 2). The correct translation is *glasleoz.* To create the plural noun *inspectors,* drop the *ker* from *zelker,* the translation of *to inspect.* Add *lek* to form a noun from the verb (Rule 9). The make the noun plural, add *oz.* The correct translation is *zellekoz.*

14. **The correct answer is choice (E).** The entire sentence translates as, "The women were spies and they injured a guard." *Kaplek* is the Artificial Language word for *man.* To make this feminine, add the suffix *nef* (Rule 1). To make it plural, add the suffix *oz.* The correct translation is *kapleknefoz.* The translation of *yev* is *he/him.* To make it feminine, add the suffix *nef* (Rule 1). To make it plural, add the suffix *oz.* The correct translation is *yevnefoz.*

15. **The correct answer is choice (C).** The translation of the complete sentence is, "The injured men are enemies from that country." *Liaker* is the translation of the infinitive *to injure.* To make this a past participle, drop the *ker* (Rule 4) and add the suffix *to* (Rule 8). To make it plural, add the suffix *oz* (Rule 2). The correct translation is *liatooz. Avelek* is the translation of *enemy.* To make it plural, add the suffix *oz* (Rule 2). The correct translation is *avelekoz.*

SUMMING IT UP

- Candidates who do not yet know Spanish or do not know it well will take the Artificial Language Test (ALT). The Artificial Language is a make-believe language with a grammatical structure similar to that of the Spanish language. The U.S. Border Patrol uses this test to predict a candidate's ability to learn Spanish at the U.S. Border Patrol Academy.

- You will be given reference materials to use during the ALT. These include Vocabulary Lists, which are like an Artificial Language dictionary. You will also receive Grammatical Rules for the Artificial Language. This document lists rules for creating words in the Artificial Language, such as past- and present-tense verbs and plural and possessive words. The Glossary of Grammatical Terms explains the parts of speech in the English language, such as verbs, nouns, pronouns, and adverbs.

- The ALT contains four types or sets of questions. For the first set (Questions 1–20), you will read a sentence in English and then an Artificial Language translation of that sentence. Three words in the translation will be underlined and numbered. You will have to decide how many of the underlined words are correctly translated. For the second set (Questions 21–30), you will select the answer choice that correctly translates an underlined word or group of words in a paragraph. For the third set (Questions 31–42), you will read a sentence translated into the Artificial Language. A word or words in this sentence will be in parentheses and in English. You have to choose the correct translation of these words. The last set (Questions 43–50) is the most difficult on the ALT. To answer these questions, you will select the correct translation of underlined words in a sentence. In parentheses after the sentence will be directions indicating which grammatical form the words should be in.

PART IV
TWO PRACTICE TESTS

ANSWER SHEET PRACTICE TEST 2

Logical Reasoning

1. Ⓐ Ⓑ Ⓒ Ⓓ Ⓔ   5. Ⓐ Ⓑ Ⓒ Ⓓ Ⓔ   8. Ⓐ Ⓑ Ⓒ Ⓓ Ⓔ   11. Ⓐ Ⓑ Ⓒ Ⓓ Ⓔ   14. Ⓐ Ⓑ Ⓒ Ⓓ Ⓔ
2. Ⓐ Ⓑ Ⓒ Ⓓ Ⓔ   6. Ⓐ Ⓑ Ⓒ Ⓓ Ⓔ   9. Ⓐ Ⓑ Ⓒ Ⓓ Ⓔ   12. Ⓐ Ⓑ Ⓒ Ⓓ Ⓔ   15. Ⓐ Ⓑ Ⓒ Ⓓ Ⓔ
3. Ⓐ Ⓑ Ⓒ Ⓓ Ⓔ   7. Ⓐ Ⓑ Ⓒ Ⓓ Ⓔ   10. Ⓐ Ⓑ Ⓒ Ⓓ Ⓔ   13. Ⓐ Ⓑ Ⓒ Ⓓ Ⓔ   16. Ⓐ Ⓑ Ⓒ Ⓓ Ⓔ
4. Ⓐ Ⓑ Ⓒ Ⓓ Ⓔ

Spanish Language Proficiency

Part I

1. Ⓐ Ⓑ Ⓒ Ⓓ Ⓔ   5. Ⓐ Ⓑ Ⓒ Ⓓ Ⓔ   9. Ⓐ Ⓑ Ⓒ Ⓓ Ⓔ   13. Ⓐ Ⓑ Ⓒ Ⓓ Ⓔ   17. Ⓐ Ⓑ Ⓒ Ⓓ Ⓔ
2. Ⓐ Ⓑ Ⓒ Ⓓ Ⓔ   6. Ⓐ Ⓑ Ⓒ Ⓓ Ⓔ   10. Ⓐ Ⓑ Ⓒ Ⓓ Ⓔ   14. Ⓐ Ⓑ Ⓒ Ⓓ Ⓔ   18. Ⓐ Ⓑ Ⓒ Ⓓ Ⓔ
3. Ⓐ Ⓑ Ⓒ Ⓓ Ⓔ   7. Ⓐ Ⓑ Ⓒ Ⓓ Ⓔ   11. Ⓐ Ⓑ Ⓒ Ⓓ Ⓔ   15. Ⓐ Ⓑ Ⓒ Ⓓ Ⓔ   19. Ⓐ Ⓑ Ⓒ Ⓓ Ⓔ
4. Ⓐ Ⓑ Ⓒ Ⓓ Ⓔ   8. Ⓐ Ⓑ Ⓒ Ⓓ Ⓔ   12. Ⓐ Ⓑ Ⓒ Ⓓ Ⓔ   16. Ⓐ Ⓑ Ⓒ Ⓓ Ⓔ   20. Ⓐ Ⓑ Ⓒ Ⓓ Ⓔ

Part II Section I

1. Ⓐ Ⓑ Ⓒ Ⓓ Ⓔ   3. Ⓐ Ⓑ Ⓒ Ⓓ Ⓔ   5. Ⓐ Ⓑ Ⓒ Ⓓ Ⓔ   6. Ⓐ Ⓑ Ⓒ Ⓓ Ⓔ   7. Ⓐ Ⓑ Ⓒ Ⓓ Ⓔ
2. Ⓐ Ⓑ Ⓒ Ⓓ Ⓔ   4. Ⓐ Ⓑ Ⓒ Ⓓ Ⓔ

Part II Section II

1. Ⓐ Ⓑ Ⓒ Ⓓ   3. Ⓐ Ⓑ Ⓒ Ⓓ   5. Ⓐ Ⓑ Ⓒ Ⓓ   6. Ⓐ Ⓑ Ⓒ Ⓓ   7. Ⓐ Ⓑ Ⓒ Ⓓ
2. Ⓐ Ⓑ Ⓒ Ⓓ   4. Ⓐ Ⓑ Ⓒ Ⓓ

Part II Section III

1. Ⓐ Ⓑ Ⓒ Ⓓ Ⓔ   3. Ⓐ Ⓑ Ⓒ Ⓓ Ⓔ   5. Ⓐ Ⓑ Ⓒ Ⓓ Ⓔ   6. Ⓐ Ⓑ Ⓒ Ⓓ Ⓔ   7. Ⓐ Ⓑ Ⓒ Ⓓ Ⓔ
2. Ⓐ Ⓑ Ⓒ Ⓓ Ⓔ   4. Ⓐ Ⓑ Ⓒ Ⓓ Ⓔ

Artificial Language

Set 1

1. Ⓐ Ⓑ Ⓒ Ⓓ Ⓔ   5. Ⓐ Ⓑ Ⓒ Ⓓ Ⓔ   9. Ⓐ Ⓑ Ⓒ Ⓓ Ⓔ   13. Ⓐ Ⓑ Ⓒ Ⓓ Ⓔ   17. Ⓐ Ⓑ Ⓒ Ⓓ Ⓔ

2. Ⓐ Ⓑ Ⓒ Ⓓ Ⓔ   6. Ⓐ Ⓑ Ⓒ Ⓓ Ⓔ   10. Ⓐ Ⓑ Ⓒ Ⓓ Ⓔ   14. Ⓐ Ⓑ Ⓒ Ⓓ Ⓔ   18. Ⓐ Ⓑ Ⓒ Ⓓ Ⓔ

3. Ⓐ Ⓑ Ⓒ Ⓓ Ⓔ   7. Ⓐ Ⓑ Ⓒ Ⓓ Ⓔ   11. Ⓐ Ⓑ Ⓒ Ⓓ Ⓔ   15. Ⓐ Ⓑ Ⓒ Ⓓ Ⓔ   19. Ⓐ Ⓑ Ⓒ Ⓓ Ⓔ

4. Ⓐ Ⓑ Ⓒ Ⓓ Ⓔ   8. Ⓐ Ⓑ Ⓒ Ⓓ Ⓔ   12. Ⓐ Ⓑ Ⓒ Ⓓ Ⓔ   16. Ⓐ Ⓑ Ⓒ Ⓓ Ⓔ   20. Ⓐ Ⓑ Ⓒ Ⓓ Ⓔ

Set 2

21. Ⓐ Ⓑ Ⓒ Ⓓ Ⓔ   23. Ⓐ Ⓑ Ⓒ Ⓓ Ⓔ   25. Ⓐ Ⓑ Ⓒ Ⓓ Ⓔ   27. Ⓐ Ⓑ Ⓒ Ⓓ Ⓔ   29. Ⓐ Ⓑ Ⓒ Ⓓ Ⓔ

22. Ⓐ Ⓑ Ⓒ Ⓓ Ⓔ   24. Ⓐ Ⓑ Ⓒ Ⓓ Ⓔ   26. Ⓐ Ⓑ Ⓒ Ⓓ Ⓔ   28. Ⓐ Ⓑ Ⓒ Ⓓ Ⓔ   30. Ⓐ Ⓑ Ⓒ Ⓓ Ⓔ

Set 3

31. Ⓐ Ⓑ Ⓒ Ⓓ Ⓔ   34. Ⓐ Ⓑ Ⓒ Ⓓ Ⓔ   37. Ⓐ Ⓑ Ⓒ Ⓓ Ⓔ   39. Ⓐ Ⓑ Ⓒ Ⓓ Ⓔ   41. Ⓐ Ⓑ Ⓒ Ⓓ Ⓔ

32. Ⓐ Ⓑ Ⓒ Ⓓ Ⓔ   35. Ⓐ Ⓑ Ⓒ Ⓓ Ⓔ   38. Ⓐ Ⓑ Ⓒ Ⓓ Ⓔ   40. Ⓐ Ⓑ Ⓒ Ⓓ Ⓔ   42. Ⓐ Ⓑ Ⓒ Ⓓ Ⓔ

33. Ⓐ Ⓑ Ⓒ Ⓓ Ⓔ   36. Ⓐ Ⓑ Ⓒ Ⓓ Ⓔ

Set 4

43. Ⓐ Ⓑ Ⓒ Ⓓ Ⓔ   45. Ⓐ Ⓑ Ⓒ Ⓓ Ⓔ   47. Ⓐ Ⓑ Ⓒ Ⓓ Ⓔ   49. Ⓐ Ⓑ Ⓒ Ⓓ Ⓔ   50. Ⓐ Ⓑ Ⓒ Ⓓ Ⓔ

44. Ⓐ Ⓑ Ⓒ Ⓓ Ⓔ   46. Ⓐ Ⓑ Ⓒ Ⓓ Ⓔ   48. Ⓐ Ⓑ Ⓒ Ⓓ Ⓔ

Practice Test 2

LOGICAL REASONING

1. Worker's compensation is designed to help workers who have been injured on the job. The goal of worker's compensation is to ensure that employees receive appropriate medical care, lost wages resulting from the injury, and rehabilitation, if necessary. An employee may be excluded from worker's compensation if an injury or a death results from willful misconduct or intoxication. Employees who are denied coverage have the right to sue their employer only if the employer intentionally causes the employee's injury or if an employer required to carry worker's compensation insurance fails to do so. Miguel A. is an employee who has suffered a head injury in a warehouse. He was not wearing a hard hat at the time of the injury even though he is required to do so.

   From the information given above, it can validly be concluded that

   (A) Miguel A. will receive worker's compensation.

   (B) Miguel A.'s employer may have intentionally caused his head injury.

   (C) Miguel A. has the right to sue his employer if he is denied compensation.

   (D) Miguel A. may be denied worker's compensation.

   (E) Miguel A. will only receive appropriate medical care.

2. The city of Middletown employs 10 snowplow operators during the winter. If these operators cannot keep up with the snow removal, the mayor may hire outside contractors to assist them. These contractors must submit detailed formal bids that include an estimate of how much the job will cost. If the mayor declares a state of emergency, he or she may immediately hire outside contractors without following a formal bidding process.

From the information given above, it can validly be concluded that

(A) the mayor declares a state of emergency each winter.

(B) the mayor usually accepts bids from contractors during a state of emergency.

(C) the mayor does not have to declare a state of emergency to hire outside contractors without a bid.

(D) the mayor does not require snowplow operators to work during a state of emergency.

(E) the mayor must declare a state of emergency to hire outside contractors without a bid.

3. Naturalization is the process by which a foreign citizen or national can become a U.S. citizen. To become a U.S. citizen, foreign citizens must demonstrate an ability to read, write, and speak English; a knowledge and understanding of U.S. history and government; and a favorable disposition toward the United States. Special circumstances allow for the naturalization of foreign citizens who do not meet all these criteria. Nadia J. is an Iranian national. She has a favorable disposition toward the United States and she reads, writes, and speaks English well. She has very little understanding of U.S. history and government.

From the information given above, it can validly be concluded that

(A) Nadia J. meets all the criteria for naturalization.

(B) Nadia J. may have to learn about U.S. history and government to be naturalized.

(C) Nadia J. may have to learn to read, write, and speak English to be naturalized.

(D) Nadia J. has special circumstances that will allow her to be naturalized.

(E) Nadia J. will not be naturalized because she is an Iranian national.

4. The California Retail Food Code has many rules regulating mobile food facilities, such as hot dog carts and taco stands. All California vendors must complete an application before opening a mobile food facility. After receiving a permit, the vendor must adhere to the Code's strict regulations to stay open. This includes maintaining proper refrigeration units, providing soap and water for employees to sanitize their hands, and eliminating the presence of any vermin in or around the vehicle. Failure to comply with these regulations could result in the immediate closure of the mobile food facility. Sandra H. just opened a mobile hot dog stand in Concord, California. The city follows the California Retail Food Code.

From the information given above, it can validly concluded that

(A) if Sandra H.'s hot dog stand is closed, then she must not have a permit.

(B) if Sandra H. has soap and water, then her hot dog stand will not be closed.

(C) if Sandra H. opened a hot dog stand in Concord, then she must have a permit.

(D) if Sandra H.'s hot dog stand is closed, then she did not follow the regulations.

(E) if Sandra H. does not have a permit for her hot dog stand, then she is not in Concord.

5. All Border Patrol candidates undergo a thorough background check before they receive a firm offer of employment. The Border Patrol conducts background checks to ensure that candidates are honest and loyal. Investigators look at every aspect of a candidate's life. Certain evidence can terminate a candidate's conditional offer of employment with the Border Patrol. Information that may affect a candidate's status includes evidence of drug or alcohol abuse, an arrest record, or involvement with criminals. Frank L. failed the background check. The Border Patrol terminated his conditional offer of employment.

From the information given above, it can validly be concluded that

(A) Frank L. may not be loyal or honest.

(B) Frank L. has abused alcohol in the past.

(C) Frank L. may be divorced several times.

(D) Frank L. is involved with criminals.

(E) Frank L. has an arrest record.

6. Line watch is one of the most important duties of Border Patrol Agents. Border Patrol Agents on line watch observe the lines between international boundaries to prevent the illegal entry of aliens into the United States. These agents also participate in signcutting. When agents participate in signcutting, they look for disturbances in the natural terrain. Such disturbances include footprints, tire tracks, and trash. Claire L. is a Border Patrol Agent stationed along the Mexican border. She notices a discarded water bottle in some brush not far from the border.

From the information given above, it CANNOT validly be concluded that

(A) Claire L. has participated in signcutting.

(B) Claire L. participates in line watch.

(C) Claire L. has detected the presence of an illegal alien.

(D) Claire L. has discovered a disturbance in the natural terrain.

(E) Claire L. wants to prevent illegal aliens from crossing the border.

7. Couples hoping to hold a wedding ceremony in a San Diego public park must fill out an application for a permit from the Office of Parks and Recreation. Applications must be approved. The application may be denied if another event is taking place on the same day. Applications must be submitted at least 15 days before the date of the event. Couples with special requests must submit their applications at least 30 days before the event. The Office of Parks and Recreation limits the number of guests to 300. Events cannot be more than 4 hours long. Exceptions to these rules are made on a case-by-case basis. Ladonna P. wants to hold a wedding ceremony in a San Diego public park.

From the information given above, it can validly concluded that

(A) if Ladonna P. submits her application 30 days before her wedding, then she has a special request.

(B) if Ladonna P. wants to hold a wedding ceremony in a San Diego public park, then she must submit an application at least 15 days before the wedding.

(C) if Ladonna P. has fewer than 300 guests at her wedding ceremony, then her ceremony has taken place in a San Diego public park.

(D) if Ladonna P.'s wedding ceremony lasts more than 4 hours, then it has not taken place in a San Diego public park.

(E) if Ladonna P. fills out an application for a permit at least 15 days before her wedding, then she will be able to hold a wedding ceremony in a San Diego public park.

8. All Border Patrol recruits must pass a second pre-employment fitness test known as the PFT-2. Recruits who fail the test will have their offer of employment revoked. Before taking the test, recruits will have their blood pressure and pulse checked. If a recruit's blood pressure or pulse is too high, then he or she will not be allowed to take the test. The Border Patrol recommends that recruits avoid smoking and drinking caffeine on the day of the test because these actions may raise blood pressure and pulse rate. Juan M. has a cup of coffee the morning of his PFT-2 test.

From the information given above, it CANNOT validly be concluded that

(A) Juan M. will not be allowed to take the PFT-2.

(B) Juan M. did not follow the Border Patrol's recommendations.

(C) Juan M. will have his blood pressure and pulse checked before the test.

(D) Juan M. will have his offer of employment revoked if he does not pass the test.

(E) Juan M.'s morning cup of coffee might affect his blood pressure and pulse rate.

9. Border Patrol agents are inspecting a farm near the Mexican border. Agents believe that the owners of the farm may have hired illegal aliens. The agents learn that the farm employs 16 laborers. Nine of the laborers are women. Ten of the laborers are legal residents of the United States. Four of the illegal aliens are from El Salvador.

From the information given above, it can validly be concluded that

(A) it is not true that some men work on the farm.

(B) it is not true that some of the women are from El Salvador.

(C) all of the women are from El Salvador.

(D) some of the women are legal residents of the United States.

(E) none of the men are legal residents of the United States.

10. Thirty Border Patrol Agents work in a certain sector in Texas. All of the agents are stationed near the Mexican border. Fifteen of the agents patrol the border on foot. Fifteen patrol either on ATVs or in SUVs. All of the agents who patrol on ATVs or who work with canines have received special training. Two of the agents work with canines. All of the agents carry firearms. Raymond K. is a Border Patrol Agent in this sector who patrols the border on an ATV.

From the information given above, it can validly be concluded that

(A) Raymond K. also patrols the border on foot.

(B) Raymond K. has received special training.

(C) Raymond K. does not work with canines.

(D) Raymond K. does not carry a firearm.

(E) Raymond K. also patrols in an SUV.

11. Recently, Border Patrol Agents in Tucson raided a drop house, a place where illegal aliens stay until smugglers feel that they can take them north without being caught. More than 60 illegal aliens were in the drop house, and some had been living in deplorable conditions inside the house for weeks. Border Patrol Agents believe the illegal aliens had been there so long because new checkpoints set up in the area by Border Patrol made it difficult for smugglers to move them. Most of the illegal aliens were from Mexico. While most were men, some women and children were also apprehended. Two U.S. citizens were apprehended and charged with human smuggling. One was also charged with smuggling illegal narcotics.

From the information given above, it CAN-NOT validly be concluded that

(A) the women and children in the drop house were from Mexico.

(B) the drop house may have also been used to smuggle narcotics.

(C) the U.S. citizens were arrested for human smuggling.

(D) new checkpoints have made smuggling more difficult.

(E) some of the male illegal immigrants were from Mexico.

12. BORSTAR is a specialized unit of the Border Patrol that responds to emergency search-and-rescue situations across the country. BORSTAR is comprised of Border Patrol Agents who volunteer to undergo specialized training. All potential BORSTAR agents must complete a five-week training course at the BORSTAR Academy. BORSTAR agents often respond to situations involving distressed Border Patrol Agents and illegal aliens. Because BORSTAR agents often work in rugged terrain, it is important for all recruits to be in excellent physical condi-tion. Ileana J. is attending the BORSTAR Academy.

From the information given above, it CAN-NOT validly be concluded that

(A) Ileana J. is a Border Patrol Agent.

(B) Ileana J. volunteered for BORSTAR.

(C) Ileana J. frequently responds to rescue missions.

(D) Ileana J. will receive special training at the academy.

(E) Ileana J. may eventually rescue Border Patrol Agents.

13. Ten students are in the Spanish program at the Border Patrol Academy. Six of the students are women. None of the students has taken a Spanish class before. Half of the students have an average that is below 70 percent. Two of the students have averages of 90 percent.

From the information given above, it can validly be concluded that

(A) all of the students with averages under 70 percent are men.

(B) some of the students with averages under 70 percent are women.

(C) all of the men in the class have taken a Spanish class before.

(D) the two students with average of 90 percent are men.

(E) some of the women have taken a Spanish class before.

14. Many states have enacted "Right to Farm" laws, which protect farmers from lawsuits filed by their neighbors. Because of this law, a farm cannot be shut down simply because a neighbor or a community is offended by the noise or smell it creates. The law states that a farm that has been operating for more than a year cannot be deemed a nuisance, even if new neighbors move into the area. Jim T. has recently moved next to a farm. He

wants the farm to be shut down. He claims that the smell is a nuisance.

From the information given above, it can validly concluded that

(A) if the farm has been operating for less than a year, it will be shut down.

(B) if the farm has been operating for less than a year, the smell is not a nuisance.

(C) if the farm has been operating for more than a year, it can be shut down.

(D) if the farm has been operating for more than a year, Jim cannot file a lawsuit.

(E) if the farm has been operating for more than a year, it cannot be deemed a nuisance.

15. At the academy, Border Patrol recruits receive driving instruction in van/utility vehicle operation, skid control, and emergency response. These courses are graded on a pass/fail basis. Once a recruit has passed all three basic courses, he or she can pursue training in driving, vehicle stops (low-risk and high-risk), night driving, 4×4 off-road driving, and SUV/van evasive driving. Rupert G. is currently taking a class in night driving.

From the information given above, it can validly be concluded that

(A) Rupert G. has completed the vehicle-stops course.

(B) Rupert G. has not taken a course in 4×4 off-road driving.

(C) Rupert G. has passed a course in emergency response.

(D) Rupert G. will not take a course in SUV/van evasive driving.

(E) Rupert G. has not passed a course in skid control.

16. It is estimated that 10.8 million illegal immigrants lived in a certain country in 2009. More than half of these immigrants arrived before the year 2000. More than 6 million were from Mexico. Although most illegal immigrants worked in the service, construction, and production industries, some worked in professional positions in business and management. Others worked in farming, transportation, and production industries. Regardless of the occupation, illegal immigrants earned less money than citizens of this country performing the same jobs.

From the information given above, it can be validly concluded that, in 2009, in the country described above

(A) it is not the case that immigrants earned the same wages as citizens performing the same job.

(B) it is not the case that some immigrants worked in professional positions in business and management.

(C) none of the immigrants worked in the transportation and production industries.

(D) most of those not employed in professional occupations were immigrants.

(E) very few immigrants worked in service, construction, and production industries.

SPANISH LANGUAGE PROFICIENCY

Part I

Directions: Read the sentence and then choose the most appropriate synonym for the underlined word.

1. Miren cómo <u>brinca</u> aquel hombre.
   - (A) saluda
   - (B) salta
   - (C) brinda
   - (D) saltea
   - (E) brisa

2. Las mujeres habían montado una empresa <u>lucrativa</u>.
   - (A) perjudicial
   - (B) lustrosa
   - (C) gravosa
   - (D) caritativa
   - (E) rentable

3. Hay una tubería de <u>desagüe</u> que corre debajo de la ciudad.
   - (A) alimentación
   - (B) drenaje
   - (C) llenado
   - (D) desaire
   - (E) aguamala

4. En esta región funciona una <u>red</u> de maleantes.
   - (A) pescador
   - (B) roja
   - (C) organización
   - (D) trampa
   - (E) atrapar

5. El terreno por aquí es bien <u>accidentado</u>.
   - (A) áspero
   - (B) llano
   - (C) suave
   - (D) choque
   - (E) atropellado

6. Desde la cumbre podemos <u>divisar</u> a nuestros compañeros.
   - (A) dividir
   - (B) ocultar
   - (C) escuchar
   - (D) adivinar
   - (E) ver

7. Los <u>recién</u> llegados se sentaron a descansar.
   - (A) recientemente
   - (B) recios
   - (C) agotados
   - (D) difícil
   - (E) otra vez

8. Mañana los espera una importante <u>tarea</u>.
   - (A) trabajo
   - (B) trago
   - (C) recreo
   - (D) descanso
   - (E) trabado

9. Entre sus <u>efectos</u> encontramos varias navajas y cuchillas.
   - (A) consecuencias
   - (B) eficiencia
   - (C) afecciones ilnesses
   - (D) pertenencias
   - (E) efectividad

10. ¿Qué <u>asuntos</u> te traen por acá?
    - (A) cuestiones
    - (B) cuestas
    - (C) juntos
    - (D) conjuntos
    - (E) asuetos

11. Ese <u>rostro</u> me es conocido.

    (A) ojo

    (B) mejilla

    (C) caro

    (D) arrastro

    (E) cara

12. No <u>cepille</u> al perro con tanta fuerza.

    (A) alimente

    (B) entrene

    (C) llame

    (D) peine

    (E) adiestre

13. <u>Olvidé</u> mis guantes en el coche.

    (A) recordé

    (B) encontré

    (C) usé

    (D) dejé

    (E) olfateé

14. No podemos abrir esto sin un <u>abridor</u>.

    (A) llavero

    (B) destapador

    (C) abrigo

    (D) despertador

    (E) puerta

15. El <u>desplome</u> de la casa fue casi inmediato.

    (A) edificación

    (B) caída

    (C) desplume

    (D) venta

    (E) levantamiento

16. Cuando llegues al <u>viaducto</u>, espéranos.

    (A) vivero

    (B) cruce

    (C) acueducto

    (D) vivienda

    (E) puente

17. Abrimos paso rápídamente entre la maleza <u>espesa</u>.

    (A) tupida

    (B) clara

    (C) especial

    (D) pesada

    (E) despejada

18. Debemos presentarnos en la <u>sede</u> a las ocho de la mañana.

    (A) oficina central

    (B) cenicero

    (C) sendero

    (D) filial

    (E) sucursal

19. Ten cuidado con los <u>peatones</u> al conducir.

    (A) conductores

    (B) semáforos

    (C) caminantes

    (D) pares

    (E) automovilistas

20. No entiendo cómo <u>alcanzaron</u> a subir hasta aquí.

    (A) pudieron

    (B) fallaron

    (C) fatigaron

    (D) fracasaron

    (E) pudrieron

Part II

Section I

Directions: Read each sentence carefully. Select the appropriate word or phrase to fill each blank space.

1. Los autos _____ iban muy _____.
   - (A) antiguas / despacias
   - (B) antiguos / despacios
   - (C) antiguo / despaciamente
   - (D) antiguos / despacio
   - (E) antiguos / espacio

2. Ayer los trabajadores _____ las herramientas _____ del camión.
   - (A) dejó / debajo
   - (B) dejaron / debajo
   - (C) dejé / sobre
   - (D) dejen / entre
   - (E) dejarán / contra

3. De pronto vimos _____ luz_____.
   - (A) una / brillante
   - (B) un / brillantes
   - (C) una / brillanta
   - (D) una / brilla
   - (E) unos / brillan

4. Vimos _____ mucha gente _____ ciudad.
   - (A) acercarse / de la
   - (B) acerca / del
   - (C) acercaban / de el
   - (D) acercó / de las
   - (E) acercaron / de lo

5. Las agentes _____ a punto _____ llegar.
   - (A) eran / pero
   - (B) estar / sin
   - (C) siendo / que
   - (D) estaban / de
   - (E) son / con

6. Creo que usaré tu cámara en _____ de la _____.
   - (A) sin / mi
   - (B) más / tuya
   - (C) como / tuyas
   - (D) revés / su
   - (E) vez / mía

7. Me _____ que Tom es _____ hombre.
   - (A) parecemos / buenos
   - (B) parecen / buena
   - (C) pareces / buenas
   - (D) parece / buen
   - (E) parezco / bueno

Section II

Directions: Read each sentence carefully. Select the one sentence that is correct.

1. **(A)** La misión de los agentes fronterizos es proteger nuestro país y defenderlo.
   (B) El misión de los agentes fronterizos es para proteger nuestro país y para defender.
   (C) La misión de los frontera agentes es a proteger nuestro país ya defenderlo.
   (D) La misión es proteger y defenderlo los agentes de nuestro país fronterizo.

2. **(A)** Este lugar, pese a su baja densidad demográfica, reviste importancia para el país.
   (B) Este lugar, pesa a su bajo densidad demográfico, revista importante de el país.
   (C) Esta lugar pesa baja densidad, importancia revista demográfica para la país.
   (D) Este densidad lugar reviste, pese su baja importancia para el país demográfica.

3. **(A)** Todos ciudadanos debe aportan su máximo esfuerzo por alcanzar el bueno de todos.
   (B) Todo el ciudadano debes aportar tu máximo esfuerzo a alcanzar bien de todos.
   (C) Todo ciudadano debe aportar su máximo esforzarse por alcanzar el bien de todos.
   (D) Todos deben aportar máximo esfuerzo pero alcanzar el bien de ciudadano.

4. **(A)** Ante la evidencia que veo, no tengo nada que decir salvo que los hechos son claros.
   (B) Antes de la evidencia que veo, yo tengo nada que decir los hechos son claros.
   (C) Ante la evidencia que veo, y no tengo que decir que los hechos claros.
   (D) Ante la evidencia que veo, son claros que tengo nada a decir salvo los hechos.

5. **(A)** ¿Lo saber ustedes quién el autor es de el artículo que leer antier?
   (B) ¿Sabemos ustedes quién el autor es de la artículo quien leemos antier?
   (C) ¿Sabes usted quiénes el autor de el artículo que leo antier?
   (D) ¿Saben ustedes quien es el autor del artículo que leímos antier?

6. **(A)** Cuando regresemos a casa, quítense las botas y cuelguen las chaquetas.
   (B) Cuándo regresaremos entre casa, quitaron las botas y colgaron las chaquetas.
   (C) Cuando cuelgaste las chaquetas regresaste casa, y quitaste las botas.
   (D) Cuando regrese con la casa, quítensen las botas y cuélguesen las chaquetas.

7. **(A)** Nosotros sabemos mucho el ciudad de Nueva York.
   (B) Nosotros conocemos muy bien la ciudad de Nueva York.
   (C) Nosotros sabemos Nueva York Ciudad muy bien.
   (D) Nosotros conocer el Nueva York ciudad mucho.

Section III

Directions: Read each sentence carefully. Select the correct word or phrase to replace the under-lined portions of the sentence. In those cases in which the sentence needs no correction, select answer choice (E).

1. Ya <u>llevamos</u> la mitad del trabajo hecho.
   - (A) estamos
   - (B) hemos
   - (C) trabajamos
   - (D) somos
   - (E) No es necesario hacer ninguna corrección.

2. ¿Por qué estaban ustedes <u>corrían</u>?
   - (A) corrieron
   - (B) corren
   - (C) corriendo
   - (D) correr
   - (E) No es necesario hacer ninguna corrección.

3. Mañana por la <u>tarde</u> comenzará a nevar.
   - (A) pasado mañana
   - (B) mañana
   - (C) cuando
   - (D) clima
   - (E) No es necesario hacer ninguna corrección.

4. Tuve una pesadilla y me desperté <u>sudaba</u>.
   - (A) sudor
   - (B) sudando
   - (C) sudar
   - (D) sudé
   - (E) No es necesario hacer ninguna corrección.

5. Dudo mucho que los caballos <u>sube</u> por aquí.
   - (A) suben
   - (B) subir
   - (C) subiendo
   - (D) suban
   - (E) No es necesario hacer ninguna corrección.

6. ¿Quiénes te dieron los informes que traes?
   - (A) Cuál
   - (B) Quién
   - (C) Cuáles
   - (D) A quién
   - (E) No es necesario hacer ninguna corrección.

7. ¿<u>Cuentas</u> libras piensan que hay aquí?
   - (A) Cuentas
   - (B) Contamos
   - (C) Cuenten
   - (D) Cuántas
   - (E) No es necesario hacer ninguna corrección.

ARTIFICIAL LANGUAGE

The Vocabulary Lists

The words on the following lists are the same; they are merely arranged differently, as they would be in a bilingual dictionary. In the first list, you can look up words in English to find their equivalent word in the Artificial Language. In the second list, you can look up words in the Artificial Language to find their equivalent word in English. During the actual test, you will have the vocabulary lists with you for consultation at all times. You should note that the words given below are not the same as those given in the actual test. Therefore, it is best not to try to memorize them before taking the actual test.

Word List Arranged Alphabetically by the English Word				Word List Arranged Alphabetically by the Artificial Language Word			
English	Artificial Language	English	Artificial Language	Artificial Language	English	Artificial Language	English
a, an	bex	skillful	janle	almanlek	government	kaplek	man
alien	huslek	that	velle	arker	to drive	kometlek	friend
and	loa	the	wir	avelek	enemy	lexker	to station
boy	ekaplek	this	volle	bex	a, an	liaker	to injure
country	failek	to be	synker	bonker	to guard	loa	and
difficult	glasle	to border	regker	browlek	river	mor	friend
enemy	avelek	to cross	chonker	chonker	to cross	pirker	to escape
friend	kometlek	to drive	arker	colle	legal	quea	of
from	mor	to escape	pirker	daqlek	jeep	regker	to border
government	almanlek	to guard	bonker	degker	to shoot	synker	to be
he, him	yev	to have	tulker	ekaplek	boy	tatker	to spy
jeep	daqlek	to identify	kalenker	failek	country	trenedlek	paper
legal	colle	to injure	liaker	frigker	to work	tulker	to have
loyal	inle	to inspect	zelker	glasle	difficult	velle	that
man	kaplek	to shoot	degker	huslek	alien	volle	this
of	quea	to spy	tatker	inle	loyal	wir	the
paper	trenedlek	to station	lexker	janle	skillful	yev	he, him
river	browlek	to work	frigker	kalenker	to identify	zelker	to inspect

Grammatical Rules for the Artificial Language

The grammatical rules given here are similar, but not identical, to those used in the ALT. Some of the suffixes (word endings) and prefixes (additions to the beginning of a word) used in the actual test differ from those used in the practice test.

During the actual test, you will have access to the rules at all times. Consequently, it is important that you understand these rules, but it is not necessary that you memorize them. In fact, memorizing them will hinder rather than help you, since there are differences between the rules in the version of the Artificial Language that appears here and the one that appears in the actual test.

You should note that the next part of this section contains a glossary of grammatical terms to assist you if you are not thoroughly familiar with the meaning of these grammatical terms.

<u>Rule 1</u>: To form the feminine singular form of a noun, a pronoun, an adjective, or an article, add the suffix <u>nef</u> to the masculine singular form. Only nouns, pronouns, adjectives, and articles take feminine endings in the Artificial Language. When gender is not specified, the masculine form is used.

Example: If a <u>male eagle</u> is a <u>verlek</u>, then a <u>female eagle</u> is a <u>verleknef</u>. If an <u>ambitious</u> man is a <u>tosle</u> man, an ambitious woman is a <u>toslenef</u> woman.

<u>Rule 2</u>: To form the plural of nouns, pronouns, adjectives, and articles, add the suffix <u>oz</u> to the correct singular form.

Example: If one <u>male eagle</u> is a <u>verlek</u>, several <u>male eagles</u> are <u>verlekoz</u>. If an <u>ambitious</u> woman is a <u>toslenef</u> woman, several <u>ambitious</u> women are <u>toslenefoz</u> women.

<u>Rule 3</u>: Adjectives modifying nouns and pronouns with feminine and/or plural endings must have endings that agree with the words they modify. In addition, an article (*a/an* and *the*) preceding a noun must also agree with the noun in gender and number.

Example: If an <u>active male eagle</u> is a <u>sojle verlek</u>, an <u>active female eagle</u> is a <u>sojlenef ver-leknef</u> and several <u>active female eagles</u> are <u>sojlenefoz verleknefoz</u>. If <u>this male eagle</u> is <u>volle verlek</u>, <u>these female eagles</u> are <u>vollenefoz verleknefoz</u>. If <u>the male eagle</u> is <u>wir verlek</u>, <u>the female eagle</u> is <u>wirnef verleknef</u> and <u>the female eagles</u> are <u>wirnefoz verleknefoz</u>. If <u>a male eagle</u> is <u>bex verlek</u>, <u>several male eagles</u> are <u>bexoz verlekoz</u>.

<u>Rule 4</u>: The stem of a verb is obtained by omitting the suffix <u>ker</u> from the infinitive form of the verb.

Example: The stem of the verb <u>tirker</u> is <u>tir</u>.

<u>Rule 5</u>: All subjects and their verbs must agree in number; that is, singular subjects require singular verbs and plural subjects require plural verbs. (See Rules 6 and 7.)

<u>Rule 6</u>: To form the present tense of a verb, add the suffix <u>em</u> to the stem for the singular or the suffix <u>im</u> to the stem for the plural.

Example: If <u>to bark</u> is <u>nalker</u>, then <u>nalem</u> is the present tense for the singular (the dog <u>barks</u>) and <u>nalim</u> is the present tense for the plural (the dogs <u>bark</u>).

<u>Rule 7</u>: To form the past tense of a verb, first add the suffix <u>zot</u> to the stem, and then add the suffix <u>em</u> if the verb is singular or the suffix <u>im</u> if it is plural.

Example: If <u>to bark</u> is <u>nalker</u>, then <u>nalzotem</u> is the past tense for the singular (the dog <u>barked</u>) and <u>nalzotim</u> is the past tense for the plural (the dogs <u>barked</u>).

<u>Rule 8</u>: To form the past participle of a verb, add the suffix <u>to</u> to the stem of the verb. It can be used to form compound tenses with the verb <u>to have</u>, as a predicate with the verb <u>to be</u>, or as an adjective.

In the last two cases, it takes masculine, feminine, singular and plural forms in agreement with the noun to which it refers.

Example of use in a compound tense with the verb to have:

If to bark is nalker and to have is tulker, then tulem nalto is the *present perfect* for the singular (the dog has barked) and tulim nalto is the *present perfect* for the plural (the dogs have barked). Similarly, tulzotem nalto is the *past perfect* for the singular (the dog had barked) and tulzotim nalto is the *past perfect* for the plural (the dogs had barked).

Example of the use as a predicate with the verb to be:

If to adopt is rapker and to be is synker, then a boy was adopted is a ekaplek synzotem rapto and many girls were adopted is ekapleknefoz synzotim raptonefoz.

Example of use as an adjective:

If to delight is kasker then a delighted boy is a kasto ekaplek and many delighted girls are kastonefoz ekapleknefoz.

Rule 9: To form a noun from a verb, add the suffix lek to the stem of the verb.

Example: If longker is to write, then a writer is a longlek.

Rule 10: To form an adjective from a noun, substitute the suffix le for the suffix lek.

Example: If pellek is beauty, then a beautiful male eagle is a pelle verlek and a beautiful female eagle is a pellenef verleknef. (Note the feminine suffix nef.)

Rule 11: To form an adverb from an adjective, add the suffix ki to the masculine form of the adjective. (Note that adverbs do not change their form to agree in gender or number with the word they modify.)

Example: If pelle is beautiful, then beautifully is pelleki.

Rule 12: To form the possessive of a noun or pronoun, add the suffix ae to the noun or pronoun after any plural or feminine suffixes.

Example: If a boglek is a dog, then a dog's collar is a boglekae collar. If he is yev, then his book is yevae book. If she is yevnef, then her book is yevnefae book.

Rule 13: To make a word negative, add the prefix fer to the correct affirmative form.

Example: If an active male eagle is a sojle verlek, an inactive male eagle is a fersojle verlek. If the dog barks is boglek nalem, then the dog does not bark is boglek fernalem.

Glossary of Grammatical Terms

This glossary will be available to you during the actual test, but it is recommended that you study the glossary before taking the test. The glossary contains basic grammatical concepts that apply to English, Spanish, and the Artificial Language. The glossary contains fairly extensive and comprehensive explanations of each grammatical concept. **The explanations in the actual test are not comprehensive. Consequently, it is particularly important that you study these explanations very carefully.**

Article: An article is a word that precedes a noun and determines whether it is a definite or indefinite noun; for instance <u>the</u> book, <u>an</u> object.

Adjective: An adjective is a word used to modify a noun or pronoun (for example, <u>intelligent</u> women). Generally, an adjective serves to answer questions such as <u>which</u>, <u>what kind of</u>, and <u>how many</u>. For example,

"<u>This</u> book" would be the adjectival answer to the question "which book?" "a <u>beautiful</u> book"
   1   2

would be the adjectival answer to the question "what kind of book?" and (3) "<u>several</u> days" would
                                                                                              3

be the adjectival answer to the question "how many days?"

In English, adjectives have only one form, regardless of the type of noun they modify. More specifically, whether a noun is feminine or masculine, singular or plural, the adjective used to modify it remains the same; for example, the adjective <u>strong</u> is exactly the same when it refers to one man, one woman, or many men. By contrast, in both Spanish and the Artificial Language, the ending of the adjective is different if the adjective is modifying a singular masculine noun, a singular feminine noun, a plural masculine noun, or a plural feminine noun.

Adverb: An adverb is a word used to modify a verb. For example, the sentence "It was produced" could be modified to express <u>where</u> it was produced by saying "It was produced <u>locally</u>."

Generally, an adverb is used to answer the questions <u>where</u> (as in the example above), <u>when</u> (as for example, "he comes <u>frequently</u>"), or <u>how</u> (as for example, "she thinks <u>logically</u>"). Adverbs sometimes are used to modify an adjective or another adverb. For example, in the sentence "She has a <u>really</u> beautiful mind," the adverb <u>really</u> modifies the adjective <u>beautiful</u>. In the sentence "She thinks <u>very</u> logically," the adverb <u>very</u> modifies the adverb <u>logically</u>. In the Artificial Language, the only adverbs used are those that modify verbs. In the Spanish language, as well as in the English language, adverbs are used to modify verbs, adjectives, and other adverbs.

Gender: As a grammatical concept, gender refers to the classification of words according to whether they are masculine, feminine, or neuter.

As stated above, Spanish takes masculine or feminine endings for nouns, adjectives, and articles. The neuter form is used sometimes to express abstraction in a more emphatic manner. The neuter form is <u>NOT</u> used in the Artificial Language. Consequently, it is very important for you to remember that in the Artificial Language <u>all</u> nouns, adjectives, and articles take either a masculine or a feminine ending according to whether the sentence refers to a male or female.

Also, all nouns and adjectives in the Artificial Language were conceived (for the sake of simplicity) to be masculine. Thus, unless the feminine gender is specified in the sentence, the masculine gender is used always.

Infinitive: An infinitive is the general, abstract form of a verb; for example, <u>to look</u>, <u>to think</u>, <u>to remember</u>, <u>to walk</u>. Once the action expressed by the verb is attached to a specific subject (a person, animal, or thing), then we say the verb is "conjugated," or linked to that subject; for example, "he/she thinks," "the dog runs," "the table broke."

In contrast to the way that an infinitive in English is preceded by the word "to" (as in "to think"), in the Artificial Language (and in Spanish), infinitives are defined by their suffix. In the version of the Artificial Language used here, this ending (or suffix) is <u>ker</u>. (In the actual test, the ending will be different.)

Noun: A noun is a word that names a person, place, thing, or abstraction; for example. <u>Lindsay</u>, <u>Chicago</u>, <u>tree</u>, <u>wisdom</u>. A noun can refer to an individual (as in <u>Lindsay</u>, an individual person, or <u>Chicago</u>, an individual place) or to a set (as in "<u>all stones</u>," "<u>all trees</u>," "<u>all cities</u>").

Prefix: A prefix always occurs at the beginning of a word. It can be a single letter or a sequence of letters; for example, <u>a</u>moral, <u>il</u>legal, <u>dys</u>functional.

A prefix is the opposite of a suffix, which always occurs at the end of a word, but both serve to change the basic word in some way. For example, <u>polite</u> is the basic word (in this case an adjective), to express the concept of behavior that conforms to accepted social norms, while adding the prefix <u>im</u> and creating the word <u>impolite</u> transforms the word <u>polite</u> into its contradictory concept. You should note that in the Artificial Language a prefix is used to create negative concept (see Rule 13). Such a rule mimics both Spanish and English, in both of which negation is usually expressed by using a negative prefix.

Pronoun: A pronoun is a word used in place of a noun; for example, "she" instead of "Lindsay," "they" instead of "the guards," "it" instead of "the stone," "himself/herself" instead of "the judge."

In both English and Spanish, there is a difference between a pronoun that stands for the subject of an action (as in "<u>She</u> threw the stone," meaning that <u>Lindsay</u> threw the stone), and a pronoun that stands for the object of an action (as in "The stone was thrown at <u>her</u>," meaning that the stone was thrown at Lindsay). By contrast, in the Artificial Language used in this manual, there is no grammatical difference between <u>he</u> and <u>him</u>, both being <u>yev</u>. Remember, however, that in the Artificial Language pronouns take feminine endings when the subject or object of the action is feminine. Accordingly, in the version of the Artificial Language given in this manual, both <u>she</u> (subject) and <u>her</u> (object) would be <u>yevnef</u> (i.e., <u>yev</u> plus the feminine suffix <u>nef</u>).

Suffix: A suffix always occurs at the end of a word. It can be a single letter or a sequence of letters, for example, cream<u>y</u>, read<u>able</u>, nice<u>ly</u>. Unlike prefixes, suffixes often change the "part of speech" (i.e., the type of word). For example, in the case of cream<u>y</u>, the suffix <u>y</u> changes the noun <u>cream</u> into the adjective <u>creamy</u>, and in the case of <u>nicely</u>, the suffix <u>ly</u> changes the adjective <u>nice</u> into the adverb <u>nicely</u>.

In addition, suffixes are used to conjugate verbs (for example, to change the present tense into the past tense: you walk, you walk<u>ed</u>) and to create the plural form of nouns (for example, boy, boy<u>s</u>). In Spanish, suffixes are used for the same purposes, but they are used for other purposes too, such as creating plural forms for adjectives and changing the gender of a word.

In the Artificial Language, suffixes are used (1) to change the part of speech (for example, Rule 11 uses a suffix to change an adjective into an adverb), (2) to conjugate verbs (for example, Rules 6 and 7 use suffixes to express present and past tenses), and (3) to create the plural forms of nouns, pronouns, adjectives, and articles (Rule 2). In addition, the Artificial Language mimics Spanish in using a suffix to express gender.

You should study all the rules on suffixes in the Artificial Language, and you should practice using these rules, but you should NOT memorize them because (1) you will have them available to you at all times during the actual test, and (2) in the actual test, some of the suffixes and prefixes are different from the ones used in this practice test.

Verb: A verb is used to express either an action or a state of being. For example, "He prepared dinner" expresses the action of making all preparations for dinner, while "He is a citizen" expresses the state or condition of being a citizen.

A condition or "state of being" can be permanent or transitory. For example, "The agent's horse is a bay mare" expresses a permanent condition for the horse (being a bay mare), while "George is at lunch" expresses a transitory condition for George (being at lunch). The Spanish language, unlike English, has two different verbs to express permanent and transitory conditions, although the Artificial Language is akin to English rather than to Spanish in its use of a single verb to express any state of being.

When a verb is linked to a subject (i.e., "conjugated"), it changes from the abstract infinitive form to a specific form such as a present tense or a past tense. The Artificial Language primarily uses only two tenses: the simple past tense and the simple present tense in the indicative mood (see Rules 6 and 7). (Verbs in the indicative mood express a real action or condition, whereas verbs in the sub-junctive mood express hypothetical actions or conditions. The subjunctive mood does not exist in the Artificial Language, but it is very important in Spanish.)

You may find that the past participle is used in the test (see Rule 8). In that case, the present perfect tense (they have crossed) and the past perfect tense (they had crossed) will be used in the Artificial Language.

Be sure to apply the rules as directed in the test material. If no rule governing the past participle is listed in the actual test material, then the past participle is treated as a simple past tense.

Test Questions

Set 1: Questions 1 Through 20

Directions: For each sentence, decide which words have been translated correctly. Use scratch paper to list each <u>numbered</u> word that is correctly translated into the Artificial Language. When you have finished listing the words that are correctly translated in sentences 1 through 4, select your answer according to the following instructions:

Mark:

    (A) if <u>only</u> the word numbered 1 is correctly translated.

    (B) if <u>only</u> the word numbered 2 is correctly translated.

    (C) if <u>only</u> the word numbered 3 is correctly translated.

    (D) if <u>two</u> or <u>more</u> of the numbered words are correctly translated.

    (E) if <u>none</u> of the numbered words is correctly translated.

Be sure to list only the <u>numbered</u> words that are <u>correctly</u> translated.

Study the sample question before going on to the test questions.

Sample Sentence

He identifies the driver.

Sample Translation

<u>Volle</u> <u>kalenim</u> wir <u>arlek</u>.
  1   2   3

The word numbered 1, <u>volle</u>, is incorrect since the translation of <u>volle</u> is <u>this</u>. The word <u>yev</u> should have been used. The word numbered 2, <u>kalenim</u>, is also incorrect because the singular form <u>kalenem</u> should have been used. The word numbered 3 is correct and should be written on your note paper. <u>Arlek</u> has been correctly formed form the infinitive <u>arker</u> (to drive) by applying Rules 4 and 9. So, only the word numbered 3 has been correctly translated. **The correct answer is choice (C).**

Now answer Questions 1 through 20 in the manner indicated. <u>Be sure to record your answers on the separate answer sheet.</u>

Sentence   **Translation**

1. The illegal aliens escaped from the guards.
Wir fercolle huslekoz pirzotim mor wiroz
   1   2   3
bonlekoz.

2. That alien's papers were from the government.
Volle huslekoz trenedlckoz synzotem mor
   1   2   3
wir almanlek.

3. The woman identified the boy.
Wir kapleknef kalenzotem wir ekaplek.
   1   2   3

4. Those men crossed the border.
Velleoz kaplekoz chronzotim wir reglek.
   1   2   3

5. Spies are enemies.
Tatlekoz synem avelek.
   1   2   3

6. He is an alien.
Yev synem bex huslekoz.
  1   2   3

7. That girl is a friend.
Volle ekapleknef synem wir kometlek.
   1   2   3

8. The guard's boy injured her.
Wir bonkerae ekaplek liaker yevnef.
     1   2   3

9. The river borders those countries.
Wir browlek reglekoz velle failekoz.
    1   2   3

10. Those aliens are not legal.
Velloz huslekoz fersynim fercolle.
     1   2   3

11. A spy shot an inspector.
Bex tatle degzotem wir zelzot.
   1   2   3

12. The loyal man escaped from the enemy.
Wir inle ekaplek pirzotim mor wir avelek.
   1   2   3

13. That woman drives skillfully.
Velle kapleknef arim janle.
   1   2   3

14. The illegal alien crossed the border.
Wir fercolle huslek chonzotim wir bonker.
          1   2   3

15. Inspectors identified the boys and girls.
Zelek kalenzotim wiroz ekaplekoz loa
   1   2
ekapleknefoz.
  3

16. The difficult men were from that country.
Wiroz glasleoz kaplekoz mor velle
   1   2
failekoz.
  3

17. Those girls worked illegally.
Velleoz ekaplek frigzotim fercolle.
       1   2   3

18. That alien has papers from the government.
Velle huslek tulem trenedlek mor wir
   1   2   3
almanlek.

19. That jeep is a spy's.
Volle daqlek synem bex tatlekoz.
   1   2   3

20. She has to identify the boy.
Yevnef tulim kalenker wir kaplek.
     1   2   3

Set 2: Questions 21 Through 30

Directions: For each question in this group, select the one of five suggested choices that correctly translates the underlined word or group of words into the Artificial Language.

While many illegal aliens try <u>to cross the border</u> on foot, some cross the border in
21

underground tunnels. Others <u>drive</u> across the border in trucks <u>and jeeps</u>. Border Patrol
22   23

Agents <u>work</u> for their country. It is their job to catch <u>illegal aliens and spies</u>. These
24   25

<u>skillful men</u> and women must inspect government papers to ensure that these
26

<u>papers are legal</u>. Agents frequently patrol the border, but they may also work in a
27

<u>border station</u>. They do whatever it takes to get the job done. Their work is difficult and
28

dangerous. They may be injured from enemies trying <u>to shoot them</u>. Border Patrol Agents
29

are loyal and are <u>the country's</u> protectors.
30

21. (A) chonker wiroz reglekoz	**25.** (A) fercolle huslekoz loa tatlekoz
(B) chonker wir reglek	(B) fercolleoz huslekoz loa tatker
(C) chonzotim wir reglek	(C) fercolleoz huslekoz loa tatlekoz
(D) chonzotem wir regle	(D) fercolleoz huslekoz loa tatleoz
(E) chonker wir regle	(E) fercolle huslek loa tatker
22. (A) arem	**26.** (A) inle kaplekoz
(B) arzotim	(B) inleoz kaplekoz
(C) arker	(C) inle kaplek
(D) arim	(D) inleki kaplekoz
(E) arzotem	(E) inlekoz kaplekoz
23. (A) loa daqlek	**27.** (A) trenedlekoz synem colleoz
(B) loa daqle	(B) trenedlekoz synim fercolleoz
(C) loaoz daqleoz	(C) trenedlek synemoz colleoz
(D) loaoz daqekoz	(D) trenedlekoz synem colle
(E) loa daqlekoz	(E) trenedlekoz synim colleoz
24. (A) frigim	**28.** (A) reglek lexlek
(B) frigker	(B) regle lexle
(C) frigzotem	(C) regker lexker
(D) frigem	(D) regle lexlek
(E) frig	(E) regker leklex

29. (A) degzotim yevoz

    (B) degzotem yevoz

    (C) degker yevoz

    (D) deglek yev

    (E) degker velleoz

30. (A) wir failekae

    (B) wir failekoz

    (C) wiroz failekoz

    (D) wir failek

    (E) wir failzot

Set 3: Questions 31 Through 42

Directions: For this group of questions, select the one answer choice that is the correct translation of the English word or words in parentheses. You should translate the entire sentence in order to determine what form should be used.

31. Wir ferinlenef kapleknef (was a spy).

    (A) synzotem bex tatker

    (B) synzotim bex tatlekoz

    (C) synem bex tatlek

    (D) synzotim bex tatlek

    (E) synzotem bex tatlek

32. Velle browlek synem (difficult to cross).

    (A) glasle chonker

    (B) glasle chonlek

    (C) glasleker chonker

    (D) glasleki chonzotem

    (E) glasle chonzotem

33. Wir janle ekaplek (escaped from the guard).

    (A) pirzotem mor wir bonker

    (B) pirem mor wir bonlek

    (C) pirzotem mor wir bonlek

    (D) pirzotim mor wir bonlekoz

    (E) pirzotim mor wir bonlek

34. (The illegal aliens) synem mor velle failek.

    (A) Wiroz fercolleoz huslek

    (B) Wir fercolle huslek

    (C) Ferwiroz fercolleoz huslekoz

    (D) Wiroz fercolleoz huslekoz

    (E) Wir fercolleoz huslekoz

35. (That inspector) synem bex kometlek.

    (A) Velleoz zellek

    (B) Velle zellek

    (C) Volle zelker

    (D) Volle zellek

    (E) Velle zelker

36. Wir bonlek degzotem (the enemy's jeep).

    (A) wir avelekoz daqlek

    (B) wir avelekoz daqlekoz

    (C) wir avelekae daqlek

    (D) wir avelek daqlek

    (E) wirae avelekae daqlek

37. (She has) kalenker wiroz huslekoz.

    (A) Yev tulem

    (B) Yevnef tulem

    (C) Yev tulker

    (D) Yevnef tulemnef

    (E) Yevnef tulim

38. Velleoz trenedlekoz synem (a legal government).

    (A) bex fercolle almanker

    (B) bex fercolle almanlek

    (C) bexoz colleoz almanlekoz

    (D) bex colle almanlek

    (E) bexznef collenef almanlek

39. Wir tatlek frigzotem (to escape) mor wir bonlek.

    (A) pirzotem
    (B) pirzotim
    (C) pirker
    (D) pirto
    (E) pirlek

40. Wir liale huslek (drove skillfully).

    (A) arzotem janle
    (B) arzotim janleki
    (C) arzotem janleki
    (D) arzotim janle
    (E) arker janleki

41. (Those boys) loa kapleknefoz synim colle.

    (A) Velle ekaplekoz
    (B) Volleoz ekaplekoz
    (C) Volle ekaplekoz
    (D) Velleoz ekaplek
    (E) Velleoz ekaplekoz

42. (The spies are) mor bex avele failek.

    (A) Wir tatlekoz synem
    (B) Wiroz tatlekoz synim
    (C) Wiroz tatkeroz synem
    (D) Wir tatlekoz synimoz
    (E) Wiroz tatlekoz synimoz

Set 4: Questions 43 Through 50

Directions: For the last group of questions, select the one answer that is the correct form of the underlined expression as it is used in the sentence. At the end of the sentence, you will find instructions in parentheses telling you which form to use. In some sentences, you will be asked to supply the correct form of two or more expressions. In this case, the instructions for these expressions are presented consecutively in the parentheses and are separated by a dash. Be sure to translate the entire sentence before selecting your answer.

43. Wiroz fercolleoz huslekoz tulker chonker wir reglek. (present perfect plural verb)

    (A) tulem chonto
    (B) tulim chonto
    (C) tulim chonzotim
    (D) tulem chonzotem
    (E) tulem chonem

44. Chonker wir reglek synker glasle. (negative singular verb)

    (A) fersynim
    (B) synimae
    (C) synim
    (D) synem
    (E) fersynem

45. Yevnef liaker wir tatker mor velle failek. (past tense—noun)

    (A) liazotem—tatlek
    (B) liaem—tatle
    (C) liazotim—tatlek
    (D) liaim—tatle
    (E) liato—tatlek

46. Wirnef huslek trenedlekoz syim mor wir failek. (feminine plural possessive noun)

    (A) huslekozae
    (B) husleknefae
    (C) husleknefoz
    (D) husleknefozae
    (E) husleknefozimae

47. Wiroz tatker tulim pirker. (plural noun—past participle as predicate)

    (A) tatlek—pirto
    (B) tatkeroz—pirzotim
    (C) tatlek—pirzotem
    (D) tatlekoz—pirto
    (E) tatleoz—pirzotim

48. Velle kapleknef kalenzotem wiroz avelek. (feminine singular adjective—plural noun)

    (A) Vellenefoz—avelekoz
    (B) Vellenefoz—avelekenefoz
    (C) Vellenef—avelekoz
    (D) Velleoz—avelekoz
    (E) Vellenef—avelek

49. Wirnefoz colle husleknefoz liaker wirnefoz ekaplek. (negative feminine plural adjective—past tense—plural feminine noun)

    (A) fercolleoz—liazotim—ekaplekoz
    (B) fercollenefoz—liazotim—ekapleknefoz
    (C) fercollenef—liazotem—ekapleknefoz
    (D) fercollenefoz—liazotem—ekapleknefoz
    (E) fercollenef—liazotim—ekapleknef

50. Bex kometlek bonlek zelzotem wirnef colle huslek trenedlekoz. (negative adjective—feminine adjective—feminine possessive noun)

    (A) ferkometle—collenef—husleknefae
    (B) ferkometlek—colle—husleknefae
    (C) ferkometle—collenefae—husleknefae
    (D) kometlenef—collenef—husleknefae
    (E) kometeknef—collenef—husleknef

ANSWER KEY AND EXPLANATIONS

Logical Reasoning

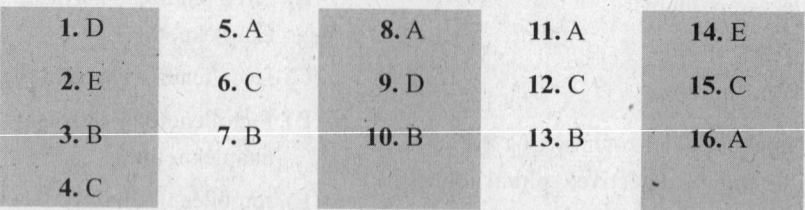

1. D	**5.** A	**8.** A	**11.** A	**14.** E
2. E	**6.** C	**9.** D	**12.** C	**15.** C
3. B	**7.** B	**10.** B	**13.** B	**16.** A
4. C				

1. **The correct answer is choice (D).** The passage says that worker's compensation may be denied if an employee's injury results from willful misconduct. Miguel A. was not wearing a hard hat at the time of his injury even though he was required to do so. Therefore, he may be denied compensation. So, choice (D) is correct. This fact also makes choice (A) incorrect. There is no evidence that his employer may have intentionally caused his injury, choice (B). Based on the information in the passage, Miguel A. will not be able to sue his employer, choice (C). There is no indication that he will receive only medical care, choice (E).

2. **The correct answer is choice (E).** The last sentence says that declaring a state of emergency allows the mayor to hire outside contractors without following the formal bidding process. There is not enough information to conclude that the mayor declares a state of emergency each winter, choice (A), or that the mayor still accepts bids from outside contractors during a state of emergency, choice (B). According to the passage, the mayor must declare a state of emergency to hire outside contractors without accepting a bid, so choice (C) is not correct. The passage says that the mayor may hire outside contractors to assist the snowplow operators. This implies that the snowplow operators work with them, so choice (D) is also incorrect.

3. **The correct answer is choice (B).** The second sentence explains that to be naturalized foreign citizens must demonstrate an ability to read, write, and speak English; a knowledge and understanding of U.S. history and government; and a favorable disposition toward the United States. Nadia's limited understanding of U.S. history and government could prevent naturalization, so choice (B) is correct. She does not meet all the criteria for naturalization, so choice (A) is incorrect. She already reads, writes, and speaks English well, so choice (C) is also incorrect. The passage does not indicate that she has special circumstances that will allow her to be naturalized or if she will not be naturalized because she is an Iranian national, so choices (D) and (E) are incorrect.

4. **The correct answer is choice (C).** The paragraph states that the City of Concord follows the California Retail Food Code. This means that Sandra H. must have a permit to open a hot dog stand, so choice (C) is correct. Sandra H.'s hot dog stand might be closed for reasons other than not having a permit or following the regulations, so choices (A) and (D) are not correct. She must meet other requirements in addition to having soap and water, so choice (B) is also not correct. She might try to open a stand in Concord without a permit, so choice (E) is incorrect.

5. **The correct answer is choice (A).** The only valid conclusion is that the investigator found evidence of something that called into question Frank's honesty or loyalty. There is not enough information to determine if Frank has abused alcohol, choice (B); is involved with criminals, choice (D); or has an arrest record, choice (E). The passage also does not indicate if Frank L. has been divorced several times or even if this is a reason that he might fail a background check, choice (C).

6. **The correct answer is choice (C).** This is an example of a test question with a negative lead statement. It asks for the conclusion that is *not* supported by the paragraph. This means that four statements are valid conclusions based on the paragraph and only one is not. According to the information in the passage, Claire L. is participating in sign-cutting, so choice (A) is true and therefore incorrect. She also must participate in line watch, choice (B), and has discovered a disturbance in the natural terrain, choice (D). As a Border Patrol Agent, it is her job to prevent illegal aliens from crossing the border, choice (E). Based on the information in the passage, you cannot conclude that she has found an illegal alien; she has found only a water bottle. Therefore, choice (C) is invalid and, therefore, the correct answer.

7. **The correct answer is choice (B).** According to the passage, if Ladonna P. wants to hold a wedding ceremony in a San Diego public park, she must submit an application for a permit at least 15 days before the date of the ceremony. While Ladonna P. must submit an application 30 days before the date if she has a special request, she might do this even if she does not have a special request, so choice (A) is not correct. Choices (C) and (D) are not correct because, although these are requirements, the passage says that exceptions to the rules are granted on a

case-by-case basis. Choice (E) is not correct because Ladonna P.'s application might be denied.

8. **The correct answer is choice (A).** This question asks for the answer choice that *cannot* be validly concluded from the information in the passage. The only statement that cannot be validly concluded is choice (A). The other answer options are true: Juan M. did not follow the Border Patrol's recommendations, choice (B), and he will have his blood pressure and pulse checked before the test, choice (C). He will lose his offer of employment if he does not pass the test, choice (D), and his morning coffee might affect his blood pressure and pulse, choice (E).

9. **The correct answer is choice (D).** If the farm has 16 laborers and 10 are residents of the United States, 6 are illegal aliens. Nine laborers are women, so at least some of the women must be legal residents of the United States. If 9 laborers are women and 16 laborers work on the farm, some laborers must be men, so choice (A) is incorrect. Some women may be from El Salvador, but since only 4 illegal aliens are from El Salvador, all of the women cannot be from that country, so choices (B) and (C) are not correct. Some of the men may be legal residents of the United States, so choice (E) is also incorrect.

10. **The correct answer is choice (B).** If Raymond K. drives an ATV, he must have received special training. Choices (A), (C), (D), and (E) are not supported by information in the passage.

11. **The correct answer is choice (A).** This is an example of a test question with a negative lead statement. It asks for the conclusion that is *not* supported by the paragraph. That means that four of the statements are valid conclusions based on the paragraph, while

one is not. The passage says that most of the illegal aliens were from Mexico. It also says that most of the illegal aliens were men. Therefore, you cannot conclude that the women and children in the drop house were from Mexico. Choices (B), (C), (D), and (E) are supported by information in the passage.

12. **The correct answer is choice (C).** This question also has a negative lead-in statement, so you have to choose the answer choice that is *not* true based on the information in the passage. While Ileana J. will participate in search-and-rescue missions when she completes her training and becomes a BORSTAR agent, the passage does not lead you to believe that she does this now. Therefore, choice (C) is the correct answer. Choices (A), (B), (D), and (E) are supported by information in the passage.

13. **The correct answer is choice (B).** There are 10 students are in the class, 6 of which are women. If half of the class has averages under 70 percent, then at least some of the women have averages that are under 70 percent. This makes choice (A) invalid. The passage says that none of the students has taken a Spanish class before, so choices (C) and (E) are incorrect. There is no way to tell if the two students with average of 90 percent are men, choice (D).

14. **The correct answer is choice (E).** The law states that a farm that has been operating for more than a year cannot be deemed a nuisance. However, even if the farm has been operating for less than a year, this does not guarantee that it will be shut down, choice (A), or that the smell is not a nuisance, choice (B). There is not even evidence to determine whether a farm that has been operating for more than a year can be shut down, choice (C). Nothing in the paragraph states that Jim

cannot file a lawsuit if the farm has been operating for more than a year, choice (D).

15. **The correct answer is choice (C).** Rupert G. can only take the night-driving course if he passed the basic driving courses first. One of these courses is skid control, so choice (C) is correct and choice (E) is incorrect. There is not enough information to tell if Rupert G. has taken a vehicle-stops course, choice (A), and the 4×4 off-road driving course, choice (B), or if he will not take a course in SUV/van evasive driving, choice (D).

16. **The correct answer is choice (A).** The passage says that regardless of occupation, illegal immigrants earned less money than citizens of this country performing the same jobs. The passage says that some immigrants worked in professional positions, so choice (B) is not correct. It also says that some worked in transportation and production, so choice (C) is incorrect. Most immigrants worked in the service, construction, and production industries, which makes choice (E) incorrect. There is not enough information in the passage to conclude that most of those not employed in professional occupations were immigrants, choice (D).

Spanish Language Proficiency

Part I

1. B	**5.** A	**9.** D	**13.** D	**17.** A
2. E	**6.** E	**10.** A	**14.** B	**18.** A
3. B	**7.** A	**11.** E	**15.** B	**19.** C
4. C	**8.** A	**12.** D	**16.** E	**20.** A

1. **The correct answer is choice (B).** The word *brinca* is a form of the verb *brincar,* which means to jump; therefore, the closest synonym is *salta,* "to jump." Choice (A), "greets," and choice (D), "sautées," are phonetically similar to the correct answer but have different meanings. Choice (C), "to toast," begins with the same syllable as *brinca,* but its meaning is unrelated. Choice (E), "breeze," also sounds similar to the target word but has a different meaning.

2. **The correct answer is choice (E).** The word *lucrativa* refers to something that brings in earnings, so the term *rentable,* "profitable," is the closest synonym. Choice (A), "detrimental," and choice (C), "costly," have meanings that refer to something unprofitable. Choice (B), "shiny," has a meaning that is unrelated to the meaning of the target word. Choice (D), "charitable," is more akin to a nonprofit operation.

3. **The correct answer is choice (B).** The word *desagüe* means a drain or drainpipe. Therefore, the closest synonym is *drenaje,* "drainage." Choice (A), "feeding," and choice (C), "filling," have meanings that are contrary to the target word. Choice (D), "snub," begins with the same prefix as *desagüe* but has an unrelated meaning. Choice (E), "jellyfish," contains the same root word *agua* as the target word but has an unrelated meaning.

4. **The correct answer is choice (C).** The word *red* means an actual net, but also any net-like organization, or network. Therefore, *organización,* "organization," is the best synonym in this sentence. Choice (A), "fisherman," has a different meaning. Choice (B), "red," sounds like the target word in English, but its meaning is unrelated in Spanish. Choice (D), "trap," and choice (E), "to catch," both may be related to a net in the literal sense, but they do not mean an organization.

5. **The correct answer is choice (A).** In this sentence, the word *accidentado* does not refer to an accident, but to a land surface that is uneven or rugged. Therefore, *áspero,* "rough," is the best synonym. Choice (B), "flat," and choice (C), "smooth," are contrary to the meaning of *accidentado.* Choice (D), "crash," and choice (E), "run over," have to do with accidents and are not related to the meaning of *accidentado* as it is used in this sentence.

6. **The correct answer is choice (E).** The term *divisar* means to spot or sight something, usually at a distance. Therefore, *ver,* "to see," is the closest synonym. Choice (A), "to divide," and choice (D), "to guess," are phonetically similar to *divisar* but have different meanings. Choice (B), "to hide," and choice (C), "to listen," have meanings that are unrelated to *divisar.*

7. **The correct answer is choice (A).** The term *recién* is an adverb referring to something that has just been done or made; therefore, *recientemente,* "recently," is the best synonym. Choice (B), "strong," is phonetically similar to *recién* but has a different meaning. Choice (C), "exhausted," choice (D), "difficult," and choice (E), "again," are not adverbs and their meanings have nothing to do with *recién.*

8. **The correct answer is choice (A).** The word *tarea* refers to a job or <u>task</u>, so *trabajo,* "job," is the best synonym. Choice (B), "drink," and choice (E), "jammed," begin with the same syllable as the correct answer but have different meanings. Choice (C), "recess," and choice (D), a "rest," may indicate a break from a task but not the task itself.

9. **The correct answer is choice (D).** The word *efectos* in this context refers to someone's personal things or <u>belongings</u>. Consequently, the best synonym is *pertenencias,* "possessions." Choice (A), "consequences," is not a synonym for *efectos* in this context. Choice (B), "efficiency," and choice (E), "effectiveness," begin with the same syllables as *efectos* but have different meanings. Choice (C), "illnesses," is unrelated to the target word.

10. **The correct answer is choice (A).** The word *asuntos* refers to someone's business or <u>matters</u>. The best synonym is *cuestiones,* "issues." Choice (B), "hills," sounds similar to the correct answer but has a different meaning. Choice (C), "together," and choice (D), "sets," have the same ending as *asuntos* but are unrelated in meaning. Choice (E), "vacation" or "day off," is likewise unrelated, although it sounds similar to *asuntos.*

11. **The correct answer is choice (E).** The term *rostro* means a person's <u>face</u>, so *cara,* "face," is the best synonym. Choice (A), "eye," and choice (B), "cheek," are only parts of the face. Choice (C), "expensive," and choice (D), a form of the verb "to drag," are phonetically similar to *cara* but have different meanings.

12. **The correct answer is choice (D).** The word *cepille* is a form of the verb *cepillar,* which means to groom or <u>brush</u>; therefore, *peine* ("comb") is the best synonym. Choices A, B, C, and E (to "feed," "train," "call," and "train," respectively) are actions a person would perform with a dog, but these words do not mean the same as *cepillar.*

13. **The correct answer is choice (D).** The verb *olvidé* is a preterit form of *olvidar,* which means to <u>forget</u> or lose something. Therefore, the best synonym is *dejé.* Choice (A), "remembered," and choice (B), "found," have meanings that are the opposite of *olvidar.* Choice (C), "used," and choice (E), "sniffed," have meanings that are unrelated to *olvidar.*

14. **The correct answer is choice (B).** The word *abridor* means a tool to open something, or an <u>opener</u>. Therefore, *destapador,* "bottle opener," is the best synonym. Choice (A), "keychain," and choice (E), "door," are related to the idea of opening something but are not openers. Choice (C), "coat," is phonetically similar to the target word but has a different meaning. Choice (D), "alarm clock," ends with the same suffix as the correct answer, but does not have the same meaning.

15. **The correct answer is choice (B).** The word *desplome* is a noun indicating a <u>collapse</u>. Therefore, *caída,* "fall," is the best synonym. Choice (A), "building," and choice (E), "raising," mean the opposite of falling. Choice (C), "plucking feathers," is phonetically similar to *desplome* but has a different meaning. Choice (D), "sale," is unrelated to the meaning of *desplome.*

16. **The correct answer is choice (E).** The word *viaducto* is commonly used to indicate a <u>bridge</u>, especially for a <u>road</u> or <u>railway</u>, over a valley. Therefore, *puente,* "bridge," is the best synonym. Choice (A), "greenhouse," choice (B), "junction," and choice (D), "housing," are unrelated to the idea of a bridge. Choice (C), "aqueduct," contains the same suffix (*ducto*) as the target word, but an aqueduct carries water rather than vehicles.

17. **The correct answer is choice (A).** The word *espesa* means <u>thick</u>, so the closest synonym is *tupida,* "dense." Choice (B), "clear," and choice (E), "unobstructed," have meanings that are contrary to the meaning of *espesa.* Choice (C), "special," and choice (D), "heavy," are phonetically similar to the target word but have different meanings.

18. **The correct answer is choice (A).** The word *sede* refers to the <u>headquarters</u> of a company or an organization, so *oficina central,* "main office," is the best synonym. Choice (B), "ashtray," and choice (C), "path," have meanings that are different from *sede.* Choice (D), "subsidiary," and choice (E), "branch office," refer to secondary offices rather than the main office.

19. **The correct answer is choice (C).** The term *peatones* means <u>pedestrians</u>. Therefore, *caminantes,* "people who are walking," is the best synonym. Choice (A), "drivers," and choice (E), "motorists," both refer to the person driving. Choice (B), "traffic lights," and choice (D), "stop signs," are objects related to driving and traffic, but they are not people.

20. **The correct answer is choice (A).** The verb *alcanzaron* is a form of *alcanzar,* which means to reach or <u>attain</u> an object or a goal. The best synonym is *pudieron,* "were able." Choice (B), "failed," and choice (D), "failed," both mean the opposite of attaining. Choice (C), "tired," and choice (E), "rotted," have meanings that are unrelated to the idea of *alcanzar.*

Part II

Section I

1. D	3. A	5. D	6. E	7. D
2. B	4. A			

1. **The correct answer is choice (D).** The adjective *antiguos* agrees with the masculine noun *autos*; and *despacio* is the correct adverb to indicate "slowly." Choices (A) and (C) use adjectives that do not agree with the noun and nonexistent forms of the adverb. Choice (B) uses the correct adjective but an incorrect adverb. Choice (E) uses the correct adjective but has a noun instead of an adverb.

2. **The correct answer is choice (B).** *Dejaron* is a preterit plural form of the verb *dejar;* and *debajo* is a preposition that is correctly followed by the article *de* to indicate "under." Choice (A) uses a singular verb form. Choices (C), (D), and (E) use incorrect verb forms and prepositions that would not be followed by *de*.

3. **The correct answer is choice (A).** The noun *luz* is feminine singular, so it takes the article *una;* and *brillante* is the adjective form that matches the noun *brillante*. Choice (B) uses an inappropriate article and a plural adjective. Choice (C) uses an inappropriate article and a nonexistent adjective. Choice (D) uses a verb instead of the adjective. Choice (E) uses an inappropriate article and a verb instead of the adjective.

4. **The correct answer is choice (A).** *Acercarse* is the proper infinitive form of the verb, and the article *la* matches the feminine noun *ciudad.* Choice (B) has no verb and uses a masculine article. Choices (C), (D), and (E)

have incorrect verb forms and articles that do not agree with the noun they accompany.

5. **The correct answer is choice (D).** The verb *estaban* is the correct form of the verb *estar,* which indicates a temporary condition; and *de* correctly completes the expression *a punto de* to indicate "about to" do something. Choices (A), (C), and (E) use forms of the verb *ser,* which indicates a permanent condition, and an incorrect phrase with *a punto.* Choice (B) uses the verb *estar* and also fails to complete the phrase correctly.

6. **The correct answer is choice (E).** The word *vez* correctly completes the prepositional phrase *en vez de,* meaning "instead of"; and *mía* is the appropriate possessive for the noun *cámara.* Choices (A), (B), (C), and (D) form the prepositional phrase incorrectly and use possessives that do not match the noun they modify.

7. **The correct answer is choice (D).** The word *parece* is the correct form of the verb *parecer;* and the adjective *buen* is the correct form of *bueno* when placed before a masculine singular noun. Choices (A), (B), (C), and (E) use incorrect verb forms and incorrect forms of *bueno.*

Section II

1. B	**3.** C	**5.** D	**6.** A	**7.** B
2. A	**4.** A			

1. **The correct answer is choice (B).** This sentence has the proper structure and is without errors. Choices (A), (C), and (D) contain various errors, including illogical structures, misplaced clauses, improper articles, and incorrect prepositions.

2. **The correct answer is choice (A).** This sentence has the proper structure and contains no errors. Choices (B) and (C) contain various errors, including illogical structures, incorrect gender, incorrect use of the phrase *pese a,* and improper verb forms. Choice (D) has several errors, including misplaced clauses, illogical structures, and incorrect gender.

3. **The correct answer is choice (C).** This sentence has the proper structure and contains no errors. Choices (A) and (B) have several errors, including missing or misused articles, improper verb forms, and incorrect word choices. Choice (D) contains misplaced clauses, illogical structures, and errors involving articles and prepositions.

4. **The correct answer is choice (A).** This sentence has the proper structure and contains no errors. Choices (B) and (D) contain several errors, including illogical structures and incorrect use of the negative. Choice (C) contains illogical structures and is not a complete sentence.

5. **The correct answer is choice (D).** This sentence has the proper structure and contains no errors. Choices (A) and (C) contain various errors, including improper verbs, incorrect pronouns, and incorrect prepositions. Choice (B) contains several errors, including improper verb placement and verb tense and an incorrect article.

6. **The correct answer is choice (A).** This sentence has the proper structure and contains no errors. Choice (B) contains incorrect prepositions and improper verb forms. Choices (C) and (D) have several errors, including misplaced clauses, improper use of the question word *cuándo,* absence of the preposition *a,* and improper verb forms.

7. **The correct answer is choice (B).** This sentence has the proper structure and contains no errors. Choices (A), (C), and (D) contain various errors, including illogical structures, incorrect word order, improper verbs, and missing or incorrect articles.

Section III

1. E	3. B	5. D	6. E	7. D
2. C	4. B			

1. **The correct answer is choice (E).** The term *llevamos* is a form of the verb *llevar*, which in this case means "to have done or completed." Choices (A), (B), (C), and (D) use the wrong verbs.

2. **The correct answer is choice (C).** *Corriendo* is the correct participle forming the compound verb *estaban corriendo*. Choices (A) and (B) use simple forms of the verb *correr*. Choice (D) uses the infinitive.

3. **The correct answer is choice (B).** This is the correct noun to indicate time: "in the morning." Choice (A) illogically reads "in the the day after tomorrow." Choices (C) and (D) use illogical words that not indicate a time.

4. **The correct answer is choice (B).** This is the gerund of the verb *sudar* as an adverb indicating *how* I awoke ("sweating"). Choices (A), (C), and (D) use other forms of the verb that are not suitable as adverbs.

5. **The correct answer is choice (D).** This is the correct subjunctive form of the verb *subir*, which is appropriate for indicating doubt. Choice (A) uses the present indicative, choice (B) uses the infinitive, and choice (C) uses the participle.

6. **The correct answer is choice (E).** The sentence is correct as written, because *quiénes* is the correct plural pronoun to use as a subject for the plural verb *dieron*. Choices (A), (B), and (C) use incorrect forms of the pronoun. Choice (D) also adds a preposition that is out of place in the sentence.

7. **The correct answer is choice (D).** *Cuántas* is a correct pronoun referring to quantity. Choices (A), (B), and (C) use forms of the verb *contar*.

Artificial Language

1. C	11. B	21. B	31. E	41. E
2. C	12. A	22. D	32. A	42. B
3. D	13. D	23. E	33. C	43. B
4. E	14. A	24. A	34. D	44. E
5. A	15. D	25. C	35. B	45. A
6. D	16. C	26. B	36. C	46. D
7. B	17. B	27. D	37. B	47. D
8. C	18. D	28. D	38. D	48. C
9. A	19. B	29. C	39. C	49. B
10. A	20. B	30. A	40. C	50. A

1. **The correct answer is choice (C).** Only the word numbered 3 is correctly translated. While *wir* is the translation of *the,* since the subject of the sentence is plural, the suffix *oz* must be added to *wir* (Rule 2). The correct translation is *wiroz.* While *fercolle* is the correct translation of the word *illegal,* since the subject of the sentence is plural, it also needs to have the suffix *oz* (Rule 2). The correct translation is *fercolleoz.*

2. **The correct answer is choice (C).** Only the word numbered 3 is correctly translated. *Volle* is the translation of the word *this. Velle* is the correct translation of *that.* The translation of the word *alien* is *huslek.* To make the word possessive, add the suffix *ae* (Rule 12). The correct translation is *huslekae.*

3. **The correct answer is choice (D).** The words 2 and 3 are correctly translated. While *wir* is the correct translation of the word *the,* because the subject of the sentence is feminine, the suffix *nef* should be added (Rule 3). The correct translation is *wirnef.*

4. **The correct answer is choice (E).** The words numbered 1, 2, and 3 in this sentence are correctly translated.

5. **The correct answer is choice (A).** Only the word numbered 1 in this sentence is correctly translated. *Synem* is the translation of *is. Synim* is the translation of *are,* since the suffix *im* indicates that the verb is plural. *Avelek* is the translation of *enemy.* To make the word plural, add the suffix *oz* (Rule 2). The correct translation is *avelekoz.*

6. **The correct answer is choice (D).** The words numbered 1 and 2 are correctly translated. The word numbered 3 is incorrect. *Huslekoz* is the translation of *aliens.* The translation of *alien* (singular) is *huslek.*

7. **The correct answer is choice (B).** Only the word numbered 2 is translated correctly. *Volle* is the translation of *this. Velle* is the translation of *that. Wir* is the translation of *the. Bex* is the translation of *a* or *an.* The correct translation of the sentence is "Velle ekapleknef synem bex kometlek."

8. **The correct answer is choice (C).** Only the word numbered 3 is correctly translated. To create the translation of *guard,* begin with *bonker,* the translation of the infinitive *to guard.* Drop the *ker* to create the verb stem (Rule 4). To make the verb a noun, add

the suffix *lek* (9). To make the noun possessive, add the suffix *ae* (Rule 12). The correct translation is *bonlekae*. To create the translation of *injured*, begin with *liaker*, the translation of *to injure*. Drop the *ker* to create the verb stem (Rule 4). To make the verb past tense, add the suffix *zot*. Then add *em* because the verb is singular (Rule 7). The correct translation is *liazotem*.

9. **The correct answer is choice (A).** Only the word numbered 1 is correctly translated. To create the present-tense noun *borders*, begin with *regker*, the translation of *to border*. Drop the *ker* to create the verb stem (Rule 4). To make the verb present tense, add *em* because the verb is singular (Rule 6). To create the translation of *those*, begin with *volle*, the translation of *this*. To make *volle* plural, add *oz* (Rule 2). The correct translation of *those* is *volleoz*.

10. **The correct answer is choice (A).** Only the word numbered 1 is correctly translated. *Fersynim* is the translation of *are not*. The translation of *is not* is *fersynem*, since the verb is singular. *Fercolle* is the translation of *illegal*. To create the translation of *legal*, drop the prefix *fer*. The correct translation is *colle*.

11. **The correct answer is choice (B).** Only the word numbered 2 is correctly translated. To create the translation of the noun *spy*, begin with *tatker*, the translation of the infinitive *to spy*. Drop the *ker* to create the verb stem (Rule 4). Add *lek* to make the verb a noun (Rule 9). The correct translation is *tatlek*. To create the noun *inspector*, begin with *zelker*, the translation of the infinitive *to inspect*. Drop the *ker* to create the verb stem (Rule 4). To make the verb a noun, add the suffix *lek*. The correct translation is *zellek*.

12. **The correct answer is choice (A).** Only the word numbered 1 is correctly translated. *Ekaplek* is the translation of *boy*. *Kaplek*

is the translation of *man*. To create the translation of *escaped*, begin with *pirker*, the translation of *to escape*. Drop the *ker* to create the verb stem (Rule 4), add *zot* to make the verb past tense, and add *em* because the verb is singular (Rule 7). The correct translation is *pirzotem*.

13. **The correct answer is choice (D).** Only the word numbered 3 is translated incorrectly. *Janle* is the translation of the adjective *skillful*. To make this an adverb, add the suffix *ki* (Rule 11). The correct translation is *janleki*.

14. **The correct answer is choice (A).** Only the word numbered 1 is translated correctly. To create the translation of *crossed*, begin with *chonker*, the translation of *to cross*. Drop the *ker* to create the verb stem (Rule 4). Add *zot* to make the verb past tense and add *em* because the verb is singular (Rule 7). The correct translation is *chonzotem*. To create the noun *border*, begin with *bonker*, the translation of *to border*. Drop the *ker* and add *lek* to make the verb a noun (Rule 9). The correct translation is *bonlek*.

15. **The correct answer is choice (D).** The words numbered 2 and 3 are correctly translated, but the word numbered 1 is not correct. To create the translation of *inspectors*, begin with *zelker*, the translation of *to inspect*. Drop the *ker* to create the verb stem (Rule 4). Add *lek* to make the verb a noun (Rule 9). To make the noun plural, add *oz* (Rule 2). The correct translation of *inspectors* is *zellekoz*.

16. **The correct answer is choice (D).** Only the word numbered 3 is incorrectly translated. *Failekoz* is the translation of *countries*. The translation of *country* is *failek*.

17. **The correct answer is choice (B).** Only the word numbered 2 is correctly translated. *Ekaplek* is the translation of *boy*. To make the translation feminine, add the suffix *nef*

(Rule 1). To make the translation plural, add the suffix *oz* (Rule 2). The translation of *girls* is *ekapleknefoz*. *Fercolle* is the translation of *illegal*. To make this an adverb, add the suffix *ki* (Rule 11). The correct translation is *fercolleki*.

18. **The correct answer is choice (D).** Only the word numbered 3 is incorrectly translated. *Trenedlek* is the translation of *paper*. To make it plural, add the suffix *oz* (Rule 2). The correct translation is *trenedlekoz*.

19. **The correct answer is choice (B).** Only the word numbered 2 is correctly translated. *Volle* is the translation of *this*. The translation of *that* is *velle*. To create the translation of *spy's*, begin with *tatker*, the translation of *to spy*. Drop the *ker* to create the verb stem (Rule 4). Add *lek* to make the verb a noun (Rule 9). To make the noun possessive, add *ae* (Rule 12). The correct translation is *tatlekae*.

20. **The correct answer is choice (B).** Only the word numbered 2 is correctly translated. *Tulim* is the translation of *have*. *Tulem* is the translation of *has*. *Kaplek* is the translation of *man*. *Ekaplek* is the translation of *boy*.

21. **The correct answer is choice (B).** The translation of the infinitive *to cross* is *chonker*. The translation of *the* is *wir*. To create the noun *border*, begin with *regker*, the translation of *to border*. Drop the *ker* to create the verb stem. To make the verb a noun, add suffix *lek* (Rule 9). The correct translation is *reglek*.

22. **The correct answer is choice (D).** To create the translation of the present-tense verb *drive,* begin with *arker,* the translation of the infinitive *to drive*. Drop the *ker* to create the verb stem (Rule 4). Add the suffix *im* because the verb is plural (Rule 6).

23. **The correct answer is choice (E).** The translation of the word *and* is *loa,* and the translation of *jeep* is *daqlek*. To make the word plural, add the suffix *oz* (Rule 2). The correct translation is *daqlekoz*.

24. **The correct answer is choice (A).** To create the present-tense verb *work*, begin with *frigker*, the translation of *to work*. Drop the *ker* (Rule 4). Add the suffix *im* because the verb is plural (Rule 6).

25. **The correct answer is choice (C).** The translation of *illegal* is *fercolle*. However, because it modifies a plural noun (*aliens*), you must add the suffix *oz* (Rule 3). The correct translation is *fercolleoz*. The translation of *alien* is *huslek*. Add *oz* to make it plural (Rule 2). The translation of *and* is *loa*. To create the plural noun *spies,* use the translation of the infinitive *to spy*, which is *tatker*. Drop the *ker* and add *lek* to make the verb a noun (Rule 9). To make the noun plural, add *oz* (Rule 2). The correct translation is *tatlekoz*.

26. **The correct answer is choice (B).** The translation of skillful is *inle*. However, in this sentence *skillful* modifies a plural noun, so you need to add the suffix *oz* (Rule 3). The correct translation is *inleoz*. The translation of *men* is created by adding *oz* to *kaplek*, the translation of *man*. The correct translation is *kaplekoz*.

27. **The correct answer is choice (D).** The translation of the word *paper* is *trenedlek*. To make the word plural, add the suffix *oz* (Rule 2). The correct translation is *trenedlekoz*. The translation of *are* is *synem* (Rule 6), and the translation of *legal* is *colle*.

28. **The correct answer is choice (D).** To create the adjective *border*, begin with *regker*, the translation of *to border*. Drop the *ker* to create the verb stem (Rule 4). To make a verb a noun, add *lek* (Rule 9). However, in this sentence, *border* is an adjective modifying *station*. According to Rule 10, to form an

adjective from a noun, drop the suffix *lek* and add the suffix *le*. The correct translation is *regle*. To create the noun *station*, use the translation of the infinitive *to station*, which is *lexker*. Drop the *ker* to create the verb stem (Rule 4). To make the verb a noun, add *lek* (Rule 9). The correct translation is *lexlek*.

29. **The correct answer is choice (C).** The translation of the infinitive *to shoot* is *degker*. To create the translation of *them*, begin with *yev*, the translation of *he/him*. Add *oz* to make this translation plural. The correct translation is *yevoz*.

30. **The correct answer is choice (A).** The translation of *the* is *wir*, and the translation of country is *failek*. To make the translation of *country* possessive, add the suffix *ae* (Rule 12). The correct translation is *failekae*.

31. **The correct answer is choice (E).** The translation of the complete sentence is, "The disloyal woman was a spy." The translation of *was* is *synzotem* (Rule 6). The translation of *a* is *bex*. To create the translation of *spy*, use the infinitive *tatker*, which is the translation of *to spy*. Drop the *ker* (Rule 4). Add the suffix *lek* to make the verb a noun (Rule 9). The correct translation is *tatlek*.

32. **The correct answer is choice (A).** The translation of the complete sentence is, "That river is difficult to cross." The translation of *difficult* is *glasle*, and the translation of *to cross* is *chonker*.

33. **The correct answer is choice (C).** The complete sentence translates as, "The skillful boy escaped from the guard." To create the translation of the past-tense verb *escaped*, begin with the translation of the infinitive *to escape*, which is *pirker*. Drop the *ker* (Rule 4). To make the verb past tense, add *zot* (Rule 7). Add *em* because the verb is singular. The correct translation is *pirzotem*. The translation of *from* is *mor*, and the translation of

the is *wir*. To create the noun *guard*, begin with *bonker*, the translation of *to guard*. Drop the *ker* (Rule 4). To make the verb a noun, add *lek* (Rule 9). The correct translation is *bonlek*.

34. **The correct answer is choice (D).** The complete sentence translates as, "The illegal aliens are from that country." The translation of *the* is *wir*, but since it modifies a plural noun, the suffix *oz* needs to be added (Rule 3). The correct translation is *wiroz*. To create the translation of *illegal*, add the prefix *fer* to *colle*, the translation of *legal*. Since the adjective modifies a plural noun, add the suffix *oz* (Rule 3). The correct translation is *fercolleoz*. The translation of *alien* is *huslek*. To make it plural, add the suffix *oz* (Rule 2). The correct translation is *huslekoz*.

35. **The correct answer is choice (B).** The entire sentence translates as, "That inspector is a friend." The translation of *that* is *velle*. To create the translation of the noun *inspector*, begin with the translation of the infinitive *to inspect*, which is *zelker*. Drop the *ker* (Rule 4). To make the verb a noun, add the suffix *lek* (Rule 9). The correct translation is *zellek*.

36. **The correct answer is choice (C).** The entire sentence translates as, "The guard shot the enemy's jeep." The translation of *the* is *wir*. The translation of *enemy* is *avelek*. To make it possessive, add the suffix *ae* (Rule 12). The correct translation is *avelekae*. The translation of *jeep* is *daqlek*.

37. **The correct answer is choice (B).** The entire sentence translates as, "She has to identify the aliens." To create the translation of *she*, add the suffix *nef* to *yev*, the translation of *he/him*. The translation of *has* is *tulem* (Rule 6).

38. **The correct answer is choice (D).** The complete sentence translates as, "Those papers are from a legal government." The

translation of *a* is *bex*, the translation of *legal* is *colle*, and the translation of *government* is *almanlek*.

39. The correct answer is choice (C). The complete sentence translates as, "The spy worked to escape from the guard." The translation of *to escape* is *pirker*.

40. The correct answer is choice (C). The translation of the complete sentence is, "The injured alien drove skillfully." To create the translation of *drove,* begin with *arker,* the translation of *to drive.* Drop the *ker* (Rule 4). Add *zot* to make the verb past tense, and then add *em* because the verb is singular (Rule 7). The correct translation is *arzotem.* The translation of the adjective *skillful* is *janle.* To make an adjective an adverb, add the suffix *ki (*Rule 11). The correct translation is *janleki.*

41. The correct answer is choice (E). The translation of the sentence is, "Those boys and girls are legal." The translation of *those* is *velleoz* (Rule 2). The translation of *boy* is *ekaplek.* To make this plural, add the suffix *oz.* The correct translation is *ekaplekoz.*

42. The correct answer is choice (B). The complete sentence translates as, "The spies are from an enemy country." The translation of *the* is *wir.* However, since *the* modifies a plural noun (*spies*), the suffix *oz* needs to be added (Rule 2). The correct translation is *wiroz.* To translate the word *spies,* take *tatker,* "to spy," drop *ker* and add *lek.* Then add *oz* to make it plural, The correct translation is *tatlekoz.* The translation of *are* is *synim* (Rule 6).

43. The correct answer is choice (B). The translation of this sentence is, "The illegal aliens have crossed the border." *Tulker* is the translation of *to have,* and *chonker* is the translation of *to cross.* To make these words the present perfect plural, drop the *ker*

from *tulker* and add *im* because the verb is plural (Rule 6). Follow Rule 8 to create the present perfect *crossed.* According to this rule, drop the *ker* and add *to.* The correct translation is *tulim chonto.*

44. The correct answer is choice (E). The translation of this sentence is, "To cross the border is not difficult." *Synker* is the translation of *to be.* To make this a singular verb, drop the *ker* (Rule 4) and add *em* because the verb is singular (Rule 6). To make the verb negative, add the prefix *fer.* The correct translation is *fersynem.*

45. The correct answer is choice (A). The translation of this sentence is, "She injured the spy from that country." To create the past-tense verb *injured,* drop the *ker* from *liaker.* Then add *zot* to make the verb past tense and *em* because the verb is singular (Rule 7). The correct translation is *liazotem.* To create the noun *spy* from *tatker,* the translation of *to spy,* drop the *ker* (Rule 4). Then add *lek* to make the verb a noun (Rule 9). The correct translation is *tatlek.*

46. The correct answer is choice (D). The translation of this sentence is, "The aliens' papers are from the government." To create the translation of the feminine plural possessive noun *aliens',* add *nef* to *huslek,* the translation of *alien* (Rule 1). Add *oz* to make it plural (Rule 2). Then add the suffix *ae* to make the noun possessive (Rule 12). The correct translation is *husleknefozae.*

47. The correct answer is choice (D). The translation of this sentence is, "The spies have escaped." To create the plural noun *spies,* drop the *ker* from *tatker,* the translation of *to spy.* Add *lek* to form a noun from the verb (Rule 9). To make the noun plural, add *oz* (Rule 2). The correct translation is *tatlekoz.* To create the past participle *escaped,* drop the *ker* from *pirker,* the translation of *to* *escape.* Then add *to* (Rule 8). The correct translation is *pirto.*

48. The correct answer is choice (C). The translation of this sentence is, "That woman identified the enemies." *Velle* is the correct translation of *that.* To make it feminine, add the suffix *nef* (Rule 1). The correct translation is *vellenef.* To make *avelek,* the Artificial Language word for *enemy,* plural, add the suffix *oz* (Rule 2). The correct translation is *avelekoz.*

49. The correct answer is choice (B). The translation of this sentence is, "The illegal aliens injured the girls." *Colle* is the Artificial Language word for *legal.* To make it negative, add the prefix *fer* (Rule 13). To make it feminine, add the suffix *nef* (Rule 1). To make it plural, add the suffix *oz* (Rule 2). The correct translation is *fercollenefoz.* To create the past-tense verb *injured* from *liaker,* the translation of *to injure,* drop the *ker* (Rule 4). To make the verb past tense, add the suffix *zot.* Then add the suffix *im* because the verb is plural (Rule 7). The correct translation is *liazotim. Ekaplek* is the Artificial Language word for *boy.* To make it feminine, add the suffix *nef* (Rule 1). To make it plural, add the suffix *oz* (Rule 2). The correct translation is *ekapleknefoz.*

50. The correct answer is choice (A). The translation of the entire sentence is, "An unfriendly guard inspected the legal alien's papers." To create the translation of the negative adjective *unfriendly,* add the prefix *fer* to *kometlek,* the Artificial Language word for *friend.* According to Rule 10, to form an adjective from a noun, drop the *lek* ending and add *le.* The correct translation is *ferkometle.* To make the adjective *colle (legal)* feminine, add the suffix *nef* (Rule 1). The correct translation is *collenef.* To make *huslek,* the Artificial Language word for *alien,* feminine, add the suffix *nef* (Rule 1). To make it possessive, add the suffix *ae* (Rule 12). The correct translation is *husleknefae.*

ANSWER SHEET PRACTICE TEST 3

Logical Reasoning

1. Ⓐ Ⓑ Ⓒ Ⓓ Ⓔ   5. Ⓐ Ⓑ Ⓒ Ⓓ Ⓔ   8. Ⓐ Ⓑ Ⓒ Ⓓ Ⓔ   11. Ⓐ Ⓑ Ⓒ Ⓓ Ⓔ   14. Ⓐ Ⓑ Ⓒ Ⓓ Ⓔ

2. Ⓐ Ⓑ Ⓒ Ⓓ Ⓔ   6. Ⓐ Ⓑ Ⓒ Ⓓ Ⓔ   9. Ⓐ Ⓑ Ⓒ Ⓓ Ⓔ   12. Ⓐ Ⓑ Ⓒ Ⓓ Ⓔ   15. Ⓐ Ⓑ Ⓒ Ⓓ Ⓔ

3. Ⓐ Ⓑ Ⓒ Ⓓ Ⓔ   7. Ⓐ Ⓑ Ⓒ Ⓓ Ⓔ   10. Ⓐ Ⓑ Ⓒ Ⓓ Ⓔ   13. Ⓐ Ⓑ Ⓒ Ⓓ Ⓔ   16. Ⓐ Ⓑ Ⓒ Ⓓ Ⓔ

4. Ⓐ Ⓑ Ⓒ Ⓓ Ⓔ

Spanish Language Proficiency

Part I

1. Ⓐ Ⓑ Ⓒ Ⓓ Ⓔ   5. Ⓐ Ⓑ Ⓒ Ⓓ Ⓔ   9. Ⓐ Ⓑ Ⓒ Ⓓ Ⓔ   13. Ⓐ Ⓑ Ⓒ Ⓓ Ⓔ   17. Ⓐ Ⓑ Ⓒ Ⓓ Ⓔ

2. Ⓐ Ⓑ Ⓒ Ⓓ Ⓔ   6. Ⓐ Ⓑ Ⓒ Ⓓ Ⓔ   10. Ⓐ Ⓑ Ⓒ Ⓓ Ⓔ   14. Ⓐ Ⓑ Ⓒ Ⓓ Ⓔ   18. Ⓐ Ⓑ Ⓒ Ⓓ Ⓔ

3. Ⓐ Ⓑ Ⓒ Ⓓ Ⓔ   7. Ⓐ Ⓑ Ⓒ Ⓓ Ⓔ   11. Ⓐ Ⓑ Ⓒ Ⓓ Ⓔ   15. Ⓐ Ⓑ Ⓒ Ⓓ Ⓔ   19. Ⓐ Ⓑ Ⓒ Ⓓ Ⓔ

4. Ⓐ Ⓑ Ⓒ Ⓓ Ⓔ   8. Ⓐ Ⓑ Ⓒ Ⓓ Ⓔ   12. Ⓐ Ⓑ Ⓒ Ⓓ Ⓔ   16. Ⓐ Ⓑ Ⓒ Ⓓ Ⓔ   20. Ⓐ Ⓑ Ⓒ Ⓓ Ⓔ

Part II Section I

1. Ⓐ Ⓑ Ⓒ Ⓓ Ⓔ   3. Ⓐ Ⓑ Ⓒ Ⓓ Ⓔ   5. Ⓐ Ⓑ Ⓒ Ⓓ Ⓔ   6. Ⓐ Ⓑ Ⓒ Ⓓ Ⓔ   7. Ⓐ Ⓑ Ⓒ Ⓓ Ⓔ

2. Ⓐ Ⓑ Ⓒ Ⓓ Ⓔ   4. Ⓐ Ⓑ Ⓒ Ⓓ Ⓔ

Part II Section II

1. Ⓐ Ⓑ Ⓒ Ⓓ   3. Ⓐ Ⓑ Ⓒ Ⓓ   5. Ⓐ Ⓑ Ⓒ Ⓓ   6. Ⓐ Ⓑ Ⓒ Ⓓ   7. Ⓐ Ⓑ Ⓒ Ⓓ

2. Ⓐ Ⓑ Ⓒ Ⓓ   4. Ⓐ Ⓑ Ⓒ Ⓓ

Part II Section III

1. Ⓐ Ⓑ Ⓒ Ⓓ Ⓔ   3. Ⓐ Ⓑ Ⓒ Ⓓ Ⓔ   5. Ⓐ Ⓑ Ⓒ Ⓓ Ⓔ   6. Ⓐ Ⓑ Ⓒ Ⓓ Ⓔ   7. Ⓐ Ⓑ Ⓒ Ⓓ Ⓔ

2. Ⓐ Ⓑ Ⓒ Ⓓ Ⓔ   4. Ⓐ Ⓑ Ⓒ Ⓓ Ⓔ

Artificial Language

Set 1

1. Ⓐ Ⓑ Ⓒ Ⓓ Ⓔ	5. Ⓐ Ⓑ Ⓒ Ⓓ Ⓔ	9. Ⓐ Ⓑ Ⓒ Ⓓ Ⓔ	13. Ⓐ Ⓑ Ⓒ Ⓓ Ⓔ	17. Ⓐ Ⓑ Ⓒ Ⓓ Ⓔ
2. Ⓐ Ⓑ Ⓒ Ⓓ Ⓔ	6. Ⓐ Ⓑ Ⓒ Ⓓ Ⓔ	10. Ⓐ Ⓑ Ⓒ Ⓓ Ⓔ	14. Ⓐ Ⓑ Ⓒ Ⓓ Ⓔ	18. Ⓐ Ⓑ Ⓒ Ⓓ Ⓔ
3. Ⓐ Ⓑ Ⓒ Ⓓ Ⓔ	7. Ⓐ Ⓑ Ⓒ Ⓓ Ⓔ	11. Ⓐ Ⓑ Ⓒ Ⓓ Ⓔ	15. Ⓐ Ⓑ Ⓒ Ⓓ Ⓔ	19. Ⓐ Ⓑ Ⓒ Ⓓ Ⓔ
4. Ⓐ Ⓑ Ⓒ Ⓓ Ⓔ	8. Ⓐ Ⓑ Ⓒ Ⓓ Ⓔ	12. Ⓐ Ⓑ Ⓒ Ⓓ Ⓔ	16. Ⓐ Ⓑ Ⓒ Ⓓ Ⓔ	20. Ⓐ Ⓑ Ⓒ Ⓓ Ⓔ

Set 2

21. Ⓐ Ⓑ Ⓒ Ⓓ Ⓔ	23. Ⓐ Ⓑ Ⓒ Ⓓ Ⓔ	25. Ⓐ Ⓑ Ⓒ Ⓓ Ⓔ	27. Ⓐ Ⓑ Ⓒ Ⓓ Ⓔ	29. Ⓐ Ⓑ Ⓒ Ⓓ Ⓔ
22. Ⓐ Ⓑ Ⓒ Ⓓ Ⓔ	24. Ⓐ Ⓑ Ⓒ Ⓓ Ⓔ	26. Ⓐ Ⓑ Ⓒ Ⓓ Ⓔ	28. Ⓐ Ⓑ Ⓒ Ⓓ Ⓔ	30. Ⓐ Ⓑ Ⓒ Ⓓ Ⓔ

Set 3

31. Ⓐ Ⓑ Ⓒ Ⓓ Ⓔ	34. Ⓐ Ⓑ Ⓒ Ⓓ Ⓔ	37. Ⓐ Ⓑ Ⓒ Ⓓ Ⓔ	39. Ⓐ Ⓑ Ⓒ Ⓓ Ⓔ	41. Ⓐ Ⓑ Ⓒ Ⓓ Ⓔ
32. Ⓐ Ⓑ Ⓒ Ⓓ Ⓔ	35. Ⓐ Ⓑ Ⓒ Ⓓ Ⓔ	38. Ⓐ Ⓑ Ⓒ Ⓓ Ⓔ	40. Ⓐ Ⓑ Ⓒ Ⓓ Ⓔ	42. Ⓐ Ⓑ Ⓒ Ⓓ Ⓔ
33. Ⓐ Ⓑ Ⓒ Ⓓ Ⓔ	36. Ⓐ Ⓑ Ⓒ Ⓓ Ⓔ			

Set 4

43. Ⓐ Ⓑ Ⓒ Ⓓ Ⓔ	45. Ⓐ Ⓑ Ⓒ Ⓓ Ⓔ	47. Ⓐ Ⓑ Ⓒ Ⓓ Ⓔ	49. Ⓐ Ⓑ Ⓒ Ⓓ Ⓔ	50. Ⓐ Ⓑ Ⓒ Ⓓ Ⓔ
44. Ⓐ Ⓑ Ⓒ Ⓓ Ⓔ	46. Ⓐ Ⓑ Ⓒ Ⓓ Ⓔ	48. Ⓐ Ⓑ Ⓒ Ⓓ Ⓔ		

Practice Test 3

LOGICAL REASONING

1. The city of Jefferson is zoned for both residential and commercial buildings. Timothy P. owns a restaurant near the beach. He hired a local band to play live music outside on Friday and Saturday nights. The city's noise ordinance requires that all restaurants stop playing outside music by 11:00 p.m. Establishments that violate the ordinance will receive a fine of $200 for the first offense and a fine of $500 for a second violation. After three violations, the city has the authority to temporarily close the establishment.

   From the information given above, it can validly be concluded that

   (A) if Timothy P. turns off the outside music by 11:00 p.m., then the city will not close his restaurant.

   (B) if the city closes Timothy P.'s restaurant, then he has violated the noise ordinance.

   (C) if the band plays outside after 11:00 p.m., then the city will close Timothy P.'s restaurant.

   (D) if the band plays outside after 11:00 p.m., then Timothy P. will be in violation of the noise ordinance.

   (E) if Timothy P. does not turn off the outside music after 11:00 p.m., then he will not receive a fine.

2. In California, police charge shoplifters with either petty theft or grand theft, depending on the value of the stolen item. Shoplifting anything worth $400 or less is considered petty theft. Shoplifting anything worth more than $400 is considered grand theft. The prosecutor may reduce a petty theft of less than $50 to an infraction. If the guilty party is a first-time offender, he or she may just have to pay a fine. A petty theft is a misdemeanor. Grand theft can be a misdemeanor or a felony. Sabrina L. was arrested for stealing a lipstick worth $27.

   From the information given above, it can validly be concluded that

   (A) Sabrina L. may be charged with grand theft.

   (B) Sabrina L. is a first-time offender.

(C) Sabrina L. has committed petty theft.

(D) the prosecutor may charge Sabrina L. with a felony.

(E) the prosecutor will reduce the charge to an infraction.

3. The Lakewood Homeowners' Association has a strict series of guidelines for its residents. All members must pay an annual fee of $2,000. The exteriors of all houses must be painted in neutral shades of green, brown, or blue. Front-lawn grass must not exceed four inches in height. Window awnings must complement the house color. Homeowners must submit a request to the Lakewood Homeowners' Association at least two weeks in advance to change any outside structure. Any member who violates the association's guidelines will receive a warning. If the problem is not resolved, the association has the right to fine the homeowner. Heidi R. is a member of the Lakewood Homeowners' Association.

From the information given above, it CAN-NOT validly be concluded that

(A) Heidi R.'s house is painted green or brown.

(B) Heidi R. must pay an annual fee of $2,000.

(C) Heidi R.'s front lawn must not be more than four inches high.

(D) Heidi R. will receive a warning if her awnings do not complement her house color.

(E) Heidi R. must submit a request to the association if she wants to paint her house.

4. Rachel Z. is pulled over by a police officer for failing to stop at a stop sign. The officer asks for her license, her registration, and proof of her insurance. The officer discovers that Rachel's license is expired. He issues her a citation for driving with an expired license.

The citation states that Rachel must get her license renewed within 10 days. Failure to do so will result in a fine of $250 and, possibly, the loss of the driver's license.

From the information given above, it can validly be concluded that

(A) if Rachel Z. does not lose her license, then she renewed her license within 10 days.

(B) if Rachel Z. renews her license within 10 days, then she will not receive a fine.

(C) if Rachel Z. loses her license, then she did not renew her license.

(D) if Rachel Z. does not renew her license, then she will not pay a fine.

(E) if Rachel Z. receives a fine, then she will not lose her license.

5. Some 500,000 immigrants were living in a certain country in 2009. Although most of these immigrants worked as laborers and migrant workers, some worked in professional occupations. For instance, many were employed in restaurant and hotel management. Very few of them worked in medicine, another professional occupation.

From the information given above, it can be validly concluded that, in 2009, in the country described above,

(A) most immigrants were employed in restaurant and hotel management.

(B) it is not the case that some of the hotel managers were immigrants.

(C) some of the hotel managers were immigrants.

(D) most of those not employed in restaurant and hotel management were immigrants.

(E) none of those employed in professional occupations were immigrants.

6. The number of Chinese immigrants arrested while illegally crossing the Mexican border into Arizona has increased in recent years. Many of the smugglers of Chinese immigrants also smuggle drugs into the United States. Most of these Chinese immigrants are from Fujian Province in southeast China. Chinese immigrants are known to pay more than immigrants from other countries to get into the United States. Arrests reports indicate that most Chinese immigrants pay smugglers $40,000 or more, often in steep monthly payments. All Chinese immigrants pay more to get into the United States than Mexican immigrants. Taila M. is a Chinese immigrant who has been arrested for trying to illegally cross the Mexican border into Arizona.

From the information given above, it can be validly concluded that,

(A) Taila M. paid a smuggler $40,000 or more in steep monthly payments.

(B) Taila M. is from the Fujian Province in southeast China.

(C) Taila M.'s smuggler also smuggled drugs into the country.

(D) Taila M.'s smuggler was arrested for smuggling immigrants.

(E) Taila M. paid more to get into the country than a Mexican immigrant.

7. Border Patrol Agents received a lead about illegal activity taking place on a beach in California. Upon investigation, they discovered a boat that was reported stolen in the harbor. They apprehended 8 illegal immigrants on the boat. Four of the illegal immigrants were men. Three of the men were from Cambodia. None of the female immigrants was from Mexico. The driver of the boat escaped. Several arrests have been made.

From the information given above, it can be validly concluded that, concerning the immigrants on this boat,

(A) none of the female immigrants was from Cambodia.

(B) some of the male immigrants were from Mexico.

(C) one of the men was not from Cambodia.

(D) it is not the case that the driver of the boat was Mexican.

(E) it is not the case that some of the immigrants were arrested.

8. Border Patrol Agents working in the Laredo Sector receive information from the command center about a broken fence in a remote area near the border. When they reach the fence, they notice several sets of tracks heading east. Eventually, the trail leads them to some brush, where they find 3 men hiding with four large bundles of marijuana. Two of the men were from Mexico. The other man was a U.S. citizen. Several arrests have been made.

From the information given above, it can be validly concluded that

(A) the 3 men broke the fence.

(B) the U.S. citizen was arrested.

(C) the drugs belonged to the Mexican immigrants.

(D) some of the men were arrested.

(E) none of the men was a drug dealer.

9. Recently, Border Patrol Agents working along the Texas border have been warned that Mexican drug cartels are using "cloned" Border Patrol vehicles to smuggle narcotics across the border. Agents have been told to be on the lookout for a suspected cloned Crown Victoria, the same vehicle used by some Border Patrol agents in this area. It is suspected that some Mexican law enforcement officials have become corrupted and now receive payments from the drug cartel. This makes the vehicles difficult to apprehend if they cross back across the Mexican border. Homeland Security cautions that cloned vehicles make the job of a Border Patrol Agent even more dangerous. Several Border Patrol Agents working near the Texas border were recently wounded by members of a Mexican drug cartel who approached them in a cloned vehicle. The Border Patrol Agents assumed the driver of the vehicle was a member of the U. S. Border Patrol. Clyde T. was one of the agents wounded in this incident.

From the information given above, it CANNOT be validly concluded that Clyde T.

(A) is not a corrupted Mexican law official.

(B) does not drive a Crown Victoria while working.

(C) was injured by a member of a cartel.

(D) has seen a cloned vehicle.

(E) works along the Texas border.

10. In the United States, both legal and illegal immigrants may be deported or excluded. Deportation affects those already living in the United States. Immigrants who are deported are forced to return to their native country. Exclusion affects those living in other countries. Those who are excluded are forbidden to enter the United States. Reasons for deportation and exclusion include threatening U.S. security, committing certain crimes, and violating immigration laws. Jorge V. has been deported to Mexico.

From the information given above, it can be validly concluded that

(A) Jorge V. committed a serious crime.

(B) Jorge V. is also excluded from the United States.

(C) Jorge V. had been living in the United States.

(D) Jorge V. violated immigration laws.

(E) Jorge V. is a threat to U.S. security.

11. Police officers were led to believe that many weapons sold at a certain gun store in California where being illegally sold to drug dealers in Mexico. Upon investigating the lead, the officers learned that all of the weapons sold illegally were either assault rifles or powerful pistols known in Mexico as "cop killers." None of the firearms manufactured by Western Guns was sold illegally. Also, none of the illegally sold weapons was 0.45 caliber.

From the information given above, it can be validly concluded that, concerning the weapons sold at the store,

(A) all of the 0.45 caliber weapons were made by Western Guns.

(B) none of the assault rifles sold illegally was made by Western Guns.

(C) some of the weapons made by Western Guns were sold illegally.

(D) all of the pistols sold illegally were 0.45 caliber.

(E) some of the weapons made by Western Guns were 0.45 caliber.

12. In Pennsylvania, simple possession of marijuana is a misdemeanor. Defendants who are found guilty of simple possession face jail time and fines of up to $5,000. To prove simple possession, the prosecution must show that the defendant knowingly and deliberately possessed the marijuana without a prescription, knew that the drug was illegal, and had actual control or possession of the drug. Wendy J. has been charged with simple possession of marijuana.

From the information given above, it can be validly concluded that

(A) if Wendy J. is not found guilty of simple possession, then she did not know the drug was illegal.

(B) if Wendy J. is found guilty of simple possession, then she is guilty of a misdemeanor.

(C) if Wendy J. is not found guilty of simple possession, then she will not have to pay a fine.

(D) if Wendy J. is found guilty of simple possession, then she may have had a prescription.

(E) if Wendy J. is not found guilty of simple possession, then she did not have control of the drug.

13. Recently, local EMS workers called on Border Patrol Agents after discovering a group of people trapped in an Arizona desert. Nine illegal immigrants were in the group. Four of the immigrants were from Mexico, 2 were from Honduras, and 3 were from Colombia. Two of the illegal immigrants from Mexico were female and were dehydrated. A U.S. citizen has been charged with smuggling the immigrants across the border.

From the information given above, it can be validly concluded that

(A) the Border Patrol arrested all of the illegal immigrants.

(B) the Border Patrol sometimes works with other agencies.

(C) none of the male immigrants was dehydrated.

(D) none of the immigrants from Honduras was female.

(E) all of the immigrants from Colombia were male.

14. Residents of the town of Kent pay school taxes every September. Taxes are mailed on the first of the month. Residents must pay their taxes by September 30th. Residents who pay late will incur fees. Residents who pay their taxes after September 30th but before October 8th will be charged a fee of $50. Residents who pay their taxes between October 8th and October 22nd will be charged a fee of $100. Those who pay between October 22nd and October 31st will be charged a fee of $200. Aimee Z. is a resident of Kent. She has paid her taxes but has incurred a fee.

From the information given above, it can be validly concluded that Aimee Z.

(A) paid her taxes after September 30th but before October 9th.

(B) paid her taxes before September 30th.

(C) will be charged an extra fee of $100.

(D) paid her taxes after September 30th.

(E) paid her taxes between October 8th and October 22nd.

15. Immigrants living in the United States legally may be deported if they are convicted of a felony or a crime involving drugs. Recently, a Haitian man was deported after pleading guilty to a drug crime in Connecticut. Three natives of the Dominican Republic, Guyana, and Mexico were also deported after being convicted of drug crimes in New York State. Carla B. was also deported to the Philippines on this day.

From the information given above, it CANNOT be validly concluded that

(A) Carla B. committed a drug crime.

(B) the native of Mexico committed a drug crime.

(C) Carla B. had been living in the United States.

(D) the native of Haiti had been living in the United States.

(E) Carla B. is a native of the Philippines.

16. Border Patrol Agents receive information about illegal activity in a parking garage. When they arrive at the scene, they find eleven cars parked in the garage. Six of the cars have expired registrations. Four of the cars with expired registrations are blue. One of the cars in the lot has a broken rear window. After searching the six cars with expired registrations, the agents find narcotics in two of the cars.

From the information given above, it can be validly concluded that

(A) all of the cars in the lot were blue.

(B) the car with the broken rear window is blue.

(C) the cars that contained narcotics had expired registrations.

(D) the cars that contained narcotics were blue.

(E) the car with the broken rear window had an expired registration.

SPANISH LANGUAGE PROFICIENCY

Part I

Directions: Read the sentence and then choose the most appropriate synonym for the underlined word.

1. Oigo a alguien que <u>llama</u> pidiendo ayuda desde los escombros.

   (A) vicuña

   (B) fuego

   (C) flama

   (D) clarín

   (E) clama

2. El plato que acaban de traer no solamente es costoso sino también <u>feísimo</u>.

   (A) hermoso

   (B) desagradable

   (C) fehaciente

   (D) corriente

   (E) carísimo

3. La señora consideró que era necesario <u>remendar</u> los zapatos antes de volver a usarlos.

   (A) remitir

   (B) remedar

   (C) averiar

   (D) desgarrar

   (E) reparar

4. Al final de la <u>jornada</u> habíamos recorrido casi la mitad del camino.

   (A) horneada

   (B) jornal

   (C) día

   (D) colmada

   (E) jornalero

5. Conozco bien a ese individuo y les aseguro que es muy <u>zorro</u>.

   (A) franco

   (B) sagaz

   (C) candido

   (D) ingenuo

   (E) mazo

6. Las autoridades están investigando las causas de esta <u>oleada</u> de fechorías.

   (A) cansada

   (B) ojear

   (C) ola

   (D) cortada

   (E) oleosa

7. El granjero laboró todo el día con su <u>yunta</u>.

   (A) junta

   (B) bueyes

   (C) cerca

   (D) máquina

   (E) yerta

8. Estas construcciones son sin duda <u>hechura</u> de los habitantes del lugar.

   (A) creación

   (B) hechizo

   (C) negocio

   (D) largura

   (E) ranura

9. Por favor <u>arrímense</u> acá para que vean mejor.

   (A) acérquense

   (B) súbanse

   (C) aléjense

   (D) apártanse

   (E) bájense

10. Pueden reconocer al hombre porque es alto y <u>orejón</u>.

    (A) oración

    (B) cansón

    (C) orejudo

    (D) cejudo

    (E) joven

11. Como el tiempo está templado, sugiero poner todo en la <u>nevera</u>.

    (A) nieva

    (B) invierno

    (C) nueva

    (D) frigorífico

    (E) nunca

12. ¿No le parece que el muro de esa casa está <u>ladeado</u>?

    (A) inclinado

    (B) ladrando

    (C) lado

    (D) alado

    (E) inculcado

13. Esta situación no es para nada <u>igual</u> a la ocurrida anteriormente.

    (A) imán

    (B) iglesia

    (C) dispar

    (D) disímil

    (E) semejante

14. Encontramos las armas en un <u>foso</u> detrás del garaje.

    (A) airoso

    (B) fósil

    (C) luz

    (D) hoyo

    (E) foto

15. El arroyo <u>baña</u> un sector amplio de la llanura.

    (A) lava

    (B) banca

    (C) enloda

    (D) río

    (E) año

16. Al ver acercarse a los agentes, los maleantes se dieron a la <u>fuga</u>.

    (A) filo

    (B) huida

    (C) arrugada

    (D) hule

    (E) hueso

17. ¡Nunca había visto un ganado tan <u>flaco</u> como de el ese señor!

    (A) rollizo

    (B) inflado

    (C) familiar

    (D) famélico

    (E) grueso

18. No pude llegar antes porque un cliente me <u>entretuvo</u> más tiempo del previsto

    (A) enfadó

    (B) entrevió

    (C) guardó

    (D) distrajo

    (E) tuvo

19. A los pocos minutos, vimos una <u>muchedumbre</u> dirigirse al centro de la ciudad.

    (A) gentío

    (B) techumbre

    (C) murciélago

    (D) gentil

    (E) muchacho

20. Todo lo que él hace y dice es en <u>guasa</u>.

    (A) sensatez

    (B) guarida

    (C) guapa

    (D) chanza

    (E) gravedad

Part II

Section I

Directions: Read each sentence carefully. Select the appropriate word or phrase to fill each blank space.

1. Tengan cuidado, no _____ eso porque _____ caliente.
   - (A) tocas / está
   - (B) tocan / están
   - (C) tocando / son
   - (D) toquen / está
   - (E) tocar / eran

2. Fuimos a la tienda _____ comprar los suministros _____.
   - (A) porque / requerimientos
   - (B) por / requeridas
   - (C) para / requeridos
   - (D) pero / requerido
   - (E) entre / requerida

3. Aquellas personas no son _____ listas _____ parecen.
   - (A) tan / como
   - (B) tan / que
   - (C) tanto / que
   - (D) tantas / como
   - (E) tanta / se

4. Los hombres _____ los implementos si fueran _____.
   - (A) usaron / suyas
   - (B) usarán / suyo
   - (C) usaban / de ti
   - (D) usarán / suya
   - (E) usarían / suyos

5. No _____ lo que necesitaban porque no me _____.
   - (A) traí / dicen
   - (B) traje / dijeron
   - (C) trayendo / dijieron
   - (D) traigo / dicieron
   - (E) traímos / decir

6. _____ entraba en la gruta, me encontré con _____ serpiente enorme.
   - (A) Pero / un
   - (B) Sino / uno
   - (C) Antes / unas
   - (D) Cuando / una
   - (E) Después / el

7. Encontré la solución a _____ problema y se _____ dije a mis compañeros.
   - (A) aquel / la
   - (B) esa / las
   - (C) la / los
   - (D) un / lo
   - (E) aquella / las

Section II

Directions: Read each sentence carefully. Select the one sentence that is correct.

1. **(A)** Nosotros determinemos el estatus necesario muy pronto de estas personas.

    (B) Nosotros que determinamos el estatus muy pronto de estas personas.

    (C) Ello es necesario que determinamos el estatus de estas personas mucho pronto.

    (D) Es necesario que determinemos el estatus de estas personas muy pronto.

2. **(A)** Por iniciative de los afectados, se decidió proceder a corregir inmediatamente el problema.

    (B) Por iniciative de los afectados decidió a corregir inmediato el problema.

    (C) Los afectados, por iniciative de proceder, decidiedon a corrigir el problema inmediatamente.

    (D) Por iniciative los afectados decidieron proceder el problema inmediatamente para corregir.

3. **(A)** Lo primero coso que debemos es desconectar estas cables.

    (B) Lo primero que nosotros debemos hacemos es desconectamos estas cables.

    (C) Lo primero que debemos hacer es desconectar estos cables.

    (D) Lo que debemos primero hacemos es disconectar estos cables.

4. **(A)** No conozco a nadie sabe cuál es la mejor manera por acondiciona motores.

    (B) Yo no conocer nadie que sabe cuál es la mejor manera de acondicionar motores.

    (C) No conozco a nadie que sepa cuál es la mejor manera de acondicionar motores.

    (D) Yo conozco a nadie que saben cuál es la mejor manera a acondicionar motores.

5. **(A)** El inspectora que se revisó atentamente los documentos la presentaron.

    (B) La inspector revisó el documento que se le presentaron atentamente.

    (C) La inspectora revisó atentamente los documentos que se le presentaron.

    (D) La inspector los revisó atentamente que le presentaron los documentos.

6. **(A)** La estrategia de la agente era avanzar con cautela mientras sus compañeros la vigilaban.

    (B) La estrategia de la agente era avanzó con cautela pero sus compañeros le vigilan.

    (C) La estrategia era mientras la agente los vigilaban avanzar por cautela sus compañeros.

    (D) La estrategia de la agente era para avanzar en cautela mientras sus compañeros lo vigilarán.

7. **(A)** Este lugar me parece tan bueno la para enramada que aquel construir.

    (B) Este lugar me parece tan bueno como aquel para construir la enramada.

    (C) Este me parece tan bueno lugar de aquel para construir la enramada.

    (D) Este lugar me parezco tanto bueno de aquel para construir la enramada.

Section III

Directions: Read each sentence carefully. Select the correct word or phrase to replace the underlined portions of the sentence. In those cases in which the sentence needs no correction, select answer choice (E).

1. Yo creo que debes <u>descansa</u> la noche antes del examen.
   - (A) descanso
   - (B) descansar
   - (C) descanses
   - (D) descansa
   - (E) No es necesario hacer ninguna corrección.

2. <u>El agua</u> de este lago está limpia como el cristal.
   - (A) Las aqua
   - (B) Agua
   - (C) Los agua
   - (D) La agua
   - (E) No es necesario hacer ninguna corrección.

3. No <u>realizaron</u> que ustedes estaban allá adentro.
   - (A) me di cuenta
   - (B) realizo
   - (C) contando
   - (D) realicé
   - (E) No es necesario hacer ninguna corrección.

4. Mañana <u>saliremos</u> de vacaciones al norte del país.
   - (A) salieron
   - (B) salirán
   - (C) saldremos
   - (D) salí
   - (E) No es necesario hacer ninguna corrección.

5. Los agentes <u>han comido</u> nada en toda la tarde.
   - (A) comen
   - (B) comieron
   - (C) no han comieron
   - (D) no han comido
   - (E) No es necesario hacer ninguna corrección.

6. Por favor <u>dice</u> quién fue el primero que vio a la víctima.
   - (A) dirán
   - (B) dijeran
   - (C) dígan
   - (D) dijeron
   - (E) No es necesario hacer ninguna corrección.

7. Nos estamos subiendo rápidamente al camión <u>fin de</u> partir cuanto antes.
   - (A) final
   - (B) a fin
   - (C) a fin de
   - (D) finalmente
   - (E) No es necesario hacer ninguna corrección.

ARTIFICIAL LANGUAGE

The Vocabulary Lists

The words on the following lists are the same; they are merely arranged differently, as they would be in a bilingual dictionary. In the first list, you can look up words in English to find their equivalent word in the Artificial Language. In the second list, you can look up words in the Artificial Language to find their equivalent word in English. During the actual test, you will have the vocabulary lists with you for consultation at all times. Nonetheless, you should note that the words given below are not the same as those given in the actual test. Therefore, it is best not to try to memorize them before taking the actual test.

Word List Arranged Alphabetically by the English Word				Word List Arranged Alphabetically by the Artificial Language Word			
English	Artificial Language	English	Artificial Language	Artificial Language	English	Artificial Language	English
a, an	bex	skillful	janle	almanlek	government	kaplek	man
alien	huslek	that	velle	arker	to drive	kometlek	friend
and	loa	the	wir	avelek	enemy	lexker	to station
boy	ekaplek	this	volle	bex	a, an	liaker	to injure
country	failek	to be	synker	bonker	to guard	loa	and
difficult	glasle	to border	regker	browlek	river	mor	friend
enemy	avelek	to cross	chonker	chonker	to cross	pirker	to escape
friend	kometlek	to drive	arker	colle	legal	quea	of
from	mor	to escape	pirker	daqlek	jeep	regker	to border
government	almanlek	to guard	bonker	degker	to shoot	synker	to be
he, him	yev	to have	tulker	ekaplek	boy	tatker	to spy
jeep	daqlek	to identify	kalenker	failek	country	trenedlek	paper
legal	colle	to injure	liaker	frigker	to work	tulker	to have
loyal	inle	to inspect	zelker	glasle	difficult	velle	that
man	kaplek	to shoot	degker	huslek	alien	volle	this
of	quea	to spy	tatker	inle	loyal	wir	the
paper	trenedlek	to station	lexker	janle	skillful	yev	he, him
river	browlek	to work	frigker	kalenker	to identify	zelker	to inspect

Grammatical Rules for the Artificial Language

The grammatical rules given here are similar, but not identical, to those used in the ALT. Some of the suffixes (word endings) and prefixes (additions to the beginning of a word) used in the actual test differ from those used in the practice test.

During the actual test, you will have access to the rules at all times. Consequently, it is important that you understand these rules, but it is not necessary that you memorize them. In fact, memorizing them will hinder rather than help you, since there are differences between the rules in the version of the Artificial Language that appears here and the one that appears in the actual test.

You should note that the next part of this section contains a glossary of grammatical terms to assist you if you are not thoroughly familiar with the meaning of these grammatical terms.

Rule 1: To form the feminine singular form of a noun, a pronoun, an adjective, or an article, add the suffix nef to the masculine singular form. Only nouns, pronouns, adjectives, and articles take feminine endings in the Artificial Language. When gender is not specified, the masculine form is used.

Example: If a male eagle is a verlek, then a female eagle is a verleknef. If an ambitious man is a tosle man, an ambitious woman is a toslenef woman.

Rule 2: To form the plural of nouns, pronouns, adjectives, and articles, add the suffix oz to the correct singular form.

Example: If one male eagle is a verlek, several male eagles are verlekoz. If an ambitious woman is a toslenef woman, several ambitious women are toslenefoz women.

Rule 3: Adjectives modifying nouns and pronouns with feminine and/or plural endings must have endings that agree with the words they modify. In addition, an article (*a/an* and *the*) preceding a noun must also agree with the noun in gender and number.

Example: If an active male eagle is a sojle verlek, an active female eagle is a sojlenef verleknef and several active female eagles are sojlenefoz verleknefoz. If this male eagle is volle verlek, these female eagles are vollenefoz verleknefoz. If the male eagle is wir verlek, the female eagle is wirnef verleknef and the female eagles are wirnefoz verleknefoz. If a male eagle is bex verlek, several male eagles are bexoz verlekoz.

Rule 4: The stem of a verb is obtained by omitting the suffix ker from the infinitive form of the verb.

Example: The stem of the verb tirker is tir.

Rule 5: All subjects and their verbs must agree in number; that is, singular subjects require singular verbs and plural subjects require plural verbs. (See Rules 6 and 7.)

Rule 6: To form the present tense of a verb, add the suffix em to the stem for the singular or the suffix im to the stem for the plural.

Example: If to bark is nalker, then nalem is the present tense for the singular (the dog barks) and nalim is the present tense for the plural (the dogs bark).

Rule 7: To form the past tense of a verb, first add the suffix zot to the stem, and then add the suffix em if the verb is singular or the suffix im if it is plural.

Example: If to bark is nalker, then nalzotem is the past tense for the singular (the dog barked) and nalzotim is the past tense for the plural (the dogs barked).

Rule 8: To form the past participle of a verb, add the suffix to to the stem of the verb. It can be used to form compound tenses with the verb to have, as a predicate with the verb to be, or as an adjective.

In the last two cases, it takes masculine, feminine, singular, and plural forms in agreement with the noun to which it refers.

Example of use in a compound tense with the verb to have:

If to bark is nalker and to have is tulker, then tulem nalto is the *present perfect* for the singular (the dog has barked) and tulim nalto is the *present perfect* for the plural (the dogs have barked). Similarly, tulzotem nalto is the *past perfect* for the singular (the dog had barked) and tulzotim nalto is the *past perfect* for the plural (the dogs had barked).

Example of the use as a predicate with the verb to be:

If to adopt is rapker and to be is synker, then a boy was adopted is a ekaplek synzotem rapto and many girls were adopted is ekapleknefoz synzotim raptonefoz.

Example of use as an adjective:

If to delight is kasker then a delighted boy is a kasto ekaplek and many delighted girls are kastonefoz ekapleknefoz.

Rule 9: To form a noun from a verb, add the suffix lek to the stem of the verb.

Example: If longker is to write, then a writer is a longlek.

Rule 10: To form an adjective from a noun, substitute the suffix le for the suffix lek.

Example: If pellek is beauty, then a beautiful male eagle is a pelle verlek and a beautiful female eagle is a pellenef verleknef. (Note the feminine suffix nef.)

Rule 11: To form an adverb from an adjective, add the suffix ki to the masculine form of the adjective. (Note that adverbs do not change their form to agree in gender or number with the word they modify.)

Example: If pelle is beautiful, then beautifully is pelleki.

Rule 12: To form the possessive of a noun or pronoun, add the suffix ae to the noun or pronoun after any plural or feminine suffixes.

Example: If a boglek is a dog, then a dog's collar is a boglekae collar. If he is yev, then his book is yevae book. If she is yevnef, then her book is yevnefae book.

Rule 13: To make a word negative, add the prefix fer to the correct affirmative form.

Example: If an active male eagle is a sojle verlek, an inactive male eagle is a fersojle verlek. If the dog barks is boglek nalem, then the dog does not bark is boglek fernalem.

Glossary of Grammatical Terms

This glossary will be available to you during the actual test, but it is recommended that you study the glossary before taking the test. The glossary contains basic grammatical concepts that apply to English, Spanish, and the Artificial Language. The glossary contains fairly extensive and comprehensive explanations of each grammatical concept. **The explanations in the actual test are not comprehensive. Consequently, it is particularly important that you study these explanations very carefully.**

Article: An article is a word that precedes a noun and determines whether it is a definite or indefinite noun; for instance <u>the</u> book, <u>an</u> object.

Adjective: An adjective is a word used to modify a noun or pronoun (for example, <u>intelligent</u> women). Generally, an adjective serves to answer questions such as <u>which</u>, <u>what kind of</u>, and <u>how many</u>. For example,

"<u>This</u> book" would be the adjectival answer to the question "which book?" "a <u>beautiful</u> book"
  1   2
would be the adjectival answer to the question "what kind of book?" and "<u>several</u> days" would
                                                 3

be the adjectival answer to the question "how many days?"

In English, adjectives have only one form, regardless of the type of noun they modify. More specifically, whether a noun is feminine or masculine, singular or plural, the adjective used to modify it remains the same; for example, the adjective <u>strong</u> is exactly the same when it refers to one man, one woman, or many men. By contrast, in both Spanish and the Artificial Language, the ending of the adjective is different if the adjective is modifying a singular masculine noun, a singular feminine noun, a plural masculine noun, or a plural feminine noun.

Adverb: An adverb is a word used to modify a verb. For example, the sentence "It was produced" could be modified to express <u>where</u> it was produced by saying "It was produced <u>locally</u>."

Generally, an adverb is used to answer the questions <u>where</u> (as in the example above), <u>when</u> (as for example, "he comes <u>frequently</u>"), or <u>how</u> (as for example, "she thinks <u>logically</u>"). Adverbs sometimes are used to modify an adjective or another adverb. For example, in the sentence "She has a <u>really</u> beautiful mind," the adverb <u>really</u> modifies the adjective <u>beautiful</u>. In the sentence "She thinks <u>very</u> logically," the adverb <u>very</u> modifies the adverb <u>logically</u>. In the Artificial Language, the only adverbs used are those that modify verbs. In the Spanish language, as well as in the English language, adverbs are used to modify verbs, adjectives, and other adverbs.

Gender: As a grammatical concept, gender refers to the classification of words according to whether they are masculine, feminine, or neuter.

As stated above, Spanish takes masculine or feminine endings for nouns, adjectives, and articles. The neuter form is used sometimes to express abstraction in a more emphatic manner. The neuter form is <u>NOT</u> used in the Artificial Language. Consequently, it is very important for you to remember that in the Artificial Language <u>all</u> nouns, adjectives, and articles take either a masculine or a feminine ending according to whether the sentence refers to a male or female.

Also, all nouns and adjectives in the Artificial Language were conceived (for the sake of simplicity) to be masculine. Thus, unless the feminine gender is specified in the sentence, the masculine gender is used always.

Infinitive: An infinitive is the general, abstract form of a verb; for example, <u>to look</u>, <u>to think</u>, <u>to remember</u>, <u>to walk</u>. Once the action expressed by the verb is attached to a specific subject (a person, animal, or thing), then we say the verb is "conjugated," or linked to that subject; for example, "he/she thinks," "the dog runs," "the table broke."

In contrast to the way that an infinitive in English is preceded by the word "to" (as in "to think"), in the Artificial Language (and in Spanish), infinitives are defined by their suffix. In the version of the Artificial Language used here, this ending (or suffix) is <u>ker</u>. (In the actual test, the ending will be different.)

Noun: A noun is a word that names a person, place, thing, or abstraction; for example. <u>Lindsay</u>, <u>Chicago</u>, <u>tree</u>, <u>wisdom</u>. A noun can refer to an individual (as in <u>Lindsay</u>, an individual person, or <u>Chicago</u>, an individual place) or to a set (as in "<u>all stones</u>," "<u>all trees</u>," "<u>all cities</u>").

Prefix: A prefix always occurs at the beginning of a word. It can be a single letter or a sequence of letters; for example, <u>a</u>moral, <u>il</u>legal, <u>dys</u>functional.

A prefix is the opposite of a suffix, which always occurs at the end of a word, but both serve to change the basic word in some way. For example, <u>polite</u> is the basic word (in this case an adjective) to express the concept of behavior that conforms to accepted social norms, while adding the prefix <u>im</u> and creating the word <u>impolite</u> transforms the word <u>polite</u> into its contradictory concept. You should note that in the Artificial Language a prefix is used to create negative concept (see Rule 13). Such a rule mimics both Spanish and English, in both of which negation is usually expressed by using a negative prefix.

Pronoun: A pronoun is a word used in place of a noun; for example, "she" instead of "Lindsay," "they" instead of "the guards," "it" instead of "the stone," "himself/herself" instead of "the judge."

In both English and Spanish, there is a difference between a pronoun that stands for the subject of an action (as in "<u>She</u> threw the stone," meaning that <u>Lindsay</u> threw the stone), and a pronoun that stands for the object of an action (as in "The stone was thrown at <u>her</u>," meaning that the stone was thrown at Lindsay). By contrast, in the Artificial Language used in this manual, there is no grammatical difference between <u>he</u> and <u>him</u>, both being <u>yev</u>. Remember, however, that in the Artificial Language pronouns take feminine endings when the subject or object of the action is feminine. Accordingly, in the version of the Artificial Language given in this manual, both <u>she</u> (subject) and <u>her</u> (object) would be <u>yevnef</u> (i.e., <u>yev</u> plus the feminine suffix <u>nef</u>).

Suffix: A suffix always occurs at the end of a word. It can be a single letter or a sequence of letters, for example, crea<u>my</u>, read<u>able</u>, nice<u>ly</u>. Unlike prefixes, suffixes often change the "part of speech" (i.e., the type of word). For example, in the case of crea<u>my</u>, the suffix <u>y</u> changes the noun <u>cream</u> into the adjective <u>creamy</u>, and in the case of <u>nicely</u>, the suffix <u>ly</u> changes the adjective <u>nice</u> into the adverb <u>nicely</u>.

In addition, suffixes are used to conjugate verbs (for example, to change the present tense into the past tense: you walk, you walk<u>ed</u>) and to create the plural form of nouns (for example, boy, boy<u>s</u>). In Spanish, suffixes are used for the same purposes, but they are used for other purposes too, such as creating plural forms for adjectives and changing the gender of a word.

In the Artificial Language, suffixes are used (1) to change the part of speech (for example, Rule 11 uses a suffix to change an adjective into an adverb), (2) to conjugate verbs (for example, Rules 6 and 7 use suffixes to express present and past tenses), and (3) to create the plural forms of nouns, pronouns, adjectives, and articles (Rule 2). In addition, the Artificial Language mimics Spanish in using a suffix to express gender.

You should study all the rules on suffixes in the Artificial Language, and you should practice using these rules, but you should NOT memorize them because (1) you will have them available to you at all times during the actual test, and (2) in the actual test, some of the suffixes and prefixes are different from the ones used in this practice test.

Verb: A verb is used to express either an action or a state of being. For example, "He <u>prepared</u> dinner" expresses the action of making all preparations for dinner, while "He is a <u>citizen</u>" expresses the state or condition of being a citizen.

A condition or "state of being" can be permanent or transitory. For example, "The agent's horse <u>is a bay mare</u>" expresses a permanent condition for the horse (being a bay mare), while "George <u>is at lunch</u>" expresses a transitory condition for George (being at lunch). The Spanish language, unlike English, has two different verbs to express permanent and transitory conditions, although the Artificial Language is akin to English rather than to Spanish in its use of a single verb to express any state of being.

When a verb is linked to a subject (i.e., "conjugated"), it changes from the abstract infinitive form to a specific form such as a present tense or a past tense. The Artificial Language primarily uses only two tenses: the simple past tense and the simple present tense in the indicative mood (see Rules 6 and 7). (Verbs in the indicative mood express a <u>real</u> action or condition, whereas verbs in the subjunctive mood express <u>hypothetical</u> actions or conditions. The subjunctive mood does not exist in the Artificial Language, but it is very important in Spanish.)

You may find that the past participle is used in the test (see Rule 8). In that case, the present perfect tense (they <u>have crossed</u>) and the past perfect tense (they <u>had crossed</u>) will be used in the Artificial Language.

Be sure to apply the rules as directed in the test material. If no rule governing the past participle is listed in the actual test material, then the past participle is treated as a simple past tense.

Test Questions

Set 1: Questions 1 Through 20

Directions: For each sentence, decide which words have been translated correctly. Use scratch paper to list each <u>numbered</u> word that is correctly translated into the Artificial Language. When you have finished listing the words that are correctly translated in sentences 1 through 4, select your answer according to the following instructions:

Mark:

    (A) if <u>only</u> the word numbered 1 is correctly translated.

    (B) if <u>only</u> the word numbered 2 is correctly translated.

    (C) if <u>only</u> the word numbered 3 is correctly translated.

    (D) if <u>two</u> or <u>more</u> of the numbered words are correctly translated.

    (E) if <u>none</u> of the numbered words is correctly translated.

Be sure to list only the <u>numbered</u> words that are <u>correctly</u> translated.

Study the sample question before going on to the test questions.

Sample Sentence	**Sample Translation**
He identifies the driver.	<u>Volle</u> <u>kalenim</u> wir <u>arklek</u>.
	1 2 3

The word numbered 1, *volle,* is incorrect since the translation of *volle* is <u>this</u>. The word *yev* should have been used. The word numbered 2, *kalenim,* is also incorrect because the singular form *kalenem* should have been used. The word numbered 3 is correct and should be written on your note paper. *Arlek* has been correctly formed from the infinitive *arker* (to drive) by applying Rules 4 and 9. So, only the word numbered 3 has been correctly translated. **The correct answer is choice (C).**

Now answer Questions 1 through 20 in the manner indicated. <u>Be sure to record your answers on the separate answer sheet.</u>

Sentence

Translation

1. The men were not injured.

Wiroz <u>kaplekoz</u> <u>synzotim</u> <u>ferliazotim</u>.
         1   2   3

2. These girls work illegally.

Vollenefoz <u>ekapleknef</u> <u>frigem</u> <u>fercolleki</u>.
           1   2   3

3. The spies shot the driver.

Wiroz <u>tatlekoz</u> <u>degzotim</u> wir arlek.
     1   2   3

4. An enemy was identified.

<u>Wir</u> avelek <u>zyzotem</u> <u>kalento</u>.
1   2   3

5. This woman and girl have legal papers.

<u>Vollenefoz</u> <u>kapleknefoz</u> loa ekapleknef <u>tulem</u>
      1   2   3
colle tranedlekoz.

6. That guard is disloyal.

<u>Velle</u> <u>bonker</u> synem <u>inle</u>.
1   2   3

7. The driver of the jeep was an illegal alien.

Wir <u>arle</u> quea wir daqlek <u>synzotem</u> bex
     1   2
<u>fercolleoz</u> huslek.
3

8. The spies escaped from the border station.

Wiroz <u>tatlek</u> <u>pirzotim</u> mor wir <u>reglek</u> lexlek.
     1   2   3

9. That government is legal.

<u>Velle</u> <u>almanlek</u> synem <u>fercolle</u>.
1   2   3

10. The skillful and friendly inspector drove the jeep.

Wir <u>janlek</u> loa <u>kometlek</u> <u>zelker</u> arzotem wir
     1   2   3
daqlek.

11. Those boys crossed the border and the river.

Velleoz <u>ekaplek</u> <u>chonzitem</u> wir <u>reglek</u> loa
       1   2   3
wir browlek.

12. The illegal aliens and the legal woman were injured.

Wiroz <u>fercolleoz</u> huslekoz loa wir colle
       1
<u>kapleknef</u> synzotim <u>liazotem</u>.
    2   3

13. The girls' escape was difficult.

Wirnefoz <u>ekapleknefoz</u> <u>pirker</u> synzotem
        1   2
<u>glasle</u>.
3

14. The driver escaped and was not injured.

Wir <u>arker</u> pirzotem loa <u>synzotemfer</u> <u>liato</u>.
     1   2   3

15. A man crossed the river to shoot the spy.

Bex kaplek <u>chonem</u> wir browlek <u>degker</u>
          1   2
wir <u>tatker</u>.
3

16. The illegal aliens' friend injured her.

Wir fercolle <u>huslekae</u> kometlek <u>liazotem</u>
               1   2

<u>yevnef</u>.
3

17. The woman inspects the identification papers.

Wirnef <u>kapleknefoz</u> <u>zelem</u> wir kalenle
             1   2

<u>trendedlekae</u>.
3

18. Illegal aliens escape from his station.

<u>Fercolle</u> huslekoz <u>pirem</u> mor yev <u>lexlek</u>.
   1   2   3

19. The friendly girl drove the jeep.

Wirnef <u>kometlek</u> ekapleknef <u>arem</u> wir
   1   2   3

daqlek.

20. Those women are not from that country.

<u>Velleoz</u> <u>kapleknefoz</u> <u>synim</u> mor velle failek.
  1   2   3

Set 2: Questions 21 Through 30

Directions: For each question in this group, select the one of five suggested choices that correctly translates the underlined word or group of words into the Artificial Language.

Protecting the <u>country's borders</u> is difficult work. Border Patrol Agents must be brave
                        21

and <u>loyal</u>. They must stop illegal aliens from crossing <u>the border</u>. Trying to identify illegal
  22   23

aliens <u>is not</u> easy. Border Patrol Agents must <u>inspect their papers</u> from the government.
     24   25

Border Patrol Agents must be on the lookout for <u>enemies and spies</u> who might try
                                      26

<u>to shoot them</u>. Some Border Patrol Agents feel lucky <u>to have</u> such an important job. They
  27   28

work <u>from border stations</u> and patrol the borders on foot and in jeeps so that illegal aliens and
     29

criminals do not <u>escape</u> across the border.
       30

21. (A) failekoz reglekoz
    (B) failekoz regkeroz
    (C) failek reglek
    (D) failekae reglekae
    (E) failekae reglekoz

22. (A) loa inlek
    (B) loa inle
    (C) loale inle
    (D) loaoz inleoz
    (E) loa inleki

23. (A) wir regker
    (B) wir regle
    (C) wir reglek
    (D) wiroz reglekoz
    (E) ferwir regle

24. (A) fersynem
    (B) synemfer
    (C) fersynim
    (D) synim
    (E) fersynzotem

25. (A) zelim yev trendedlek
    (B) zelem yevoz trenedlekoz
    (C) zelker yevoz trenedlekoz
    (D) zelim yevoz trenedlekoz
    (E) zelim yevoz tranedlekae

26. (A) avelekoz loa tatkeroz
    (B) avelekoz loa tatlekoz
    (C) avelekae loa tatlekae
    (D) avelek loa tatker
    (E) avelek loa tatlek

27. (A) degker yev
    (B) degker volle
    (C) deglek yevoz
    (D) degle kaplekoz
    (E) degker yevoz

28. (A) tulker
    (B) tulim
    (C) tulem
    (D) tulzotem
    (E) tulzotim

29. (A) more reglek lexlek
    (B) mor regleoz lexlekoz
    (C) mor regle lexkeroz
    (D) mor regle lexlekoz
    (E) mor reglek lexlekoz

30. (A) pirker
    (B) pirem
    (C) pirzotim
    (D) pirim
    (E) pirzotem

Set 3: Questions 31 Through 42

Directions: For this group of questions, select the one answer choice that is the correct translation of the English word or words in parentheses. You should translate the entire sentence in order to determine what form should be used.

31. (That man) fersynem bex fercolle huslek.
    (A) Velle kaplek
    (B) Velle kaplekoz
    (C) Volle kaplek
    (D) Velleoz kaplek
    (E) Velle ekaplek

32. (She crossed) wir browlek.
    (A) Yevnef chonzotemnef
    (B) Yev chonzotim
    (C) Yevnef chonzotem
    (D) Yevnef chonzotim
    (E) Yev chonto

33. Velle huslek synem (a friend).
    (A) wir kometlek
    (B) bex kometlek
    (C) bex kometlekoz
    (D) bexoz kometlekoz
    (E) wirnef kometleknef

34. Wiroz bonlekoz (have inspected) volleoz trenedlekoz.
    (A) tulker zelto
    (B) tulim zelzotim
    (C) tulem zelzotem
    (D) tulem zelto
    (E) tulim zelto

35. Velle tatlek (injured the inspector).
    (A) liaim wir zellek
    (B) liazotem wir zellek
    (C) liazotem wir zelle
    (D) liazotim wir zellek
    (E) liato wir zelker

36. Wir (men's papers) synim fercolle.
    (A) kaplekozae trenedlekoz
    (B) kaplek trenedlek
    (C) kaplekae trenedlekae
    (D) kaplekoz trenedlekoz
    (E) kaplek trenedlekae

37. Wiroz (men and women) synzotim mor regle lexlek.
    (A) kaplek loa kapleknef
    (B) ekaplek loa ekapleknef
    (C) kaplekoz loa kapleknefoz
    (D) kaplekoz loa kapleknef
    (E) ekaplekoz loa kapleknefoz

38. Velle (guard's station) synem colle.
    (A) bonlekoz lexlek
    (B) bonlekoz lexlekoz
    (C) bonlek lexlek
    (D) bonlekae lexlek
    (E) bonkerae lexlek

39. Yev (has to drive) bex daqlek.
    (A) tulker arker
    (B) tulem arker
    (C) tulem arzotem
    (D) tulim arker
    (E) tulim arzotim

40. Vellenef kapleknef (was injured).
    (A) synzotem liato
    (B) synzotem liazotem
    (C) synzotim liazotim
    (D) synzotim liato
    (E) synzotem liaem

41. Wiroz (spies shot) wir bonlek.

  (A) tatkeroz degzotim

  (B) tatlekoz degzotem

  (C) tatlek degim

  (D) tatlekim degim

  (E) tatlekoz degzotim

42. Wirnefez ekapleknefoz (escaped from the inspector).

  (A) pirker mor wir zelker

  (B) pirzotim mor wir zellek

  (C) pirzotim mor wir zelkeroz

  (D) pirem mor wir zellekoz

  (E) pirzotem mor wir zellek

Set 4: Questions 43 Through 50

Directions: For the last group of questions, select the one answer that is the correct form of the underlined expression as it is used in the sentence. At the end of the sentence, you will find instructions in parentheses telling you which form to use. In some sentences, you will be asked to supply the correct form of two or more expressions. In this case, the instructions for these expressions are presented consecutively in the parentheses and are separated by a dash. Be sure to translate the entire sentence before selecting your answer.

43. Wirnef kapleknef tulker kalenker wir avelek. (present perfect singular verb)

  (A) tulim kalenzotim

  (B) tulem kalento

  (C) tulim kalento

  (D) tulem kalenzotem

  (E) tulker kalento

44. Velle bonlek synem kometlek. (negative adjective)

  (A) ferkometlek

  (B) ferkomet

  (C) kometlefer

  (D) ferkometle

  (E) kometle

45. Velle lexker zelker synim inle. (possessive noun—plural noun)

  (A) lexlek—zellek

  (B) lexlekae—zellekoz

  (C) lexae—zellekoz

  (D) lexkerae—zellekoz

  (E) lexleoz—zellekoz

46. Wir zelker arzotim wir daqlek. (feminine plural adjective—feminine plural noun)

  (A) Wirnef—zelleknef

  (B) Wirnefoz—zeltonefoz

  (C) Wirnefoz—zelkernefoz

  (D) Wirnefoz—zelleknefoz

  (E) Wiroz—zellekoz

47. Wirnef ekaplek synim colle huslekoz loa yevoz chonker wir reglek. (feminine plural noun—past tense)

  (A) ekapleknefoz—chonto

  (B) ekapleknef—chonzotem

  (C) ekapleknefoz—chonzotim

  (D) ekapleknefae—chonzotim

  (E) ekapleknefae—chonzotem

48. Wir bonlek tulem <u>kalenker</u> wir <u>avelek</u>. (past participle predicate—plural noun)

(A) kalenki—avelek

(B) kalento—avelekoz

(C) kalentooz—avelekoz

(D) kalenzotem—avelek

(E) kalenzotim—avelekoz

49. Wiroz <u>inle</u> <u>kaplek</u> synzotim mor wir almanlek loa tulzotim <u>chonker</u> wir reglek. (negative plural adjective—plural noun—past participle as predicate)

(A) ferinleoz—kaplekoz—chonto

(B) ferinle—kaplekoz—chonzotem

(C) ferinleoz—kapleknef—chonzotim

(D) inleoz—kaplek—chonzotem

(E) inleoz—ekaplekoz—chonto

50. Bex <u>avelek</u> <u>huslek</u> tulzotem colle trenedlekoz loa synzotem <u>kometlek</u>. (feminine singular adjective—feminine noun—feminine adverb)

(A) aveleknef—husleknef—kometlenefki

(B) avelenef—huslekoz—kometlek

(C) avelenef—husleknef—kometlenefki

(D) avelekoz—husleknef—kometleknef

(E) avele—huslek—kometleknef

ANSWER KEY AND EXPLANATIONS

Logical Reasoning

1. D	**5.** C	**8.** D	**11.** B	**14.** D
2. C	**6.** E	**9.** B	**12.** B	**15.** A
3. A	**7.** C	**10.** C	**13.** B	**16.** C
4. B				

1. **The correct answer is choice (D).** The only thing you know for sure is that Timothy will be in violation of the noise ordinance if the band plays outside after 11:00 p.m. The city might close his restaurant for a different reason, so choices (A) and (B) are incorrect. Choice (C) is also incorrect because the city may give him only a fine if the band plays outside after 11:00 p.m.

2. **The correct answer is choice (C).** Because Sabrina L. stole a lipstick that was only $27, she has committed a petty theft. She would have to steal something worth more than $400 to be charged with grand theft, choice (A). The passage does not indicate if she is a first-time offender, choice (B). The prosecutor would not charge her with a felony for this crime, choice (D), and there is not enough information to determine if the prosecutor will reduce the charge to an infraction, choice (E).

3. **The correct answer is choice (A).** You cannot conclude that Heidi's house is painted green or brown. According to the passage it might also be blue. Since Heidi is a member of the homeowners' association, you can conclude that she must pay an annual fee of $2,000, choice (B), she must keep her grass under four inches high, choice (C), and she must submit a request to the association if she wants to paint her house, choice (E). Because she is a member, you can also conclude that Heidi will receive a warning if her awnings do not complement the color of her house, choice (D).

4. **The correct answer is choice (B).** Rachel will not receive a fine if she renews her license within 10 days. There is no way to determine if she will lose her license if she does not pay the fine, because this is merely a possibility. This makes choices (A) and (E) invalid. Rachel might lose her license for a different reason, so choice (C) is also incorrect. Rachel will have to pay a fine if she does not renew her license, so choice (D) is invalid as well.

5. **The correct answer is choice (C).** The passage says that many immigrants were employed in restaurant and hotel management. Therefore, at least some of them were. According to the passage, most immigrants worked as laborers and migrant workers, so choice (A) is not correct. Since the passage says that many immigrants were employed in restaurant and hotel management, choice (B) is also incorrect. There is not enough information in the passage to conclude that most of those not employed in restaurant and hotel management were immigrants, only that most immigrants were laborers and migrant workers, so choice (D) is also incorrect. The passage says that some immigrants were employed in professional occupations, so choice (E) is incorrect.

6. **The correct answer is choice (E).** The passage says that all Chinese immigrants pay more than Mexican immigrants to get into the United States. Therefore, you can conclude that Taila paid more than a Mexican immigrant. The passage does not say how much she paid, so choice (A) is not correct. While the passage says that most Chinese immigrants are from the Fujian Province, it does not say where Taila is from, so choice (B) is also incorrect. We do not know anything about Taila's smuggler, so choices (C) and (D) are also incorrect.

7. **The correct answer is choice (C).** The passage says that 4 of the illegal immigrants were men and that 3 of the men were from Cambodia. This means that one of the male immigrants was not from Cambodia, so choice (C) is correct. The passage does not indicate if any of the women were from Cambodia, so choice (A) is incorrect. The passage also says that none of the female immigrants was from Mexico, but it does not indicate where the fourth male immigrant was from, so choice (B) is also incorrect. Nothing is said about the driver of the boat except that he escaped, so choice (D) is incorrect. The passage says that several arrests were made and that the driver escaped, so it is likely that at least some of the immigrants were arrested; therefore, choice (E) is also incorrect.

8. **The correct answer is choice (D).** The only conclusion you can draw is that some of the men were arrested, since the passage says several arrests have been made. The fence may have been broken before the 3 men passed through it, so choice (A) is not correct. The passage does not say that all 3 men were arrested, so we do not know if the U.S. citizen was arrested, choice (B). We also do not know who owned the drugs, choice (C). The men were probably drug dealers

based on the information in the passage, so choice (E) is also incorrect.

9. **The correct answer is choice (B).** To correctly answer this question, you have to choose the conclusion that *cannot* be made based on the information in the passage. Choice (B) is correct; you cannot conclude that Clyde T. does not drive a Crown Victoria while working. The passage says that many agents in this area drive this type of car. The passage also does not give any information about the type of vehicle Clyde T. drives on the job. The passage says that Clyde T. was an agent wounded in the incident, so choice (A) is not correct. You can conclude that he was injured, choice (C) and that he has seen a cloned vehicle, choice (D). Since he was working along the Texas border at the time of the attack, choice (E) is also a valid conclusion and therefore incorrect.

10. **The correct answer is choice (C).** The passage says the deportation affects immigrants already living in the United States. Since Jorge V. was deported, he must have been living in the United States. There is not enough information in the passage to know whether he committed a serious crime, choice (A); has also been excluded from the United States, choice (B); has violated immigration laws, choice (D); or is a threat to U.S. security, choice (E).

11. **The correct answer is choice (B).** The passage says that none of the firearms made by Western Guns was sold illegally. Therefore, none of the assault rifles sold illegally could have been manufactured by Western Guns. The passage does not indicate if Western Guns manufactures 0.45 caliber weapons, so choices (A) and (E) are incorrect. Choice (C) is incorrect because the passage says all weapons manufactured by Western Guns were sold legally. Choice (D) is incorrect,

because all of the 0.45 caliber weapons were sold legally.

12. **The correct answer is choice (B).** The only valid conclusion based on the information in the passage is choice (B). The passage says that simple possession of marijuana is a misdemeanor. Therefore, if Wendy is found guilty of simple possession, she is guilty of a misdemeanor. Because she is found not guilty does not necessarily mean that she did not know the drug was illegal, choice (A); that she will not have to pay a fine, choice (C); or that she was not in control of the drug, choice (E). If she had a prescription, she would not be found guilty of simple possession, so choice (D) is incorrect.

13. **The correct answer is choice (B).** The only conclusion you can draw from the information in the passage is that the Border Patrol sometimes works with other agencies, such as local EMS workers. The passage only indicates that a U.S. citizen has been charged with smuggling, so choice (A) is not correct. The passage says that 2 females from Mexico were dehydrated, but it does not mention whether any male immigrants were dehydrated, so choice (C) is not correct. The passage does not indicate whether the immigrants from Honduras and Colombia were male or female, so choices (D) and (E) are not correct.

14. **The correct answer is choice (D).** The passage does not say how much money Aimee Z. had to pay, only that she has incurred a fee. This means that she paid her taxes late, so choice (D) is correct. There is not enough information in the passage to indicate the amount of the fee or when she paid her taxes, so choices (A), (C), and (E) are incorrect. If she paid her taxes before September 30th, choice (B), she would not have incurred a fee.

15. **The correct answer is choice (A).** To correctly answer this question, you have to choose the conclusion that *cannot* be made based on the information in the passage. The passage says only that Carla B. was deported. We cannot conclude that she committed a drug crime, especially since the passage says immigrants may also be deported for committing a felony. Choices (B), (C), (D), and (E) are logical conclusions based on the information in the passage.

16. **The correct answer is choice (C).** The passage says that after searching the six cars with expired registrations, they found narcotics in two of the cars. This means that the cars that contained narcotics had expired registrations. Four of the cars with expired registrations were blue, but the passage does not say if these were the cars that contained narcotics, so choice (D) is incorrect. The passage does not indicate that all of the cars in the parking lot were blue, choice (A), only that four of the cars with expired registrations were blue. It also does not indicate whether the car with a broken rear window was blue, choice (B), or had an expired registration, choice (E).

answers practice test 3

Spanish Language Proficiency

Part I

1. E	5. B	9. A	13. E	17. D
2. B	6. C	10. C	14. D	18. D
3. E	7. B	11. D	15. A	19. A
4. C	8. A	12. A	16. B	20. D

1. **The correct answer is choice (E).** The word *llama* has several meanings, but in this sentence it is a form of the verb *llamar* meaning to <u>call</u>, so the best synonym is *clama,* "calls out." Choice (A), "vicuña," is an animal similar to a *llama.* Choice (B), "fire," and choice (C), "flame," are similar to another meaning of *llama.* The meaning of Choice (D), "bugle," is different from the meaning of *llama.*

2. **The correct answer is choice (B).** The word *feísimo* is a superlative of *feo* and refers to something that is very unpleasant, ugly, or <u>bad-tasting</u>, so the term *desagradable,* "unpleasant," is the closest synonym. Choice (A), "beautiful," indicates the opposite of *feo.* Choice (C), "reliable," and choice (D), "current," have meanings unrelated to the meaning of *feísimo.* Choice (E), "carísimo," uses the same suffix as the target word, but the meaning is different.

3. **The correct answer is choice (E).** The word *remendar* means to <u>mend</u> or fix something. Therefore, the closest synonym is *reparar,* to "fix" or "repair." Choice (A), to "send," is unrelated to the meaning of *remendar.* Choice (B), to "mimic," is also unrelated to the meaning of the target word. Choice (C), to "damage," and choice (D), "tear," have meanings that are contrary to the idea of mending something.

4. **The correct answer is choice (C).** The word *jornada* refers to a <u>day</u>, especially with reference to an activity such as a day's work or a day's walk. Therefore, *día,* "day," is the best synonym. Choice (A), a "batch of baking," is phonetically similar to *jornada,* but its meaning is unrelated. Choice (B), "day's wage," and choice (E), "day-laborer," both come from the same root as *jornada,* but they do not have the same meaning or indicate an activity. The meaning of choice (D), "filled," is unrelated.

5. **The correct answer is choice (B).** The word *zorro* means a <u>fox</u>, both literally and in the sense of a sly or crafty person. Therefore, *sagaz,* "astute," is the best synonym. Choice (A), "frank," choice (C), "credulous," and choice (D), "naïve," are contrary to the meaning of *zorro.* Choice (E), "mallet," has no relation to the target word.

6. **The correct answer is choice (C).** The term *oleada* refers to the surge of a <u>wave</u> and, in this sentence, is used figuratively. Therefore, *ola* ("wave") is the closest synonym. Choice (A), "tired," and choice (D), "cut," have the same ending as the target word but their meanings are unrelated. Choice (B), "to have a look," and choice (E), "oily," are phonetically similar to *oleada* but have different meanings.

7. **The correct answer is choice (B).** The term *yunta* means a yoke or pair of <u>oxen</u>, so *bueyes,* "oxen," is the best synonym. Choice (A), "board" or "committee," choice (C), "close," choice (D), "car," and choice (E), "stiff," all have meanings that have nothing to do with *yunta*.

8. **The correct answer is choice (A).** The word *hechura* refers to that which has been <u>made or built</u> by someone, so *creación,* "creation," is the best synonym. Choice (B), "bewitchment," sounds phonetically similar to *hechura* but has a different meaning. Choice (C), "business," also has a different meaning. Choice (D), "length," and choice (E), "slit," have the same ending as the target word but different meanings.

9. **The correct answer is choice (A).** The word *arrímense* is a form of the verb *arrimarse,* which means <u>to move closer</u>, so the best synonym is *acérquense,* "come closer." Choice (B), "move up higher," and choice (E), "move lower," both refer to moving in a certain direction, but not necessarily closer. Choice (C), "move away," and choice (D), "move farther off," mean the opposite of *arrímense.*

10. **The correct answer is choice (C).** The word *orejón* refers to either a person or an animal with <u>big ears</u>. Therefore, the best synonym is *orejudo,* "long-eared." Choice (A), "prayer," sounds similar to *orejón* but has a different meaning. Choice (B), "tiresome," choice (D), "bushy-browed," and choice (E), "young," can also describe a person, but they do not refer to ears.

11. **The correct answer is choice (D).** The term *nevera* means any kind of a <u>cooler</u>. Therefore, *frigorífico* ("refrigerator") is the best synonym. Choices (A), "it is snowing," and choice (B), "winter," both have the same root as *nevera* but have different meanings. The meanings of choice (C), "new," and

choice (E), "never," are different from the target word.

12. **The correct answer is choice (A).** The word *ladeado,* from the root word *lado,* "side," means to be <u>slanted</u> to one side. Therefore, *inclinado,* "tilted," is the best synonym. Choice (B), "barking," and choice (D), "winged," are phonetically similar to *ladeado* but have different meanings. Choice (C), "side," is the root word for *ladeado* but is not its synonym. Choice (E), to "instill," also has a meaning that is unrelated to *ladeado.*

13. **The correct answer is choice (E).** The word *igual* refers to something that is <u>the same</u> or equal. Therefore, the best synonym is *semejante,* "similar." Choice (A), "magnet," and choice (B), "church," have meanings that are unrelated to *igual.* Choice (C), "different," and choice (D), "unalike," have meanings that are contrary to *igual.*

14. **The correct answer is choice (D).** The word *foso* means a ditch or <u>pit</u>, so the term *hoyo,* "hole," is the best synonym. Choice (A), "graceful," has the same suffix as the root word but a different meaning. Choice (B), "fossil," and choice (E), "photograph," begin with the same syllable as the correct answer, but their meanings are unrelated. Choice (C), "light," has a different meaning.

15. **The correct answer is choice (A).** The word *baña* is a form of the verb *bañar,* which means <u>to bathe</u> or, in this sentence, to <u>wash over</u>. Therefore, *lava,* "washes," is the best synonym. Choice (B), "dries," means the opposite of *baña.* Choice (C), "muddies," may relate to a stream but does not mean "to wash over." Choice (D), "river," is not a synonym of the target word. Choice (E), "year," is unrelated to the meaning of *baña.*

16. **The correct answer is choice (B).** The word *fuga* means <u>flight</u> in the sense of an escape; therefore, *huida,* "flight," is the

best synonym. The meanings of choice (A), "blade,", choice (C), "wrinkled," choice (D), "rubber," and choice (E), "bone," are not related to *fuga*.

17. **The correct answer is choice (D).** The word *flaco* refers to a person or an animal that is extremely skinny, so the closest synonym is *famélico*, "thin" or "scrawny." Choice (A), "plump," choice (B), "puffed up," and choice (E), "thick-set," mean the opposite of *flaco*. Choice (C) has the same initial syllable, but its meaning is not related to the target word.

18. **The correct answer is choice (D).** The word *entretuvo* is a form of the verb *entretener*, which means to entertain, but also to delay someone or prevent him or her from doing something. Therefore, *distrajo*, "distracted," is the best synonym. Choice (A), "annoyed," and choice (B), "glimpsed," have the same prefix as *entretuvo* but have different meanings, choice (C), "kept," but in the sense of securing something or putting it away. Choice (E), "had," comes from the same root as *entretuvo* but has a different meaning.

19. **The correct answer is choice (A).** The term *muchedumbre* refers to a multitude of something, especially people Therefore, *gentío*, "crowd," is the best synonym. Choice (B), "roof," and choice (C), "bat," have meanings that are unrelated to the target word. Choice (D), "gentil," and choice (E), "box," have meanings that are unrelated to the meaning of *muchedumbre*.

20. **The correct answer is choice (D).** The word *guasa* means a joke or fooling around, so the best synonym is *chanza*, "joke" or "prank." Choice (A), "reasonableness," and choice (E), "seriousness," indicate the opposite of a joke. Choice (B), "lair" or "den," and choice (C), "good-looking," begin with the same syllable as the correct answer but have different meanings.

Part II

Section I

1. D	**3.** A	**5.** B	**6.** D	**7.** D
2. C	**4.** E			

1. **The correct answer is choice (D).** *Toquen* is a subjunctive verb and therefore appropriate for a negative mandate; and *está* is the correct form of the verb *estar,* indicating a temporary condition. Choices (A) and (B) use the indicative mood instead of the subjunctive and an incorrect form of *estar.* Choices (C) and (E) also fail to use the subjunctive and have forms of the verb *ser*, which indicates a permanent condition.

2. **The correct answer is choice (C).** *Para* is the correct preposition to indicate where one goes, and the adjective *requeridos* agrees in gender and number with the noun it modifies. Choices (A) and (D) use a conjunction instead of a preposition and adjectives that do not agree with the noun they modify. Choices (B) and (E) use the wrong preposition and adjectives that do not match the noun.

3. **The correct answer is choice (A).** Only Choice (A) uses the expression *tan . . . como* to form a comparison. Choices (B), (C), (D), and (E) all form the comparison incorrectly.

4. **The correct answer is choice (E).** *Usarían* is the proper conditional form of the verb *usar*, and the possessive pronoun agrees with the noun *implementos* in gender and number. Choices (A), (B), (C), and (D) use verb forms other than the conditional and an incorrect form of the possessive.

5. **The correct answer is choice (B).** The verb *traer* is irregular, and *traje* is the correct preterit form; likewise, *dijeron* is the correct preterit form of the irregular verb *decir*. Choices (A) and (E) use nonexistent forms of the verb *traer* and inappropriate forms of *decir*. Choices (C) and (D) use inappropriate forms of *traer* and nonexistent forms of *decir*.

6. **The correct answer is choice (D).** The word *Cuando* is a proper conjunction to use at the beginning of a sentence, and the article *una* agrees with the feminine singular noun *serpiente*. Choices (A), (B), (C), and (E) begin with an incorrect conjunction and use articles that do not match the noun they accompany.

7. **The correct answer is choice (D).** The noun *problema* is masculine although it ends in -*a*. Therefore, it takes a singular, masculine indefinite article. Even though *la solución* is a singular, feminine noun, the neutral *lo* is used to modify it as it is an abstract concept. The first word in choice (A) is correct, because it is a demonstrative adjective modifying a singular, masculine noun. However, *la* cannot be used to refer to an abstract concept. Choices (B), (C), and (E) use feminine pronouns for *problema* and pronouns that do not agree with *solución* in gender and/or number.

Section II

1. D	3. C	5. C	6. A	7. B
2. A	4. C			

1. **The correct answer is choice (D).** This sentence has the proper structure and contains no errors. Choices (A) and (C) contain various errors, including illogical structures, misplaced clauses, and incorrect verb forms. Choice (B) is not a complete thought.

2. **The correct answer is choice (A).** This sentence has the proper structure and contains no errors. Choices (B), (C), and (D) contain various errors, including illogical structures, misplaced clauses, incorrect verb forms, and improper adverbs.

3. **The correct answer is choice (C).** This sentence has the proper structure and contains no errors. Choices (A), (B), and (D) have various errors, including illogical structures, incorrect verbs, and incorrect gender.

4. **The correct answer is choice (C).** This sentence has the proper structure and contains no errors. Choices (A), (B), and (D) have several errors, including illogical structures, incorrect use of the negative, absence of the personal *a,* incorrect prepositions, and improper verb forms.

5. **The correct answer is choice (C).** This sentence has the proper structure and contains no errors. Choices (A), (B), and (D) contain various errors, including illogical structures, misplaced clauses, and articles and nouns that do not agree.

6. **The correct answer is choice (A).** This sentence has the proper structure and contains no errors. Choices (B), (C), and (D) have various errors, including illogical structures, misplaced clauses, incorrect verbs and pronouns, and incorrect prepositions.

7. **The correct answer is choice (B).** This sentence has the proper structure and contains no errors. Choices (A), (C), and (D) contain various errors, including illogical structures, incorrect use of the comparison, and incorrect verb forms.

Section III

1. B	3. A	5. D	6. C	7. C
2. E	4. C			

1. **The correct answer is choice (B).** *Descansar* is used as a noun, so the infinitive form is correct. Choices (A) and (D) use the indicative, and choice (C) uses a subjunctive form of the verb.

2. **The correct answer is choice (E).** The word *agua,* although feminine, takes a masculine article for phonetic reasons. Choices (A), (C), and (D) use incorrect articles. Choice (B) leaves out the article.

3. **The correct answer is choice (A).** This is the correct form of the expression *darse cuenta* to indicate that the person realizes something. Choices (B) and (D) use the false cognate *realizar* (to "execute or carry out"). Choice (C) uses an illogical verb.

4. **The correct answer is choice (C).** This is the correct future tense of the irregular verb *salir.* Choices (A) and (D) use the past tense, which is inappropriate here. Choice (B) uses a nonexistent form of the verb.

5. **The correct answer is choice (D).** *No . . . nada* is a proper way to indicate the negative. Choices (A) and (B) use a single negative, which is incorrect. Choice (C) uses an incorrect form for the verb participle.

6. **The correct answer is choice (C).** This is the correct imperative form of the verb *decir.* Choice (A) uses the future tense, choice (B) uses a subjunctive form of the verb, and choice (D) uses the preterit tense.

7. **The correct answer is choice (C).** This is the correct expression *a fin de* to express why something is done. Choices (A) and (D) use incorrect terms instead of the expression. Choice (B) leaves out the word *de,* which is part of the expression.

Artificial Language

1. A	11. C	21. E	31. A	41. E
2. C	12. D	22. B	32. C	42. B
3. D	13. C	23. C	33. B	43. B
4. D	14. C	24. A	34. E	44. D
5. A	15. B	25. D	35. B	45. B
6. A	16. C	26. B	36. A	46. D
7. B	17. B	27. E	37. C	47. C
8. B	18. C	28. A	38. D	48. B
9. D	19. A	29. D	39. B	49. A
10. E	20. D	30. D	40. A	50. C

1. **The correct answer is (A).** Only the word numbered 1 is correctly translated. To create the translation of *were not*, add the prefix *fer* to *synzotim*, the translation of *were*. The correct translation is *fersynzotim*. *Ferliazotim* is the translation of *uninjured*, not *injured*. To create the translation of *injured*, begin with *liaker*, the translation of *to injure*. Drop the *ker* to create the verb stem (Rule 4). According to Rule 8, since the verb is a past participle, add the suffix *to* the verb stem. The correct translation is *liato*.

2. **The correct answer is (C).** Only the word numbered 3 is correctly translated. *Ekapleknef is* the translation of *girl*. To make this translation plural, add the suffix *oz* (Rule 2). The correct translation is *ekapleknefoz*. To create the present-tense verb *work*, begin with *frigker*, the translation of the infinitive *to work*. Drop the *ker* to create the verb stem (Rule 4). Add the suffix *im* because the verb is plural (Rule 6). The correct translation is *frigim*.

3. **The correct answer is (D).** All of the words in this sentence are correctly translated.

4. **The correct answer is (D).** The words numbered 2 and 3 are correctly translated. *Wir* is the translation of *the*. The translation of *an* is *bex*.

5. **The correct answer is (A).** Only the word numbered 1 is correctly translated. *Kapleknefoz* is the translation of *women*. To make this translation of *woman*, drop the suffix *oz* (Rule 2). The correct translation is *kapleknef*. *Tulem* is the translation of *has*. The suffix *em* indicates that it is singular (Rule 6). The subject of this sentence is plural, however—"woman and girl." The correct translation of *have* is *tulim*.

6. **The correct answer is (A).** Only the word numbered 1 is correctly translated. To create the translation of the noun *guard*, begin with *bonker*, the translation of the infinitive *to guard*. Drop the *ker* to create the verb stem. To make a verb a noun, add the suffix *lek* (Rule 9). The correct translation is *bonlek*. *Inle* is the translation of the word *loyal*. To create the translation of *disloyal*, add the prefix *fer*. The correct translation is *ferinle*.

7. **The correct answer is (B).** Only the word numbered 2 is correctly translated. To cre-

ate the translation of the noun *driver*, begin with *arker*, the translation of the infinitive *to drive*. Drop the suffix *ker* to create the verb stem (Rule 4). Add the suffix *lek* to make the verb a noun (Rule 6). The correct translation is *arlek*. In this sentence, the word *illegal* modifies *alien*, which is singular. Therefore, you do not need the suffix *oz* at the end of *fercolle*, the translation of *illegal*.

8. **The correct answer is (B).** Only the word numbered 2 is correctly translated. *Tatlek* is the translation of the word *spy*. To make this plural, add the suffix *oz* (Rule 2). *Reglek* is the correct translation of *border*. However, in this sentence, border is an adjective modifying *station*. According to Rule 10, to form an adjective from a noun, drop the suffix *lek* and add the suffix *le*. Therefore, the correct translation is *regle*.

9. **The correct answer is (D).** The words numbered 1 and 2 are correctly translated. *Fercolle* is the translation of *illegal*. The translation of *legal* is *colle*.

10. **The correct answer is (E).** None of the words in this sentence is correctly translated. The translation of *skillful* is *janle*. To create the translation of *friendly*, begin with the translation of the noun *friend*, which is *kometlek*. To make the noun an adjective, drop the suffix *lek* and add the suffix *le*. The correct translation is *kometle*. To create the translation of *inspector*, begin with *zelker*, the translation of *to inspect*. Drop the *ker* to create the verb stem (Rule 4). Then add *lek* to make the verb a noun (Rule 9). The correct translation is *zellek*.

11. **The correct answer is (C).** Only the word numbered 3 is correctly translated. *Ekaplek* is the translation of *boy*. The correct translation of *boys* is *ekaplekoz* (Rule 2). To create the translation of *crossed*, begin with *chonker*, the translation of *to cross*. Drop the *ker* (Rule 4), and add *zot* to make the verb

past tense. Because the verb is plural, add the suffix *im* (Rule 7). The correct translation is *chonzotim*.

12. **The correct answer is (D).** The words numbered 1 and 2 are correctly translated. *Were injured* is a past participle. According to Rule 8, the suffix *to* should be added to the verb stem. The verb stem is *lia*, so the correct translation is *liato*.

13. **The correct answer is (C).** Only the word numbered 3 is correctly translated. While *ekapleknefoz* is the translation of *girls*, to make this possessive, the suffix *ae* should be added. The correct translation is *ekapleknefozae*. To create the noun *escape*, begin with *pirker*, the translation of *to escape*. Drop the *ker* to create the verb stem (Rule 4). To make the verb a noun, add the suffix *lek* (Rule 9). The correct translation is *pirlek*.

14. **The correct answer is (C).** The word numbered 3 is the only word that is correctly translated. To create the noun *driver*, begin with *arker*, the translation of the infinitive *to drive*. Drop the *ker* to create the verb stem (Rule 4). Add the suffix *lek* to make a verb a noun (Rule 9). The correct translation of *driver* is *arlek*. While *synzotem* is the translation of *was*, to create the translation of *was not*, the prefix *fer* must be added. The correct translation is *fersynzotem*.

15. **The correct answer is (B).** Only the word numbered 2 is correctly translated. To create the translation of *crossed*, start with *chonker*, the translation of *to cross*. Drop the *ker* (Rule 4) and add *zot* to make the verb past tense. Then add *em* because the verb is singular. The correct translation is *chonzotem*. To create the noun *spy*, use *tatker*, the translation of *to spy*. Drop the *ker* and add *lek* to make the verb a noun (Rule 6). The correct translation is *tatlek*.

16. **The correct answer is (C).** Only the word numbered 3 is correctly translated. To create the plural of *alien*, add the suffix *oz* to *huslek* (Rule 2). To make this possessive, add the suffix *ae*. The correct translation is *huslekozae*. To create the verb *injured*, use the translation of *to injure*, which is *liaker*. Drop the *ker* (Rule 4) and add *zot* to make the verb past tense. The correct translation is *liazot*.

17. **The correct answer is (B).** Only the word numbered 2 is correctly translated. The translation of *woman*, which is singular, is *kapleknef*. To make the translation of *paper*, *trenedlek*, plural, add the suffix *oz*. The correct translation is *trenedlekoz*.

18. **The correct answer is (C).** Only the word numbered 3 is correctly translated. While *fercolle* is the translation of *illegal*, in this sentence, the subject is plural. According to Rule 3, adjectives modifying nouns with plural endings must agree with the words they modify. The correct translation is *fercolleoz*. Since the subject of the sentence is plural, the verb must also be plural. The verb *pirem* is the singular translation of *escape*. The correct translation is *pirem* (Rules 4 and 6).

19. **The correct answer is (A).** The word numbered 1 is the only word that is correctly translated in this sentence. The translation of friend is *kometlek*. To create the translation of the adjective *friendly*, follow Rule 10. Drop the *lek* and add the suffix *le*. The correct translation is *kometle*. To create the translation of *drove*, use the translation of the infinitive *to drive*, which is *arker*. Drop the *ker* (Rule 4), add *zot* to make the verb past tense, then add *em* because the verb is singular (Rule 7). The correct translation is *arzotem*.

20. **The correct answer is (D).** The words numbered 1 and 2 are correctly translated.

To create the translation of the words *are not*, add the prefix *fer* to *synim*, the translation of *are*. The correct translation is *fersynim*.

21. **The correct answer is (E).** The translation of *country* is *failek*. To make this translation possessive, add the suffix *ae* (Rule 12). The correct translation is *failekae*. To create the noun *border*, begin with *regker*, the translation of *to border*. Drop the *ker* (Rule 4), and add *lek* to make the verb a noun (Rule 9). To make the translation plural, add the suffix *oz* (Rule 2). The correct translation is *reglekoz*.

22. **The correct answer is (B).** The translation of the conjunction *and* is *loa*. The translation of *loyal* is *inle*.

23. **The correct answer is (C).** The translation of *the* is *wir*. The translation of *border* is *reglek* (Rules 4 and 9).

24. **The correct answer is (A).** The translation of *is* is *synem* (Rule 6). To create the translation of *is not*, add the suffix *fer* (Rule 13). The correct translation is *fersynem*.

25. **The correct answer is (D).** To create the translation of the present-tense verb *inspect*, begin with *zelker*, the translation of the infinitive *to inspect*. Drop the *ker* (Rule 4) and add *im* because the verb is plural (Rule 6). To create the translation of *their*, add *oz* to *yev*, the translation of *he/him*. The translation of *paper* is *trenedlek*. To make this translation plural, add *oz* (Rule 2). The correct translation is *trenedlekoz*.

26. **The correct answer is (B).** The translation of *enemy* is *avelek*. To make this translation plural, add the suffix *oz* (Rule 2). The translation of *and* is *loa*. To create the noun *spy*, begin with *tatker*, the translation of the infinitive *to spy*. Drop the *ker* and add *lek* to make the verb a noun (Rule 9). Add *oz* to make the noun plural (Rule 2). The correct translation is *tatlekoz*.

27. The correct answer is (E). The translation of the infinitive *to shoot* is *degker*. To create the translation of *them*, add the suffix *oz* to *yev*, the translation of *he/him*. The correct translation is *yevoz*.

28. The correct answer is (A). The translation of *to have* is *tulker*.

29. The correct answer is (D). The translation of *from* is *mor*. To create the noun *border*, begin with *regker*, the translation of the infinitive *to border*. Drop the *ker* (Rule 4) and add *lek* to make the verb a noun (Rule 9). To make a noun an adjective (Rule 10), drop the *lek* and add *le*. The correct translation is *regle*. To create the plural noun *stations*, begin with *lexker*, the translation of the infinitive *to station*. Drop the *ker* (Rule 4) and add *lek* to make the verb a noun (Rule 9). To make the noun plural, add *oz* (Rule 2). The correct translation is *lexlekoz*.

30. The correct answer is (D). To create the present-tense noun *escape*, begin with *pirker*, the translation of the infinitive *to escape*. Drop the *ker* (Rule 4). Add *im* because the verb is plural (Rule 6). The correct translation is *pirim*.

31. The correct answer is (A). The translation of *that* is *velle*, and the translation of *man* is *kaplek*. The correct translation is *velle kaplek*. The complete sentence translates as, " That man is not an illegal alien."

32. The correct answer is (C). The translation of *he* is *yev*. To make this the translation of *she*, add the suffix *nef* (Rule 1). To create the translation of *crossed*, begin with *chonker*, the translation of *to cross*. Drop the *ker* (Rule 4). To make the verb past tense, add the suffix *zot* (Rule 7). Because the verb is singular, add the suffix *em*. The correct translation is *yevnef chonzotem*. The complete sentence translates as, "She crossed the river."

33. The correct answer is (B). The translation of *a* is *bex,* and the translation of *friend* is *kometlek*. The correct translation is *bex kometlek*. The complete sentence translates as, "That alien is a friend."

34. The correct answer is (E). To create the translation of *have,* begin with *tulker,* the translation of *to have*. Drop the *ker* and add *im* because the verb is plural. In this sentence, *inspected* is a past participle. To create the past participle (Rule 8), drop the suffix *ker* and add *to*. The correct translation is *tulim zelto*. The entire sentence translates as, "The guards have inspected those papers."

35. The correct answer is (B). To create the translation of *injured,* begin with *liaker,* the translation of *to injure*. Drop the *ker* (Rule 4) and add *zot* to make the verb past tense. Then add *em* because the verb is singular (Rule 7). The translation of *the* is *wir*. To create the noun *inspector,* begin with *zelker,* the translation of *to inspect*. Drop the *ker* (Rule 4). To make the verb a noun, add the suffix *lek* (Rule 9). The correct translation is *liazotem wir zellek*. The entire sentence translates as, "That spy injured the inspector."

36. The correct answer is (A). The translation of *man* is *kaplek*. To make this plural, add the suffix *oz* (Rule 2). To make the translation possessive, also add the suffix *ae* (Rule 12). The translation of *paper* is *trenedlek*. To make this plural, add the suffix *oz*. The correct translation is *kaplekozae trenedlekoz*. The complete sentence translates as, "The men's papers are illegal."

37. The correct answer is (C). The translation of *man* is *kaplek*. To make this plural, add the suffix *oz* (Rule 2). The translation of *and* is *loa*. To create the translation of *women,* add the suffixes *nef* and *oz* to *kaplek* (Rules 1 and 2). The correct translation is *kapleknefoz*. The complete sentence translates as, "The men and women were from the border station."

38. The correct answer is (D). To create the noun *guard,* begin with *bonker,* the translation of the infinitive *to guard.* Drop the *ker* (Rule 4). To make the verb a noun, add the suffix *lek* (Rule 9). To make the noun possessive, add the suffix *ae* (Rule 12). The correct translation is *bonlekae.* To create the noun *station,* begin with *lexker,* the translation of *to station.* Drop the *ker* (Rule 4). To make the verb a noun, add the suffix *lek* (Rule 9). The correct translation is *lexlek.* The entire sentence translates as, "That guard's station is legal."

39. The correct answer is (B). The translation of *has* is *tulem* (Rule 6), and the translation of *to drive* is *arker.* The whole sentence translates as, "He has to drive a jeep."

40. The correct answer is (A). The translation of *was* is *synzotem* (Rule 7). To create the translation of the past participle *injured,* begin with *liaker,* the translation of *to injure.* Drop the *lek* (Rule 4), and then add the suffix *to* (Rule 8). The correct translation is *liato.* The complete sentence translates as, "That woman was injured."

41. The correct answer is (E). To create the plural noun *spies,* use the translation of the infinitive *to spy,* which is *tatker.* Drop the *ker* (Rule 4). To make the verb a noun, add the suffix *lek* (Rule 9). To make the noun plural, add the suffix *oz* (Rule 2). The correct translation is *tatlekoz.* To create the past-tense verb *shot,* use the translation of the infinitive *to shoot,* which is *degker.* Drop the *ker* (Rule 4). To make the verb past tense, add the suffix *zot,* and then add the suffix *im* because the verb is plural (Rule 7). The correct translation is *degzotim.* The

complete sentence translates as, "The spies shot the guard."

42. The correct answer is (B). To create the past-tense verb *escaped,* use the translation of the infinitive *to escape,* which is *pirker.* Drop the *ker* (Rule 4). Add the suffix *zot* to make the verb past tense. Then add the suffix *im* because the verb is plural. The correct translation is *pirzotim.* The translation of *from* is *mor* and the translation of *the* is *wir.* To create the translation of the noun *inspector,* begin with the translation of *to inspect,* which is *zelker.* Drop the *ker* (Rule 4). To make the verb a noun, add the suffix *lek* (Rule 9). The correct translation is *zellek.* The entire sentence translates as, "The girls escaped from the inspector."

43. The correct answer is (B). The translation of this sentence is, "The woman has identified the enemy." To create the word *has,* drop the *ker* from *tulker,* the translation of *to have.* Rule 6 states that to create the present-tense of a verb, add *em* if the verb is singular. The correct translation is *tulem.* Follow Rule 8 to create the present perfect singular tense of *kalenker, to identify.* Drop the *ker* and add the suffix *to.* The correct translation is *kalento.*

44. The correct answer is (D). The translation of the entire sentence is, "That guard is unfriendly." *Kometlek* is the Artificial Language word for *friend.* To make it negative, add the prefix *fer* (Rule 13). According to Rule 10, to form an adjective from a noun, drop the *lek* ending and add *le.* The correct translation is *ferkometle.*

45. The correct answer is (B). The translation of this sentence is, "That station's inspectors are loyal." To create the noun from *lexker,* the Artificial Language word for *to station,* drop the *ker* (Rule 4) and add *lek* (Rule 9). To make the noun an adjective drop the *lek* and add *le.* To make it possessive, add the suffix *ae* (Rule 12). The correct translation is *lexlekae*. To create a noun from *zelker,* the Artificial Language word for *to inspect,* drop the *ker* (Rule 4). Then add *lek* to make the verb a noun (Rule 9). To make the noun plural, add the suffix *oz* (Rule 2). The correct translation is *zellekoz.*

46. **The correct answer is (D).** The translation of this sentence is, "The inspectors drove the jeep." The Artificial Language word for *the* is *wir.* To make it feminine, add *nef* (Rule 1). To make it plural, add *oz* (Rule 2). The correct translation is *wirnefoz.* To create the plural noun *inspectors,* drop the *ker* from *zelker,* the Artificial Language word for *to inspect.* To form a noun from a verb, add *lek* (Rule 9). To make the noun feminine, add *nef* (Rule 2) and to make it plural, add *oz* (Rule 1). The correct translation is *zelleknefoz.*

47. **The correct answer is (C).** The translation of this sentence is, "The girls are legal aliens and they crossed the border." *Ekaplek* is the translation of *boy.* To make it feminine, add the suffix *nef* (Rule 1). To make it plural, add the suffix *oz* (Rule 2). The correct translation is *ekapleknefoz.* To create the past-tense verb *crossed,* drop the *ker* from *chonker,* the Artificial Language word for *to cross.* Add the suffix *zot* to make the verb past tense, and then add *im* because the verb is plural (Rule 7). The correct translation is *chonzotim.*

48. **The correct answer is (B).** The translation of the complete sentence is, "The guard has identified the enemies." To create the past participle of *kalenker,* which means *to identify,* drop the *ker* and add the suffix *to* (Rule 8). The correct translation is *kalento.* To create the plural noun *enemies,* add *oz* to *avelek.* The correct translation is *avelekoz.*

49. **The correct answer is (A).** The translation of the sentence is, "The loyal men were from the government and had crossed the border."

Inle is the Artificial Language word for *loyal.* To make this negative, add the prefix *fer* (Rule 13). To make it plural, add the suffix *oz* (Rule 3). The correct translation is *ferinleoz. Kaplek* is the Artificial Language word for *man.* To make this plural, add the suffix *oz* (Rule 2). The correct translation is *kaplekoz.* To create the past participle *crossed* from *chonker,* the Artificial Language word for *to cross,* drop the *ker* and add the suffix *to* (Rule 8). The correct translation is *chonto.*

50. **The correct answer is (C).** The translation of the sentence is, "An enemy alien had legal papers and was friendly." To create an adjective from the noun *enemy,* which is *avelek,* drop the *lek* and add *le* (Rule 11). To make this feminine, add the suffix *nef* (Rule 1). The correct translation is *avelenef.* The Artificial Language word *huslek* means *alien.* To make this feminine, add the suffix *nef.* The correct translation is *husleknef.* To create the adverb *friendly,* begin with *kometlek,* the Artificial Language word for *friend.* To make the noun an adjective, drop the *lek* and add *le.* To make the word feminine, add the suffix *nef.* To make the adjective an adverb, add the suffix *ki.* The correct translation is *kometlenefki.*

APPENDIX

Department of Homeland Security Federal
Employment Programs

Department of Homeland Security Federal Employment Programs

The Department of Homeland Security, in conjunction with other Federal agencies, offers a variety of programs for individuals interested in Federal employment. These opportunities are open to full- and part-time students from high school to graduate school, as well as to qualified professionals.

STUDENT TEMPORARY EMPLOYMENT PROGRAM (STEP)

The Student Temporary Employment Program (STEP) provides students with part- or full-time employment during the academic year and summer vacations. Students are free to work in a variety of fields because the program does not require the work to relate to students' academic or career goals.

To be eligible, students must be enrolled in high school, vocational school, college, or graduate school. Generally, all students must be U.S. citizens. However, the hiring agency can make exceptions for non-U.S. citizens on a case-by-case basis.

Federal agencies can make appointments to the STEP program at any time during the year. These appointments can last for up to one year. An agency may extend a position as long as the student remains in school. Employment with the hiring agency ends once the student has completed his or her degree. In addition to their salaries, students in the STEP program are also eligible for annual and sick leave.

Students should contact the Federal agency that they are interested in working with to see if it participates in the STEP program. More information is available at the Office of Personnel Management's (OPM) Web site.

STUDENT CAREER EXPERIENCE PROGRAM (SCEP)

Individuals in the Student Career Experience Program gain work experience in positions that relate to their academic interests and career goals. SCEP positions are open to undergraduate and graduate students at participating colleges and universities. Students interested in SCEP must be U.S. citizens or nationals. This program requires the full cooperation of the student, the hiring agency, and the academic institution. Many positions are paid and some offer academic credit toward the student's degree. Students in this program are also entitled to annual and sick leave.

Students who participate in SCEP are eligible for permanent positions after graduation. These students must complete 640 hours of work experience in the SCEP program before completing their degrees. They must also maintain an excellent academic record and demonstrate outstanding performance on the job.

Interested students must enroll in their school's cooperative education programs. If the institution does not have a cooperative education program, the hiring agency can make formal arrangements to hire exceptional students.

For more information on the SCEP program, students should contact their school's career services department. Additional information is available online at the OPM's Web site.

STUDENT VOLUNTEERS PROGRAM (SVP)

High school and college students can also gain work experience related to their fields of study through the Student Volunteers Program (SVP). This program allows students to investigate various career opportunities while earning academic credit for their internship. These positions are unpaid and students are not eligible for annual or sick leave.

This program requires the full cooperation of the student, the hiring agency, and educational institution. For more information, students should contact their school's career services department. Students can also contact the Federal agency they are interested in working with for additional information or requirements. OPM is not required to post positions for student volunteers.

CUSTOMS AND BORDER PROTECTION (CBP) EXPLORER PROGRAM

The Customs and Border Protection (CBP) Explorer Program is available to high school and college students between the ages of 14 and 21. This program offers young people hands-on experience in Federal law enforcement. Although this program is unpaid, students who participate may be eligible for scholarships from several Federal agencies.

The goal of this program is to expose young people to the career options available within the CBP and provide these students with the encouragement they need to achieve their career goals. Students receive extensive training before assisting federal agents in activities like surveillance operations, vessel searches, and crowd control.

Interested students need to have at least a "C" average and must obtain permission from a parent or guardian to participate in the program. More information on the program is available from your state's CBP post adviser.

FEDERAL CAREER INTERN PROGRAM

The Federal Career Intern Program is a two-year formal training and development program. This program is open year round to eligible candidates and is not limited to students. Hiring agencies accept applications from students and professionals from a variety of employment and educational backgrounds.

Interns who complete the program successfully are eligible for permanent employment within the hiring agency. These interns will not need to undergo the traditional hiring process once they graduate from the program. Interns are usually hired at grade levels GS-5, 7, and 9, depending on their prior experience. Interns receive pay, annual and sick leave, and are eligible for other benefits such as health insurance.

Hiring agencies post their own listings for Federal internships. The OPM is not required to post these listings. Interested individuals should contact the agency that they are interested in working with for additional information on possible internships.

THE PRESIDENTIAL MANAGEMENT FELLOW (PMF)

The Presidential Management Fellow (PMF) is an exclusive two-year paid fellowship for graduate students. The OPM, in conjunction with participating agencies, developed the PMF to encourage students from various academic backgrounds to seek Federal employment.

This intense program requires 160 hours of formal classroom training, completion of a four- to six-month developmental assignment, and adherence to an individual development plan developed by the student and the hiring agency. After completing the fellowship, participants receive permanent positions within the Federal government. Fellows are not required to complete a probationary period once they secure permanent positions.

Students enrolled in an advanced degree program at an accredited university are eligible for the fellowship. All students must be U.S. citizens or nationals, but there are exceptions to this restriction. Students from other countries should contact the OPM about eligibility requirements. Non-U.S. citizens selected for the PMF will not be eligible for permanent Federal employment at the conclusion of the fellowship unless they apply for citizenship.

PMF officials adhere to a strict timetable. Because the PMF receives thousands of applications every year, it is important that all applicants review this timetable to ensure that their applications and nominations are received on time and in the proper order.

After completing a standard application, interested students must also receive a nomination from their university's dean, chairperson, or academic director. Individual institutions must determine their own nomination process for qualified students. Nominees must then undergo a selection process during which PMF officials will assess their academic and professional credentials.

All acceptable nominees must undergo an in-person assessment during the application period. There are ten assessment locations across the country where PMF officials interview nominees and assess their skills. Nominees must travel to one of these locations and find suitable accommodations at their own expense.

During the assessment, officials will assess each nominee's life experiences, critical thinking skills, and writing abilities. After selecting the finalists, the PMF officials require all students to complete any remaining graduate degree requirements (though graduation is not necessary) before their appointment to a Federal agency. In certain cases, agencies will also require the completion of a background investigation before the finalist begins working.

Graduate students who are interested in the PMF should contact their school's career services center about obtaining additional information on the nomination procedure.

IMPORTANT WEB SITES

The following Web sites provide additional information on Federal fellowships, internships, and student programs.

- The Customs and Border Protection Web site— http://www.cbp.gov/
- The Office of Personnel Management Web site—http://www.opm.gov
- The Presidential Management Fellows Web site— https://www.pmf.opm.gov/
- USA Jobs—Student Jobs— http://www.usajobs.gov/studentjobs/

NOTES

NOTES